WARFARE IN THE ROMAN REPUBLIC

WARFARE IN THE ROMAN REPUBLIC

From the Etruscan Wars to the Battle of Actium

Lee L. Brice, Editor

ABC-CLIO

Santa Barbara, California • Denver, Colorado • Oxford, England

Library of Congress Cataloging-in-Publication Data

Warfare in the Roman Republic : from the Etruscan Wars to the Battle of Actium / Lee L. Brice, editor.

     pages cm

  Includes bibliographical references and index.

  ISBN 978-1-61069-298-4 (alk. paper) — ISBN 978-1-61069-299-1 (ebook)

1. Rome—History, Military. 2. Military art and science—Rome—History.

3. Military history, Ancient. I. Brice, Lee L.

  DG89.W38 2014

  355.020937'09014—dc23   2013048640

ISBN: 978-1-61069-298-4
EISBN: 978-1-61069-299-1

18 17 16 15 14 1 2 3 4 5

This book is also available on the World Wide Web as an eBook.
Visit www.abc-clio.com for details.

ABC-CLIO, LLC
130 Cremona Drive, P.O. Box 1911
Santa Barbara, California 93116-1911

This book is printed on acid-free paper ∞
Manufactured in the United States of America

to
Frank L. Holt,

. . . inspirational teacher and friend,
with affection.

Contents

Documents, 213

Introduction

Standing as we do in the shadow of the 2,510th anniversary of the traditional founding of the Roman Republic and on the eve of the 2,500th anniversary of Rome's wars against Veii, it seems a good time to consider the continuing interest in the warfare of the Roman Republic. Among all the topics I teach, few institutions capture students' interests and imagination more than the Roman Army. Whether because they have seen it in video games and film or have read about stories of the legions or the leaders, many students are familiar with and fascinated by the Roman military. The conquest of much territory that we still recognize, the sense of a professional military that is the forerunner of our modern armies, and the leaders all draw students, both young and old, to the army. Despite all the changes that have occurred in warfare, ancient Roman military history continues to attract attention of all sorts. The variety of reasons for this interest can tell us much about the topics that I address in this volume.

One overarching reason for interest in Roman warfare is the vitality of the field. Students often joke with me that ancient history should be easy because it is ancient. Like many people, they think that it does not change because it is so old. Given how much warfare has changed, they are convinced that the military history of Rome is even more stuck in an unchanging past than most types of ancient history. In a way, they are correct. The reasons for this are not hard to locate. Much of what has been written about Roman warfare in the last two centuries has focused heavily on battle narratives and consideration of famous personalities (Brice and Roberts 2011). This type of military history has carried the label "drums and trumpets" because of its traditional focus on battle narratives. Much of what we call the drums-and-trumpets style of work is stuck in old methods and styles, which is why students who think that ancient military history does not change are correct, to an extent. Despite that, it remains immensely popular with general readers.

As a type of scholarly history, drums and trumpets is often antiquated in its methods. As a result, military history is no longer as popular with academic historians as it was before the mid-20th century. This attitude by other historians has been the trend for much of the last four decades. The opprobrium is largely because scholars in other fields assume that military history is still all drums and trumpets and remain unaware of methodological advances in the study of warfare. The reality is that military history, including the history of ancient warfare, is changing all the time.

Just as historians in other specializations started drawing on new methods and engaging in more social history, postcolonial history, and cultural history after 1945, so did military historians, even if they did so a bit later than everyone else. This led to the emergence of a war-and-society approach that became increasingly popular. By 1970 historians could refer to a new military history that drew heavily on the social sciences and other fields to consider warfare in new ways. Even traditional or drums-and-trumpets history has changed thanks to John Keegan's *Face of Battle* (1976). His soldiers' perspective bottom-up approach to the sharp end of battle has affected many discussions of battles and campaigns even in ancient history (Brice and Roberts 2011). More recently, other specialized fields of study have opened up military history. Conflict archaeology, crowd psychology, game theory, and forensic anthropology are examples of fields having an enormous impact on the way historians approach ancient warfare. In these ways we have new topics of detailed study such as mutiny, battlefield physiology, and gender as well as new ways of looking at traditional topics such as logistics, economics, combat motivation, and death. The result is that military history is more popular in the classroom than it used to be (Wheeler 2011; Brice 2014), but more important, this new work has made some drums-and-trumpets histories much better. It has also had an impact on ancient history.

The methodological changes are just as true of military historians of ancient Roman warfare as of modern warfare. In addition to changes in the field of military history, there have been similar developments in ancient history and classical studies that have changed the way we look at Roman warfare. Archaeologists, for example, uncover new artifacts, sites, and sources such as new inscriptions that illustrate features of Roman career paths. Specialists in various fields using new laboratory sciences reveal previously unavailable data, including the ways in which particular weapon use can appear in the skeletal remains of users and victims. Historians employ new ways of looking at old and new evidence to reveal lost information, examine neglected topics, or elaborate new interpretations. As a result, the field of ancient history, including military history, is a far cry from my students' misconceptions of it as static; it is an exciting and dynamic field of study that advances constantly and attracts continued interest (Brice 2014). While some readers are drawn by activity in the field, others are drawn by the appeal of the content.

A traditional reason for the continuing fascination with ancient military history is the inspirational quality found in famous leaders and battles of the past. Julius Caesar served this function ever since his death. Caesar inspired Romans such as Augustus, Trajan, and Justinian and continues to inspire modern generals worldwide. Other Roman generals have provided inspiration to modern readers, even if less so than Caesar, but so have some battles. As can be seen in the title of Greg Daly's, book *Cannae: The Experience of Battle in the Second Punic War* (2001), some ancient battles have a reputation for inspiration. The Western tradition still often presents Caesar's Gallic Wars as triumphs of civilization over barbarians, while Cannae is in a long tradition of glorious defeats. Roman conquest of much of the world and then the military's role in maintaining the peace inspired numerous European empires to model themselves on Rome or portray themselves as having done so. Inspiration has provided a strong attraction for many readers, but education has also remained an important role for ancient warfare.

Traditional military history, which focused on battles and leaders has typically had a strong educational element—training leadership skills through biographies of famous commanders. Even portions of careers and leaders' command decisions have been subject to discussion and analysis when entire biographies have been unavailable or unsuitable. Some leaders' biographies have been studied in search of a distinct recipe for success or failure in warfare that authors could isolate, as if there was one particular set of skills and experience that if learned would lead to consistent success in warfare. Ancient Roman warfare has provided a number of leaders who have been the subject of such analysis. Caesar is the most obvious example, but we cannot ignore Scipio Africanus, Scipio Aemilianus, Pompey, and Antony, among so many others. Regardless of their success in locating the elusive recipe, authors such as H. Scullard (1970) and Barry Strauss (2012) continue to present the lives and actions of important ancient leaders for the leadership and historical lessons we may draw from their careers.

Readers have found battles and campaigns popular topics for military education, too. Modern works devoted to battles were popularized in the 19th century. These works have lost none of their popularity since and have expanded to include books, articles, and videos devoted to campaigns, operational histories, and wars. While many of these works entertain, they also have the goal of teaching military skills, including tactics, strategy, and operational arts. Methods of combat and warfare have changed, but the human aspect of land combat has actually changed little. Airplanes may be able to demolish a patch of ground, but as Caesar demonstrated in 58–51 BCE in Gaul, infantry must hold territory to win the conflict. Also, men in combat in ancient and modern armies still react to combat stress in many similar ways. Ancient Roman battles such as Cannae, Cynoscephalae, and Pharsalus have long been the subject of military education within and outside the military, since there is much that students and enthusiasts can learn about leadership and military skills from these engagements. There is, of course, much more to learn from ancient warfare than traditional military skills.

Warfare is also an important topic for readers because it was a fact of life in ancient Rome. While it is popular to look at the Roman Republic as a highpoint of civilization with its art, architecture, literature, and law, it is important to remember that Rome's wealth, which was unusual in the ancient world, made those achievements possible. Most ancient peoples did not participate in or enjoy the benefits of Republican Rome; indeed, many ancient peoples' closest tie to Rome was through warfare.

Ancient warfare was a feature of life common to all the ancient Mediterranean, across all regions, tribes, cities, and levels of society. Every person's life would have been affected by warfare, not just as an officer, soldier, or camp follower but also as a victim, a relative of a victim, a taxpayer, or even a resident participating in military and related institutions. Because of the potential sacrifice, warfare was the most important civic activity anyone could engage in at any level. Participating in the military was an expectation if not a requirement for every member of the Roman community who could afford to purchase weapons. Later, even as the poor had opportunities to serve, the expectation of service did not diminish. There were institutions in most cities designed to prepare would-be soldiers for fighting. In poorer communities where hunting was a part of life, these skills often translated into warfare as light-armed infantry. Warfare also provided some men with economic opportunities as soldiers serving in Italy or abroad. Since warfare was so common in Italy, war remains one of the few ubiquitous cultural ties available for historians and interested readers wishing to understand features of ancient culture and society shared by all Romans. This truism is another reason that Roman warfare remains important and interesting to a diverse audience.

The last reasons that ancient Roman warfare remains popular are the enduring entertainment quality of its stories and the recognition that it remains relevant. Caesar's life is a stunning story of achievement against immense odds coupled with the tragedy of his assassination. Regardless of the historical knowledge that we glean from the sources about him, it is also an entertaining story. Not surprisingly, Caesar has inspired many novels, works of art, television episodes, films, and computer games. His war in Gaul is difficult to understand without knowing about the wars of expansion fought in the second century; the immensity of his achievement is difficult to appreciate without knowledge of the ways in which Roman warfare changed over time. The stories of Paullus at Cannae, Caesar at Alesia, and Antony at Actium have entertained readers since the ancient world. The struggles of these commanders and soldiers against great odds and human flaws make their stories timeless. The ways in which later authors write their history in styles similar to the military histories of Polybius have contributed to giving these stories from Rome continued life.

The present volume is testament that ancient history does change, sometimes dramatically. The timeline may not change much, but I have selected other aspects of this book with recent work in mind. There are some reference entries that would not have appeared in the past, and the contents of all the entries reflect modern work on Roman warfare. The selection of primary documents has been made to illustrate specific aspects of Roman warfare, especially in terms of how warfare changed over time. Charts are one feature of this volume where I have striven for a level of honesty with readers. Ancient authors were not capable of or even interested in recording numbers that we can trust and put in charts. Therefore, I have provided charts that readers can use as starting points for more investigation into warfare. The bibliography also reflects recent work. Even the selection of terms in the glossary has been heavily influenced by changes in the ways historians approach ancient warfare.

In writing the entries, I have tried to adhere to some standardization in treating terms and names drawn from an ancient language. Latin and Greek words are transliterated and italicized if not in common usage. In transliterating ancient words and names, I have stuck to traditional Anglicized practice, such as substituting the letter "C" for the Greek letter "Kappa" in all cases and using a "G" at the beginning of the Roman names Gaius and Gnaeus. Roman names can be a mouthful, but through historical usage over the last 1,000 and more years, many individuals are known by a common name. So that readers can identify these common names quickly, in each entry for a person I have underlined the first appearance of the person's common name, such as <u>Pompey</u> for Gnaeus Pompeius Magnus, and then used the common name throughout the rest of the book.

Reflecting the difference between the modern rank of general and the various types of commanding officers in the ancient world, I have consistently preferred using the word "commander" for chief military officers. I have also preferred to use the term "Roman military" rather than "Roman Army," since the military was an institution that included numerous armies under different commanders. The array of information and the updated nature of it make this volume a useful reference tool for readers with diverse interests.

In closing, I need to acknowledge various debts. I am indebted to my editor Padraic (Pat) Carlin of ABC-CLIO. He has assisted me in locating various items and bringing the final work together, but most important, his faith in the project and support helped keep the project on target. I am indebted to my students in several years' worth of classes at my own institution and at Illinois State University. They were not afraid to ask tough questions, hold my feet to the fire, and respond to the topics with curiosity and enthusiasm. I am as always grateful to the many teachers who have attended the Dupage Valley Social Studies Conference year after year and have heard some of this material in advance and whose observations always improve the final project. Thanks to Kevin Coon and the consortium of schools who have made the Dupage conference possible. I am deeply grateful to Dr. Georgia Tsouvala of Illinois State University, who has reviewed parts of the manuscript and made various suggestions. Her encouragement, insights, and endless patience made the project feasible and improved it along the way. Any factual errors that remain are entirely my own responsibility. Finally, I am immensely indebted to my professor and friend Frank L. Holt, whose focus on history and storytelling done well inspired me. His insistence on proper methodology and clear writing have kept me on the straight and narrow path of wisdom while nurturing a strong enthusiasm for history and teaching. This volume is dedicated to him with gratitude and genuine affection.

Lee L. Brice
Normal, Illinois
September, 2013

A

Actium, Battle of

The Actian Campaign was the result of the increasing friction between Octavian and Antony culminating in a declaration of war by the Roman Senate against Cleopatra. Gathering their forces in 32 BCE, Antony and Cleopatra may have brought as many as 500 ships (including transports) and a land force as large as 100,000 legionary and allied soldiers. Antony made his primary base at Patras in northwestern Peloponnese and dispersed garrisons to key points along the western coast.

Octavian amassed his forces in Brundisium on the Italian coast. His naval commander, Agrippa, probed the Peloponnese in early 31 and secured important coastal bases that he used to disrupt Antony's sea routes of supply and communication. Octavian moved his entire force across the Adriatic and set up base on the Actium Peninsula at the entrance of the Gulf of Ambracia.

Through a series of maneuvers, Agrippa forced Antony into an inhospitable location along the same gulf as Octavian. There, Antony was blockaded by land and sea. Losing many men to desertion and disease, he eventually decided to try a breakout. This decision forced him to rely entirely on his navy.

Ancient accounts of the battle are so poor that a narrative is difficult to construct. The battle occurred on September 2. Antony had around 230 ships, only a few of which were large, heavy ships, while Octavian responded with around 400 ships. The bulk of each fleet was made up of fours and fives, the commonly popular ship in this period. Each commander added legionaries to bolster the ship crews and thus may have employed

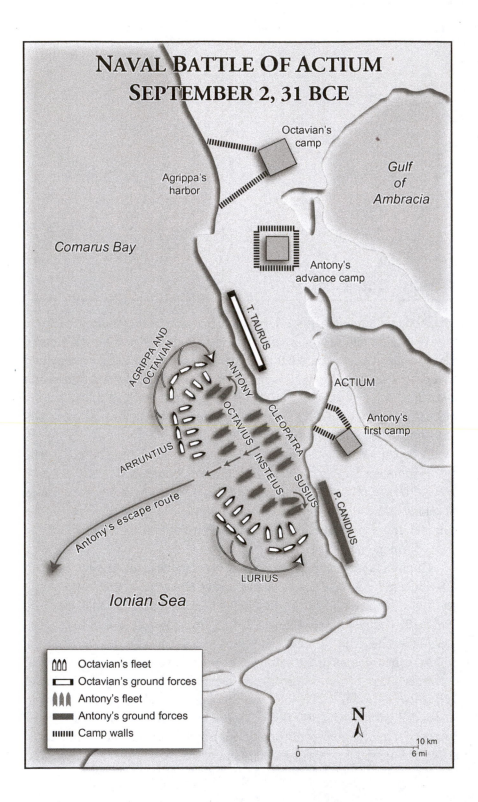

NAVAL BATTLE OF ACTIUM
SEPTEMBER 2, 31 BCE

Octavian's camp

Gulf of Ambracia

Agrippa's harbor

Comarus Bay

Antony's advance camp

T. TAURUS

AGRIPPA AND OCTAVIAN

ANTONY

ACTIUM

OCTAVIUS

CLEOPATRA

Antony's first camp

ARRUNTIUS

INSTEIUS

SUSIUS

P. CANIDIUS

Antony's escape route

LURIUS

Ionian Sea

Octavian's fleet
Octavian's ground forces
Antony's fleet
Antony's ground forces
Camp walls

N

0   10 km
0   6 mi

60,000 or more men on board. Antony's crews did not stow their masts and sails on shore but instead kept them aboard their ships so that they might take advantage of the usual daily breeze and outrun their opponents once they broke through the enemy line. Agrippa knew Antony's strategy from deserters and from the presence of sails on enemy ships.

Agrippa set his line farther out and ordered the men not to take the offensive, thus forcing the enemy to row farther than they had planned before engaging. Antony's men became exhausted, and Agrippa was able to capitalize with his experience and greater number of ships. Cleopatra, whose ships had been in reserve on the left to stop encirclement, took advantage of a gap in Octavian's lines to break through and sail south. This flight precipitated chaos as Antony's remaining ships tried to follow. In the end, only Cleopatra's squadron made it out under sail, followed by a few ships led by Antony. Most of Antony's fleet was destroyed or surrendered. His land force, which had not engaged, surrendered a short time later.

Octavian subsequently ordered the construction of Nicopolis ("Victory City") on the site of his former headquarters. The monuments included immense displays of the bronze prows (rams) of captured ships. Stonecutters had to remove enough rock from the monument blocks to hold the base of each ram. These archaeologically recovered cuttings in the shape of rams are one of our only sources for estimating the size of many of the ships.

Antony never recovered from Actium. He fled to Egypt, where he tried to rally supporters and his remaining forces. Octavian invaded Egypt in July of 30. The Battle of Actium may not have resulted in the immediate end of fighting, but it ended the Second Triumvirate and was the last serious fight of the civil war.

Spencer C. Tucker and Lee L. Brice

See also: Antonius, Marcus; Civil War III; Cleopatra VII; Fleet, Roman; Julius Caesar Octavianus, Gaius; Triumvirate, Second; Vipsanius Agrippa, Marcus

References

Carter, John M. *The Battle of Actium: The Rise and Triumph of Augustus Caesar.* London: Hamilton, 1970.

Murray, William. *The Age of Titans: The Rise and Fall of Great Hellenistic Navies.* Oxford: Oxford University Press, 2012.

Murray, William M., and P. M. Petsas. *Octavian's Campsite Memorial for the Actium War: Transactions of the American Philosophical Society,* Vol. 79. Philadelphia: American Philosophical Society, 1989.

Aemilius Lepidus, Marcus

Marcus Aemilius <u>Lepidus</u>, born circa 88 BCE, was a member of a prominent patrician family. Despite his father having been named an enemy of the state, Lepidus had a typical early political career.

During the civil war that began in 49, Lepidus as praetor in Rome supported Caesar, and as governor of Nearer Spain in 48–47 Lepidus maintained Caesar's position in the region. In return Caesar supported him for consul and master of the horse in 46, a post in which Lepidus replaced Antony. Lepidus remained master of the horse until Caesar's assassination and seems to have been key to controlling the troops in and near the city after the murder.

Since his post had ended, Lepidus went to govern Nearer Spain and Narbonensis. After Antony's loss at Mutina in 43 he joined Lepidus in Gaul, and both men were declared public enemies. At Bononia in October that year, Lepidus and Antony joined Octavian to establish the Second Triumvirate.

When Antony and Octavian moved against the assassins in 42, Lepidus governed Rome. He was little help to Octavian in settling soldiers returned from Philippi and then in the Perusine War. After several years of proving himself ineffectual, Lepidus was sent to govern Africa.

When Octavian crushed Sextus Pompey in 36, Lepidus lent assistance in Sicily. He miscalculated, however, when he declared the victory and Sicily his own. Octavian convinced Lepidus' troops to change sides and dismissed him back to Rome. Lepidus, lucky perhaps to remain alive, stayed at home until his death in 12. The removal of Lepidus from power made conflict between Antony and Octavian more likely.

Lee L. Brice

See also: Antonius, Marcus; Civil War I; Civil War II; Julius Caesar, Gaius; Julius Caesar Octavianus, Gaius; Philippi, Battle of; Pompeius Magnus, Sextus; Triumvirate, Second

References

MacKay, Christopher. *The Breakdown of the Roman Republic: From Oligarchy to Empire.* Cambridge: Cambridge University Press, 2009.

Osgood, Josiah. *Caesar's Legacy: Civil War and the Emergence of the Roman Empire.* Cambridge: Cambridge University Press, 2006.

Weigel, Richard. *Lepidus, the Tarnished Triumvir.* London: Routledge, 1992.

Aemilius Paullus, Lucius

Lucius Aemilius Paullus was born in the late third century BCE into an old patrician family. His father, L. Aemilius Paullus, was one of the two commanders at the Battle of Cannae in 216 and died there. One of his sons was adopted into the Scipio family and became Scipio Aemilianus. Little is known of Paullus' life or career before the 190s, when he served as military tribune.

Elected praetor for 191, Paullus served his term in Spain and continued there for several more years, winning a victory. He was consul and proconsul serving in southern Gaul in 182–181, during which he won a major victory. He was consul again in 168 and received command against Perseus of Macedon.

On arriving in Greece, Paullus found the soldiers poorly trained and undisciplined, so he spent some time restoring order and training the units. He moved against Perseus and tried to surround him with a secret flanking maneuver, but when Paullus lost the surprise, Perseus moved quickly north. Paullus followed, and the two sides met at Pydna in June 168. Paullus kept his nerve despite an initial bad start and won the battle handily, his cavalry chasing the survivors.

The battle effectively ended the Third Macedonian War. Afterward Paullus extorted wealth from cities that had supported Perseus; he sacked Epirus. He celebrated a triumph but pursued no further military activity.

Lee L. Brice

See also: Cannae, Battle of; Cornelius Scipio Aemilianus Africanus, Publius; Macedonian Wars; Pydna, Battle of; Spanish Wars

References

Eckstein, Arthur. *Rome Enters the Greek East: From Anarchy to Hierarchy in the Hellenistic Mediterranean, 230–170 BC.* Oxford, UK: Wiley-Blackwell, 2008.

Harris, W. V. *War and Imperialism in Republican Rome, 327–70 B.C.* Oxford: Oxford University Press, 1985.

Hoyos, Dexter, ed. *A Companion to Roman Imperialism.* Leiden: Brill, 2012.

Agrippa, Marcus Vipsanius. *See* Vipsanius Agrippa, Marcus

Allies, Roman

The process that led to Roman control of Italy south of the Po River by 396–265 BCE resulted in a network of alliances between Rome and the cities and peoples of Italy. It is inappropriate to call it a system of alliances, because doing so suggests more regularity and interconnectedness than actually existed. Italian allies were called *socii*. The alliance network evolved over time but typically shared some common features.

Some cities, such as Veii, and much of Latium became part of the Roman territory proper with full citizenship. Other cities, colonies, and peoples received varying levels of partial citizenship with certain rights. Most allies enjoyed no such rights and were tied to Rome either by friendship because they sought Roman alliance or through treaties. The nature of these relationships varied depending on how much resistance Rome had to overcome.

Generally, in return for security, peace, freedom from taxation, and some internal independence, allies surrendered control over foreign policy and had to provide and equip troops for Rome's wars. According to Polybius, by the third century each ally had a specific number of men it was required to provide and equip in war; thus, Roman leaders could measure the manpower reserves. The manpower requirement meant that Rome could draw upon an immense manpower reserve when it needed to do so. This fact was a key reason why Rome could lose battles and still win wars.

Allied units were organized as *ala* (pl., *alae*) by 311 and fought alongside the legions, on the flanks. Originally, each *ala* included cavalry and infantry totaling about the same as a legion but entirely noncitizen. Roman officers usually led these units. With allies providing troops at a ratio of one to one or more to legionaries, it is easy to understand Hannibal's strategy of detaching Italian allies in the Second Punic War.

Rome never explicitly promised to give allies citizenship, but there was an unstated expectation of that reward for loyalty. During the Second Punic War the relationship between allies and Rome changed, leading to increasing frustration by the end of the second century. In 91 the allies' frustration erupted into the Social War, which went badly for Rome at first because the allies knew how Rome fought. The war mostly ended when

Rome granted full citizenship to all allies who stopped fighting and eventually to all Italian allies. As a result, former allies were now legionaries, swelling the legionary manpower pool.

Rome also made alliances with states and peoples outside Italy, but these allies functioned differently from a military standpoint and are typically called *auxilia*. Non-Italian allies usually provided local specialist units such as cavalry and archers. In the first century, only allied cavalry units were called *alae,* and they completely displaced Roman cavalry. Allied units of these local types were critical to Pompey and Caesar in their campaigns and to all sides in the civil wars.

Allies remain the forgotten element in Roman military history. Providing half or more of most Roman armies before 91 and continuing to play a role outside Italy afterward, the allies made it possible for Rome to acquire an empire and retain it.

Lee L. Brice

See also: Julius Caesar, Gaius; Polybius; Pompeius Magnus, Gnaeus; Punic Wars; Rome; Social War

References

Cornell, T. J. *The Beginnings of Rome: Italy and Rome from the Bronze Age to the Punic Wars (1000–264 BC).* London: Routledge, 1995.

Keppie, Lawrence J. F. *The Making of the Roman Army: From Republic to Empire.* Updated ed. Norman: University of Oklahoma Press, 1998.

Rosenstein, N., and R. Morstein-Marx, eds. *A Companion to the Roman Republic.* Oxford, UK: Blackwell, 2010.

Anthony, Mark. *See* Antonius, Marcus

Antonius, Marcus

Marcus Antonius, commonly known as Mark Antony, was born around 82 BCE into a plebeian family. His father, Creticus, died while Antony was young, and his mother, Julia, was a distant relative of Julius Caesar. As a young adult, Antony followed a typical political path, first gaining military experience.

Antony quickly made a name for himself as a resourceful and talented leader. He served as a cavalry officer and then as commander in military campaigns in Judaea and Egypt during 57–54. Caesar learned of Antony and made him an associate. Over the next several years, Antony participated in the concluding phase of Caesar's conquest of Gaul.

When a civil war erupted in 49 between Caesar and Pompey, Antony was a tribune of the plebeians and loyally backed Caesar until he was forced to flee. Antony served in Italy in 49, and Caesar left him in charge of Italy that year. Antony fought in Greece in 48, commanding Caesar's left at the Battle of Pharsalus. Afterward Caesar made him his master of the horse and sent him to stabilize Italy. However, Caesar eventually became dissatisfied with Antony's rule over Italy and removed him from that position in late 47.

In early 44 Antony returned to Caesar's inner circle as a consul, just in time to be in an advantageous position when Caesar was assassinated in March. Antony used every means at his disposal to remain in power, and in June 44 the Senate granted him governorship of several regions in Gaul.

This idealized bust of Marcus Antonius was carved after his death. He was one of Caesar's lieutenants and a member of the Second Triumvirate. An accomplished commander, he made a number of political missteps that led to his suicide in 30 BCE. (Bettmann/Corbis)

Antony used the assassination of Caesar to agitate the Roman people against the assassins, especially Marcus Junius Brutus and Gaius Cassius Longinus. At the time, Antony's talent for brilliant oratory as well as his successes on the battlefield caused his stature as a popular leader to grow. Despite the popular support that he initially enjoyed, Antony fell afoul of competition for power in Rome and was forced by the Senate to march out. In addition, Octavian, Caesar's adopted son, emerged as a rival to

Antony. A coalition of forces, including Octavian's legions, defeated Antony at Mutina in 43, forcing him to withdraw to the southern part of Gaul.

Despite the loss, Antony linked up with Lepidus in southern Gaul. After negotiating with Octavian, in November 43 the three men formed a five-year pact called the Second Triumvirate. The threesome quickly disposed of their enemies, including Cicero, to secure their hold on power. The following year Antony distinguished himself in the Battle of Philippi, at the end of which Brutus and Cassius both committed suicide.

After Philippi, the triumvirs agreed to divide the empire, with Antony receiving control over the eastern provinces. He went east to raise money for the soldiers. While in the east, he became reacquainted with Cleopatra VII of Egypt. He needed her wealth and grain, while she needed his protection to retain her independence. What may have begun as a mutually beneficial relationship became romantic by late 41. After Antony's wife, Fulvia, and his brother, Lucius Antonius, had ignited and lost the Perusine War in 41–40, Antony returned to Italy where, now a widower, he married Octavia, Octavian's sister, to seal the peace in the triumvirate.

However, Antony sent his wife back to Italy in 37 and resumed his relationship with Cleopatra. He used funds and supplies from Egypt in his invasion of Parthia in 36, but the invasion ended in near catastrophe. The defeat in Parthia and his treatment of Octavia hurt Antony's reputation in Rome.

In 34 Antony staged a ceremony in which Cleopatra was pronounced as queen of kings, and the children they had also received royal titles. In Roman circles, many regarded Antony's actions as an affront. Octavian and Antony launched propaganda attacks on one another in 34–32. In 32 the propaganda led to Rome declaring war on Cleopatra. Antony still had loyal supporters; it was far easier for Octavian to portray Cleopatra as a threat to Rome.

Both sides gathered forces in western Greece, and by September 31 Agrippa, Octavian's naval commander, had blockaded Antony and Cleopatra at Actium. In the ensuing Battle of Actium, Antony lost much of his fleet, but some ships broke out and sailed to Egypt. His large land army surrendered without fighting. Back in Egypt they tried to put up a defense the following summer, but Octavian's forces captured Alexandria. Realizing that further resistance was futile, Antony committed suicide in Alexandria in 30.

Antony's death effectively ended the Roman civil wars that had dragged on from 49 to 30 and led directly to the emergence of the Roman Empire. Antony was vilified in Octavian's propaganda but was later romanticized in Western literature, thus making the real man difficult to separate from the legend.

Mark Haviland

See also: Actium, Battle of; Aemilius Lepidus, Marcus; Cassius Longinus, Gaius; Civil War II; Civil War III; Cleopatra VII; Gallic Wars; Julius Caesar, Gaius; Julius Caesar Octavianus, Gaius; Junius Brutus, Marcus; Parthian Empire; Pharsalus, Battle of; Philippi, Battle of; Pompeius Magnus, Gnaeus; Pompeius Magnus, Sextus; Triumvirate, Second; Vipsanius Agrippa, Marcus

References

MacKay, Christopher. *The Breakdown of the Roman Republic: From Oligarchy to Empire.* Cambridge: Cambridge University Press, 2009.
Osgood, Josiah. *Caesar's Legacy: Civil War and the Emergence of the Roman Empire.* Cambridge: Cambridge University Press, 2006.
Southern, Pat. *Mark Antony.* Charleston, SC: Tempus, 1998.

Detail of *lorica hamata* armor and an oval *scutum* from the base of Trajan's Column, originally in Trajan's Forum, Rome. (Lee L. Brice)

Arms and Armor, Roman

Evidence for military equipment before 60 BCE is extremely limited; therefore, historians draw heavily from paintings, reliefs, and archaeological remains to analyze early equipment. At all times increasing body armor was expensive and heavy, so most soldiers used less before Marius' reforms.

During the early Roman period before the late third century, Roman soldiers seem to have been equipped with an Italian version of Greek hoplite equipment, including helmets, elongated shields, chest protection, spears or javelins, swords, and perhaps greaves. Since Roman citizens were expected to provide their own gear, equipment varied greatly in quantity, quality, and adornment depending on a soldier's wealth. Men who could afford it purchased a metal cuirass (chest plate), while the less wealthy would perhaps have a stiff linen corselet or some variant in between. Skirmishers (*velites*) carried javelins and small shields with little or no armor, while the other three ranks (*hastati, principes,* and *triarii*) were more heavily armored.

According to Polybius, the armament carried by legionaries by the end of the Second Punic War was more recognizable, including a helmet, often of the Montefortino type; an oval shield two and a half feet wide and four feet long called a *scutum;* greaves; two heavy javelins called a *pilum* (pl. *pila*); and a short Spanish sword commonly called the *gladius.* The *triarii* may have carried a stabbing spear instead of *pila,* while the skirmishers carried a small round shield and javelins. By the early second century, all soldiers who could afford it wore chain mail body armor called *lorica hamata,* while the poorer improvised with a metal chest plate. Allies seem to have been similarly equipped.

These were an effective combination. The shield, helmet, and greaves gave a great deal of protection to soldiers, and the *lorica hamata* was worth its greater price and weight. The weight of the *lorica* is an underappreciated burden on soldiers that would exhaust them in exchange for the protection. The *pila* were thrown before engaging, and then soldiers employed the double-edged short sword to stab at opponents from behind the shield. There were in a practical sense no left-handed soldiers—everyone held the sword in their right hand. Proper shield position was to stand with the left foot forward, bracing the bottom of the shield held in the left hand, and with the right leg back, with the foot parallel to the shoulders. The shield was not just for defense. It was supposed to be used as a weapon to smash into an opponent and gain an advantage.

After Marius' reforms of the military, legionary equipment gradually became standardized as the state provided more of it, and the legionary organization had dropped the distinctive three-line maniples in favor of cohorts. Every legionary wore a Monteforino-type helmet that provided protection for the neck and cheeks as well as the skull. Shields were made of wood laminate and were oblong, four or so feet long and around two feet wide, with a long metal boss on the front. Everyone except the skirmishers had such a shield and greaves. Skirmishers seem to still have carried smaller round shields. The *pilum* became the standard javelin, and it now had a weakened shaft pin that would break on impact with rocks and shields so that it could not be thrown back. Every legionary carried two *pila*. Everyone carried a *gladius* instead of a stabbing spear. This was the recognizable legionary. Marius had also introduced gladiator-style training to the military. In addition to having to learn weapon use, men were required to maintain their weapons and pay for any replacements if they lost their equipment.

After the Social War there were no Italian allies to carry distinctive-looking gear, so the legion looked standardized. There were *auxilia,* but these provided their own armor and weapons since they were specialized units.

Legionary arms and armor were, by the first century, the result of a long process of adoption and adaptation to the needs of extended fighting against an array of opponents. The combination was extremely effective, as demonstrated by Roman success.

Lee L. Brice

See also: Artillery; Legion, Cohort; Legion, Manipular/Polybian; Marius, Gaius; Polybius; Training

References

Bishop, M. C., and J. C. Coulston. *Roman Military Equipment: From the Punic Wars to the Fall of Rome.* 2nd ed. Oxford, UK: Oxbow, 2011.

James, Simon. *Rome and the Sword: How Warriors and Weapons Shaped Roman History.* London: Thames and Hudson, 2011.

Tritle, Lawrence A., and J. Brian Campbell, eds. *The Oxford Handbook of Classical Military History.* Oxford: Oxford University Press, 2012.

Artillery

Invented by Greeks during the mid-fourth century BCE, torsion catapults were an important element in Roman sieges. These weapons used springs made of rope coils to store the energy that propelled two throwing arms. Because the amount of stored energy could be much greater than in tension catapults, these weapons had greater range (300 yards or more) and could fire rocks (*ballistae*) or arrow-tipped bolts (scorpions). The length of the springs determined the range and size of the projectile so that a variety of sizes evolved.

Romans adopted the catapult from the Greeks, perhaps as early as the third century, and continued to improve its design. The *ballistae* threw stones and came in many different sizes capable of throwing a stone as large as 200 pounds, though they normally threw smaller stones. Scorpions shot arrow-like bolts at a tremendous range. There were manuals on building *ballistae* and scorpions and formulas for the length of springs and the weight of shot or bolts. In the Roman military catapults seem to have been built and maintained by specialists.

During the Roman Republic, artillery was used exclusively in siege operations. The range of artillery made it useful for intimidation, providing cover fire for soldiers assaulting walls, and firing on an enemy assault. Artillery probably was less useful in knocking down hardened walls, but there are examples of artillery knocking down weak walls and towers, and it was effective in wearing down enemy morale. Although there is no example in our sources of Romans using a *ballista* in open battle during the Republic, it proved effective in this role later.

Lee L. Brice

See also: Siege

References

Marsden, Eric W. *Greek and Roman Artillery: Historical Development.* Oxford, UK: Clarendon, 1969.

Sabin, Philip, Hans Van Wees, and Michael Whitby, eds. *The Cambridge History of Greek and Roman Warfare,* Vol. 2. Cambridge: Cambridge University Press, 2007.

Augustus. *See* Julius Caesar Octavianus, Gaius

B

Brutus, Marcus Junius. *See* Junius Brutus, Marcus

C

Caesar, Gaius Julius. *See* Julius Caesar, Gaius

Camp Followers. *See* Slaves and Camp Followers

Cannae, Battle of

During the Second Punic War Hannibal had invaded Italy in 218 and won a string of victories against Roman forces as he marched down the east coast. His army included mercenary infantry from Spain and North Africa as well as a large cavalry force augmented with recruits from among the Gauls of northern Italy. In response to the defeats, Rome selected Fabius Maximus as dictator for six months. Realizing Hannibal's capability in battle, Fabius sought a strategy of avoiding battle but shadowing and harassing Carthaginian forces. Because of this strategy he came to be known as "Cunctator" (the Delayer).

Impatient, in 216 the Romans replaced Fabius with two consuls, Gaius Terentius Varro and Lucius Aemilius Paullus. Normally Varro and Paullus would have had independent commands. This time the Senate ordered them to combine their forces in order to meet and defeat Hannibal once and for all. Together they commanded eight enlarged legions (5,000 infantry and 300 cavalry rather than 4,000 infantry and 200 cavalry). The troops received minimal training before moving into the field to tackle Hannibal, who was then in Apulia on the Adriatic coast. Counting their allied forces, Varro and Paullus commanded as many as 87,000 men, including a larger infantry force, but had fewer cavalry than Hannibal, who had as many as 50,000 Carthaginian and allied troops (40,000 infantry and 10,000 cavalry).

The two Roman commanders may not have gotten along, but as tradition dictated, they alternated command daily. Varro, who had the command one summer day when it looked like Hannibal was at a disadvantage, ordered both armies to engage. The consuls led their forces onto an open plain on the right bank of the Aufidus River, Paullus having detached some 10,000 of his men to guard his camp. Varro positioned the Roman cavalry on both flanks, and since his forces were far superior in numbers, he apparently arranged the infantry in a more compact center mass than was the custom, with short distances between the maniples in deep formation. Varro seemed to have intended to drive through the Carthaginian center, smashing it and then mopping up the Carthaginian wings in turn. Polybius' story that the two commanders quarreled may have been an exaggeration stimulated by the Scipio family.

Hannibal drew up his army in a linear formation. His superior cavalry was on the flanks. The infantry was in the center, and Hannibal placed his best-trained African heavy infantry on either side, with the center formed of Spanish and Gallic infantry in a convex position. His strategy was to pull back his center slowly and lure the Roman army into a trap while his cavalry eliminated the Roman cavalry.

The Romans pushed forward into Hannibal's planned withdrawal and appeared to be successful initially. With the Romans apparently having broken through, Hannibal ordered his African infantry on each side of the line to wheel in. His cavalry then returned from their pursuit of the Roman cavalry and closed behind the close-packed Roman infantry, who were blinded by the dust kicked up on the dry plain. Many men, including the consul Paullus, died in the melee. Over the next several days the Carthaginians attacked both Roman camps and killed or captured many more Romans; only about 14,500 men got away, Varro among them. The Carthaginian side lost 5,700 dead, of whom 4,000 were Celts, but two or three times this number were probably wounded. Hannibal's double envelopment of a numerically superior enemy was remarkable.

Following the battle, a number of Roman allies (mostly Greek cities) in southern Italy joined Hannibal, but he did not march on Rome. The Romans redoubled their efforts and returned to Fabius' policies, harassing Hannibal

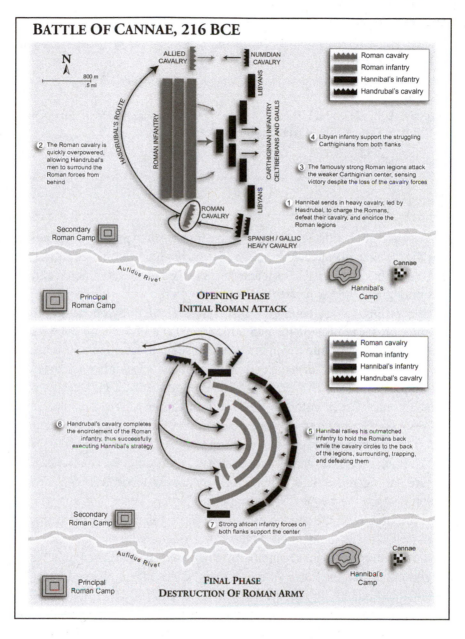

BATTLE OF CANNAE, 216 BCE

OPENING PHASE
INITIAL ROMAN ATTACK

Roman cavalry
Roman infantry
Hannibal's infantry
Handrubal's cavalry

2 The Roman cavalry is quickly overpowered, allowing Handrubal's men to surround the Roman forces from behind

4 Libyan infantry support the struggling Carthiginians from both flanks

3 The famously strong Roman legions attack the weaker Carthiginian center, sensing victory despite the loss of the cavalry forces

1 Hannibal sends in heavy cavalry, led by Hasdrubal, to charge the Romans, defeat their cavalry, and encirlce the Roman legions

ALLIED CAVALRY   NUMIDIAN CAVALRY

LIBYANS

ROMAN INFANTRY

CARTHIGINIAN INFANTRY CELTIBERIANS AND GAULS

LIBYANS

HASDRUBAL'S ROUTE

ROMAN CAVALRY

SPANISH / GALLIC HEAVY CAVALRY

Secondary Roman Camp

Principal Roman Camp

Aufidus River

Cannae

Hannibal's Camp

FINAL PHASE
DESTRUCTION OF ROMAN ARMY

Roman cavalry
Roman infantry
Hannibal's infantry
Handrubal's cavalry

6 Handrubal's cavalry completes the encirclement of the Roman infantry, thus successfully executing Hannibal's strategy

5 Hannibal rallies his outmatched infantry to hold the Romans back while the cavalry circles to the back of the legions, surrounding, trapping, and defeating them

7 Strong african infantry forces on both flanks support the center

Secondary Roman Camp

Principal Roman Camp

Aufidus River

Cannae

Hannibal's Camp

N
800 m
.5 mi

and now his allies too. Cannae was a disaster for Rome, but Rome was able to recover as a result of its alliance network, most of which did not defect.

Spencer C. Tucker

See also: Allies, Roman; Fabius Maximus Verrucosus, Quintus; Hannibal; Punic Wars

References

Daly, G. *Cannae: The Experience of Battle in the Second Punic War.* London: Routledge, 2001.

Hoyos, Dexter, ed. *A Companion to the Punic Wars.* Oxford, UK: Wiley-Blackwell, 2011.

Lazenby, J. F. *Hannibal's War: A Military History of the Second Punic War.* Norman: University of Oklahoma Press, 1998.

Carthage

The city-state of Carthage, a North African port north of present-day Tunisia, was the first Phoenician colony west of Egypt, having been settled from Tyre in the eighth century BCE. Carthage developed extensive commercial interests throughout the Mediterranean, especially in the western regions.

According to our sources, when Tyre fell to Babylon in the sixth century, Carthage became the natural leader of the Phoenician colonies in North Africa, Sicily, and Spain but does not seem to have led an empire in the traditional sense. Carthage certainly exercised great influence over the colonies, most of which were not politically independent in the same way contemporary Greek colonies were. Within the city were a council and judges who administered the state. The military commanders were important posts elected separately from the top two city leaders.

Carthage was militarily active at sea, enforcing its dominance of certain sailing routes and allying with Etruscans to occasionally defeat Greek fleets in the western Mediterranean. Perhaps because Rome had no maritime interests, the two cities had amicable relations for more than a century. Carthage maintained its position of economic prominence until the third century, when it succumbed to the Romans during the Punic Wars. Beginning in 264, the Punic Wars were waged due to complicated issues of expansion, regional hegemony, and territorial control. Over the course of the wars Carthage's military prominence dissipated, but it remained commercially effective. The final war ended in 146 with Scipio Aemilianus sacking and razing Carthage, selling the inhabitants into slavery, and even spreading salt on the site to symbolically ensure its permanent infertility.

Rome absorbed the territory as the province of Africa. During the first century, Rome created a colony on the site that became a wealthy and important city in the province.

Mike Dixon-Kennedy

Ruins of Carthage, present-day Tunisia. The city of Carthage was destroyed by the Romans following the siege of 149–146 BCE. The Romans established a colony on the site in 122 BCE, which grew to be an important port city. (Itanart/Dreamstime.com)

See also: Cornelius Scipio Aemilianus Africanus, Publius; Hannibal; Punic Wars; Punic Wars, Causes of the; Punic Wars, Consequences of the

References

Hoyos, Dexter. *The Carthaginians.* London: Routledge, 2010.

Hoyos, Dexter, ed. *A Companion to the Punic Wars.* Oxford, UK: Wiley-Blackwell, 2011.

Cassius Longinus, Gaius

Gaius Cassius Longinus was born circa 85 BCE in Rome. Nothing is known for certain about his career before he became quaestor under Crassus in 54. Cassius was still serving with Crassus in 53 but survived the defeat at Carrhae and organized the survivors to defend Syria.

Cassius returned to Rome in 50 and supported Pompey in the civil war that began the following year. After Pharsalus, Cassius requested and received clemency from Caesar. Cassius was praetor in 44 and acted as one of the leaders in the assassination plot against Caesar. When Cassius and the other assassins departed Italy, Cassius made his way to Syria, where local commanders defected to him and he prepared for civil war. Although his fortunes rose after Antony's defeat in the spring of 43, when the Second Triumvirate formed in October of that year, they declared Cassius a public enemy.

Cassius and Brutus gathered a larger army and squeezed the eastern provinces for supplies and wealth to pay the soldiers. They marched into Thrace in 42, meeting Antony and Octavian in October at Philippi. In the first day of the battle, Cassius lost to Antony and committed suicide before learning that Brutus had won against Octavian.

Lee L. Brice

See also: Antonius, Marcus; Civil War II; Civil War III; Julius Caesar, Gaius; Julius Caesar Octavianus, Gaius; Junius Brutus, Marcus; Licinius Crassus, Marcus; Philippi, Battle of; Triumvirate, Second

References

MacKay, Christopher. *The Breakdown of the Roman Republic: From Oligarchy to Empire.* Cambridge: Cambridge University Press, 2009.

Osgood, Josiah. *Caesar's Legacy: Civil War and the Emergence of the Roman Empire.* Cambridge: Cambridge University Press, 2006.

Cavalry

During much of the Roman Republic, cavalry seems to have been of mixed effectiveness in Roman warfare. Reasons for this record can be found in the expense of horses, the topography, the dominance of legions, and the bias of the sources. During the period down to the early first century BCE, Roman cavalry consisted of citizens who provided their own horses and enjoyed a higher status as a result. When employed in tasks for which they were suited, such as scouting, pursuit, and flank attack cavalry could make a difference. After the early first century Rome employed non-Italian allied *auxilia* cavalry.

Sources discuss cavalry activity occasionally in the wars of the early Republic, but the information we receive is so shrouded in nostalgia that it is of little value. We learn more in the middle Republic during Rome's expansion but still not a great deal of detail. Roman cavalry certainly played a role in the Punic Wars, fighting and scouting in Sicily as well as in Italy, but it seems to have performed less effectively than local cavalry in Gaul, Spain, and North Africa. Roman cavalry was ineffective in actual

Allied (*auxilia*) Roman cavalry on the left chasing armored Dacian cavalry. Rome employed primarily allied cavalry by the early-first century BCE. Detail from Trajan's Column, in Trajan's Forum, Rome. (Lee L. Brice)

battle against Hannibal's cavalry and receives little mention with Scipio, but it does seem to have performed well in scouting.

Once Romans encountered foreign cavalry and made treaties with foreign states that had good cavalry, they came to rely on cavalry more regularly. Despite this reliance, Roman cavalry still appear in most war and battle narratives until the Social War. From then on, Roman citizen cavalry units seem to have been disbanded. The units may have been eliminated due to manpower crisis during the Social War, but it is not clear why they were not re-formed after the war.

Cavalry could be armed with a variety of weapons, including javelins or a heavy spear or sword (or both). Their defensive equipment included a helmet and a small shield as well as a cuirass. This period predated the use of saddle, stirrups, and horseshoes. Since riders lacked saddles and stirrups, they could not really act as shock cavalry. A second disadvantage of cavalry was logistical; horses required more water, fodder, and care than their riders and could be a drain on a force under siege or in difficult terrain.

Despite these limitations on equipment, there were a variety of tasks, both independent and in support of infantry, in which cavalry engaged. The tasks for which cavalry most commonly was used were scouting and raiding as well as pursuit, harassment of enemy detachments, and flank protection/attack, all of which could be defensive or offensive actions.

Since legions were vulnerable on their flanks, commanders would place cavalry on the flanks of their battle line. In this position the cavalry played a critical role at Cannae, Zama, and Pharsalus. Heavy infantry that stood its ground could defeat or at least frustrate cavalry, such as at Pharsalus, so cavalry was better employed in hit-and-run and surprise maneuvers.

The traditional view that Rome eliminated citizen cavalry due to its ineffectiveness has been shown recently to be incorrect. There are numerous instances when Roman cavalry performed well, despite limitations common to all cavalries. Numidian, Gallic, Spanish, and Thessalian cavalry were all employed by Rome and its enemies before the second century, and all were recognized as high-quality units. The exclusive adoption of allied cavalry was probably the result of various factors, including expense, flexibility, availability, and familiarity with enemies and regions subject to Roman expansion.

The presence of cavalry in nearly every Roman warfare narrative that survives demonstrates the important potential of cavalry. It is of little surprise, then, that the use of *auxilia* cavalry continued long after the end of the Republic.

Lee L. Brice

See also: Cannae, Battle of; Hannibal; Julius Caesar, Gaius; Pharsalus, Battle of; Parthian Empire; Punic Wars; Social War; Zama, Battle of

References

Keppie, L. J. F. *The Making of the Roman Army: From Republic to Empire.* Updated ed. Norman: University of Oklahoma Press, 1998.

McCall, J. *The Cavalry of the Roman Republic: Cavalry Combat and Elite Reputations in the Middle and Late Republic.* London: Routledge, 2002.

Celts

The Celts were an ancient population that dominated Northern and Western Europe prior to the Roman Empire. The Celtic peoples consisted of a conglomeration of independent groups that were culturally connected. Defining the Celts is problematic, as the various sources—archaeological, linguistic, and historical—do not always agree. The evidence reveals a sophisticated culture that had its origins in the 14th century BCE and transformed over time, reaching a peak in the La Tène culture when Celts settled from Ireland to Anatolia, engaged in long-distance trade, and had already demonstrated the battle prowess that would impress classical writers down to the Roman invasions of Britain.

Recorded Roman encounters with Celtic culture first occurred when a raiding group sacked Rome circa 387. From then on, Romans remained vigilant about Celtic incursions and often found themselves fighting Celtic (Gallic) bands allied with their opponents in Etruria. Celts of northern Italy, the Gauls, were a continual threat during the fourth and third centuries. There was significant Gallic war beginning in 225 that required extraordinary Roman mobilization. The Gauls joined Hannibal and Hasdrubal during the Second Punic War. Rome began seriously subjugating the Celtic regions in the area between the Po River and the Alps after 225 and had finished the process by the first century. Celtic preeminence in Europe waned with Roman advances into northern Italy and then Spain and the conquest of most of Gaul.

As did other commanders in the first century, Caesar relied heavily on allied (*auxilia*) Celtic cavalry during his wars. He also provides much of our literary evidence about Celtic culture in the first century. Celtic peoples were part of the empire's fabric by the end of the Roman Republic and were even serving in the Senate and the military.

James Emmons

See also: Gallic Wars; Julius Caesar, Gaius; Punic Wars

References

James, Simon. *The World of the Celts.* London: Thames and Hudson, 2005.
Rankin, David. *Celts and the Classical World.* 2nd ed. London: Routledge, 1996.

Centurions

Centurions were the primary junior-rank officers of the Roman legions. As they were leading at the century level, the centurions were the officers with whom each soldier was probably most familiar and were key to successful management of the legion in battle and in camp. Polybius is our best source for these officers of the middle Roman Republic.

There were 60 centurions for a legion, each responsible for a century. The century was an administrative unit, not a combat unit, so centurions were responsible for all aspects of managing their century as well as for training, discipline, and the like. In combat, the two centurions of each maniple worked together to lead the unit, the centurion on the right being the higher rank. The highest-ranking centurion led the maniple of *triarii* stationed farthest right and was called *centurio primi pili*. Each centurion was assisted by an *optio* of lower rank, who would stand behind the century, and a variety of staff. Although it was once common for historians to characterize centurions as the equivalent of modern noncommissioned officers, such a label is anachronistic and inapplicable, given their responsibilities.

The commander (or rarely the military tribunes) selected centurions from the ranks. They were experienced soldiers who had proven their mettle and could read. By the time of Caesar there was a promotion pattern within legions, as centurions could be promoted through cohorts from 10th to 1st, and it was common to be promoted into a different legion. In return for the greater responsibilities, they received more pay. Despite this difference in pay, centurions were from the ranks and tended to side with their soldiers in mutinies. Octavian tried to counteract this pattern by granting centurions so many benefits that they would be separated from the soldiers by a huge status gulf and would no longer identify with them, a plan that eventually met with success.

Centurions were important unit leaders in combat, so they always suffered the greatest casualties as a percentage of officers in hard fighting, as demonstrated repeatedly in Caesar's *Commentaries*. Caesar paid special attention to centurions not only in combat but also when he was in camp or on the verge of disciplinary trouble, which suggests their importance in successful command.

Lee L. Brice

See also: Discipline; Julius Caesar, Gaius; Julius Caesar Octavianus, Gaius; Legion, Cohort; Legion, Manipular/Polybian; Legionary Commanders; Mutiny; Polybius; Training; Tribunes, Military

References

Brice, Lee L. "Disciplining Octavian: An Aspect of Roman Military Culture during the Triumviral Wars, 44–30 BCE." In *Warfare and Culture in World History,* edited by Wayne Lee, 35–60. New York: New York University Press, 2011.

Caesar. *War Commentaries of Caesar.* Translated by Rex Warner. New York: New American Library, 1960.

Keppie, L. J. F. *The Making of the Roman Army: From Republic to Empire.* Updated ed. Norman: University of Oklahoma Press, 1998.

Polybius. *Histories.* Translated by R. Waterfield and B. McGing. Oxford: Oxford University Press, 2010.

Cinna, Lucius Cornelius. *See* Cornelius Cinna, Lucius

Civil War I

Sulla was elected as consul for 88 BCE and given command by the Senate of the war against Mithradates VI. This was recognition of Sulla's success in the Social War; however, a tribune, Sulpicius, proposed and passed a law to give the command to Marius. He had achieved military greatness earlier and was seeking one last glorious campaign. Because tradition rather than law defined the Senate's powers, what Sulpicius did was irregular but legal. Sulla returned to his legions in Campania.

Marius sent officers to take command of Sulla's legions, but Sulla's soldiers stoned them to death. Sulla then harangued the legions on how his honor and the Senate had been attacked but, more important, also said that Marius and his soldiers would enjoy the booty of a foreign war. The soldiers voted to support him if he marched on Rome. Many of them had been poor citizens before volunteering for the military, so they welcomed opportunities to enrich themselves with booty from a foreign war and were inclined to support a commander who provided such opportunities. Sulla marched on Rome, where Sulpicius fled and was killed as Marius fled to Africa, and restored order. Sulla forced Cinna, consul for 87, to uphold Sulla's position. Sulla's march on Rome was the beginning of Civil War I, and it is unlikely that anyone expected it or its repercussions.

When Sulla departed for his war, Cinna changed his position and proposed laws against Sulla's acts. Cinna was forced to flee Rome and sought support among former allies of Rome. Marius, who had been in North Africa raising an army among the communities where his veterans had been settled, joined him. Together they marched on Rome, eliminating opposition along the way. Once in control, they purged many enemies, declared Sulla and his officers outlaws, and had themselves made consuls for 86. Marius died several weeks into office, leaving Cinna in nominal charge of the Republic to prepare for Sulla's eventual return. In 84 while preparing to resist Sulla, the men mutinied and murdered Cinna. The remaining consul, Carbo, made arrangements to face Sulla.

Sulla had defeated Mithradates several times but heard about Cinna's activities and so allowed Mithradates to get away and then signed a peace treaty that resolved nothing. Having settled things in the east sufficiently for the time being, Sulla sailed for Italy. Crassus and Pompey joined him in

Chart 1 Key Events of the First Roman Civil War, 88–82 BCE

Event Name	Date	Region/ Locale	Key Commanders (if known)	Combatant numbers*	Victor**
Mithradates VI invades Roman Asia and Greece	88	Bithynia, Greece	Mithradates VI, Archelaus, Neoptolemus vs. Nicomedes, M. Aquilius, C. Cassius, Q. Oppius, Q. Sentius,	40,000+ men, 10,000 cavalry vs. 3+ legions, auxilia	Mithradates
First Mithradatic War Starts	June 88	Rome	L. Cornelius Sulla	6 legions	—
Marius Given Command	Summer 88	Rome	G. Marius	—	—
Sulla marches on Rome and "restores order"; Civil war	Summer 88	Rome	Sulla, L. Licinius Lucullus vs. G. Marius	6 legions	Sulla
Marius departs Rome	Summer 88	Rome	—	—	—
Sulla leaves for Greece	Fall 88	Brundisium	Sulla, L. Licinius Lucullus	6 legions	—
Roman defense of Greece	Fall 88–87	Greece	Archelaus vs. Q. Bruttius Sura	3 legions vs. ?	Bruttius/ S
Sulla arrives in Central Greece	Spring 87	Greece	Lucullus, Sulla	6 legions, auxilia	—
Cinna leaves Rome amid rioting	Spring 87	Rome	L. Cornelius Cinna, Q. Sertorius	—	—
Siege of Athens	87–March 1, 86	Greece	Sulla, C. Curio vs. Aristion, Archelaus	? vs. ?	Sulla
Siege of Piraeus	87–Spring 86	Greece	Sulla vs. Archelaus,	? vs. ?	Sulla
Marius returns from Africa	Late 87	Italy	Marius (elder), G. Marius (younger)	6000 men	—

Event Name	Date	Region/Locale	Key Commanders (if known)	Combatant numbers*	Victor**
Cinna acquires legions	Late 87	Campania	Cinna, Sertorius, A. Claudius Pulcher	2+ legions, auxilia	Cinna/M
Second march on Rome and siege	87	Rome	Cinna, Sertorius, Marius (elder), Gn. Papirius Carbo vs. Gn. Octavius, Pompeius Strabo, Q. Caecilius Metellus Pius	7+ legions, auxilia vs. ? legions	—
Capture of Ostia	87	Near Rome	Marius (elder), G. Marius (younger)	3 legions vs. ?	Marius
Assault on Janiculum Hill	Late 87	Rome	Marius (elder), vs. Octavius, Pompeius Strabo	2–3 legions, auxilia vs. ? legions	Octavianus/S
Fall of Rome	Late 87	Rome	Cinna, Sertorius, Marius (elder), vs. Octavius, Metellus	7+ legions vs. 3+ legions	Cinna/M
Battle of Chaeronea	Spring 86	Central Greece	Sulla, L. Murena, L. Hortensius vs. Archelaus Taxiles	3 legions, cavalry, auxilia vs. 30,000–45,000 infantry, cavalry	Sulla
Flaccus is sent east vs. Sulla	Summer 86	Rome	L. Valerius Flaccus, C. Flavius Fimbria	2 legions	

(*Continued*)

Chart 1 Key Events of the First Roman Civil War, 88–82 BCE (Continued)

Event Name	Date	Region/ Locale	Key Commanders (if known)	Combatant numbers*	Victor**
Battle of Orchomenos	Summer 86	Central Greece	Sulla, L. Murena, L. Hortensius vs. Archelaus Taxiles	4? legions, cavalry, auxilia vs. 80,000 infantry, cavalry, chariots	Sulla
Sulla opens peace overtures	Late 86	Greece	Sulla and Mithradates VI	—	—
Flaccus pushes into Asia	Late 86–85	Thrace	L. Valerius Flaccus, C. Flavius Fimbria	2 legions	Flaccus/ M
Flaccus is murdered by Fimbria	Spring 85	Nicomedia	L. Valerius Flaccus vs. C. Flavius Fimbria	2 legions	Fimbria/ M
Battle of Tenedos	85	Aegean	Lucullus, Rhodians vs. Neoptolemus	fleet vs. fleet	Lucullus/ S
Battle of Rhyndacus	85	Anatolia	Fimbria vs. Taxiles, Mithradates (younger)	2 legions vs. ? infantry, cavalry	Fimbria/ M
Siege of Pitane	85	Anatolia	Fimbria vs. Mithradates VI, Mithradates (younger)	2 legions vs. cavalry, fleet	Mithradates
Peace of Dardanus	August 85	Anatolia	Mithradates VI and Sulla	—	—
Sulla is in Asia	85–84	Anatolia	Sulla, Murena, Curio, Lucullus vs. Greek cities in Anatolia Coast	3 legions, auxilia, fleet vs. ?	Sulla

Event Name	Date	Region/ Locale	Key Commanders (if known)	Combatant numbers*	Victor**
Cinna is murdered by troops	Spring 84	Ancona, Italy	Cinna dead, Carbo sole consul	2 legions?	—
Sulla sails back to Italy	Summer 84	—	Sulla	3 legions	—
Sulla arrives at Brudisium, met by supporters	Late 83	Italy	Sulla, Metellus, M. Licinius Crassus, Gn. Pompey, L. Marcius Philippus vs. Carbo,	3–10 legions, auxilia, fleet	Sulla
Battle of Mt. Tifata	Late 83	Campania	Sulla vs. G. Norbanus	6 legions, auxilia vs. ?	Sulla
Scipio's troops defect at Teanum	Late 83	Campania	Sulla vs. L. Cornelius Scipio Asiaticus	6 legions vs. ?	Sulla
Siege of Capua	Winter 83/82	Campania	Sulla vs. Norbanus	3? legions vs. ?	—
Capture of Sardinia	Spring 82	Sardinia	L. Marcius Philippus	2 legions	Philippus/ S
Battle of Asio River	March 82	Picenum	Metellus, Pompey vs. G. Carrinas	3–4 legions, auxilia vs. ?	Metellus/ S
Battle of Sacriportus	April 82	Latium	Sulla vs. G. Marius (younger)	8 legions vs. 9 legions	Sulla
Siege of Praeneste	Spring 82– Nov. 82	Latium	Q. Lucretius Ofella vs. Marius, Censorinus, Carbo, Lamponius, Pontius, Gutta, Carrinas, Damasippus	? vs. 10+ legions, auxilia (three relief efforts)	Sulla

(*Continued*)

31

Chart 1 Key Events of the First Roman Civil War, 88–82 BCE (Continued)

Event Name	Date	Region/ Locale	Key Commanders (if known)	Combatant numbers*	Victor**
Battle of Sena Gallica	April–May 82	Cisalpine Gaul	Pompey, Metellus vs. G. Marcius Censorius	3–4 legions vs. ?	Metellus/ S
Battle of Saturnia	Summer 82	Umbria	Sulla vs. Carbo	? vs. ?	Sulla
Battle of the Glanis River	Summer 82	Etruria	Sulla vs. Carbo	cavalry vs. cavalry	Sulla
First Battle of Clusium	Summer 82	Umbria	Sulla vs. Carbo	? vs. ?	Draw
Battle Near Spoletium	Summer 82	Etruria	Crassus, Pompey vs. Carrinas	? vs. ?	Crassus/ S
Battle of Faventia	Sept. 82	Cisalpine Gaul	Metellus vs. Norbanus	5 legions vs. 5 legions	Metellus/ S
Battle of Placentia	Sept. 82	Cisalpine Gaul	M. Tarentius Varro Lucullus vs. L. Qunictius	2 legions vs. 5	Lucullus/ S
Capture of Ariminum	Fall 82	Picenum	Metellus vs. Norbanus	5 legions vs. 1 legion	Metellus/ S
Battle of Colline Gates	Nov. 1, 82	Rome	Sulla, Crassus vs. Pontius, Gutta, Carrinas, Damasippus	? legions, auxilia vs. ? legions, auxilia	Crassus & Sulla
Sicilian War	Spring–Fall 81	Sicily	Pompey vs. M. Perperna, M. Brutus, Carbo	6 legions, fleet vs. ? legions, fleet	Pompey/ S

Event Name	Date	Region/Locale	Key Commanders (if known)	Combatant numbers*	Victor**
African War	Fall 81–80	Africa, Numidia	Pompey, Bogud vs. Gn. Domitius Ahenobarbus, Iarbas	6 legions, auxilia, fleet vs. 20,000 soldiers, auxilia	Pompey/ S
Sertorian War	80–72	Spain	Metellus, Pompey vs. Sertorius, Perperna	3–5 legions vs. 2–3 legions, auxilia	Pompey/ S

* Legion size unknown; theoretically 5,000–6,200 men at full strength; 10 cohorts = 1 legion. Roman sources often do not always report numbers for both sides.

** M = Marian supporters victory; S = Sullan victory.

Source: Arthur Keaveney, *Sulla: The Last Republican*, 2nd ed. (London: Routledge, 2005).

late 83 when he arrived in Brundisium. Sulla then fought his way north over the next year, finding Marius' son his greatest opposition. Finally, in November 82 Sulla met the opposition outside Rome's Colline Gate. Samnites had bolstered the Marian opposition. The battle did not go smoothly for Sulla, who was commanding his left and center, but Crassus, in command of his right, won and then turned left to strike the forces that were trying to overcome Sulla. The result was a hard-won military victory for Sulla and the end of military opposition in Italy. Marius' son committed suicide, and Carbo fled to Sicily.

The combat part of this civil war had ended in 82, but the civil war could not truly be called complete until Sulla had finished fixing what he perceived as the problems that had led to civil war. He was appointed dictator to repair the Republic for as long as necessary. Sulla proscribed his enemies, including some senators, and packed the Senate with supporters. During the following year he had a series of laws passed formalizing the Senate's powers and made sure that a tribune could never again take a commander's power away. He settled his veterans on land seized from communities that had opposed him, especially around Samnium. Sulla sent Pompey to Sicily and Africa and later to Spain to eliminate Marian opposition forces, a task at which Pompey turned out to be skilled. Finally, having restored the Republic as he saw best, Sulla resigned in 80.

Marius had enlisted poor citizens into his army, giving men who had nothing to lose a chance to gain much through combat. But it was Sulla who first used these soldiers for his personal ends. The first civil war during the Roman Republic appears to have started in 88 BCE as a result of a clash between leaders with strong personalities, but the root of the clash lay in the haphazard nature of the Roman political system. Sulla's precedent was not lost on later commanders.

Lee L. Brice

See also: Cornelius Cinna, Lucius; Cornelius Sulla Felix, Lucius; Licinius Crassus, Marcus; Marius, Gaius; Mithradates VI; Pompeius Magnus, Gnaeus; Senate; Sertorius, Quintus; Social War

References

Breed, Brian, Cynthia Damon, and Andreola Rossi, eds. *Citizens of Discord: Rome and Its Civil Wars.* Oxford: Oxford University Press, 2010.

Keaveney, Arthur. *The Army in the Roman Revolution.* London: Routledge, 2007.

Keaveney, Arthur. *Sulla, the Last Republican.* 2nd ed. London: Routledge, 2005.

MacKay, Christopher. *The Breakdown of the Roman Republic: From Oligarchy to Empire.* Cambridge: Cambridge University Press, 2009.

Civil War II

Caesar had been governor of Gaul for 10 years since 59 BCE, an irregular post made possible by his participation in the First Triumvirate. As governor, Caesar fought a successful and extremely profitable war, but as of 49 his term would end, and he would lose immunity from prosecution for crimes he may have committed as consul in 59. He planned on running in 50 for consulship the following year, but to do so he needed to resign as governor and return to Rome, a step that would also end his immunity. Caesar tried to negotiate a compromise with the Senate that would permit him to run for election without leaving Gaul, but this was rejected due to optimate opposition. Pompey, who had earlier been a friend and son-in-law of Caesar, sided increasingly with the optimates in the Senate. When they rejected the last compromise offer, they asked Pompey to protect the state. Citing the opposition as an attack on his dignity, Caesar with one legion crossed the Rubicon River, the border of his province, in January 49 and ignited civil war.

Caesar moved south quickly, capturing cities and pardoning opponents as he went. Pompey withdrew from Rome before the end of the month and then evacuated Italy for Greece in March. Caesar, temporarily dictator and elected consul, arranged affairs in Rome and marched quickly to Spain to neutralize the Pompeian legions there before he could move against Pompey, who was building his strength. The lightning campaign in Spain was not easy but succeeded in defeating the Pompeian legions there and forcing the political leadership to flee. Caesar also laid siege to Massilia. With the western provinces secure, he could turn east.

Caesar was able to get his army to Greece by 48 and blockaded Pompey at Dyrrhachium in northern Greece, despite a shortage of supplies. When Pompey broke out and turned the tables on him, Caesar withdrew to Thessaly even though there was another Macedonian force farther north. Pompey enjoyed superiority in forces and supplies, so he made camp not far from Caesar at Pharsalus. Although he could have stayed put and won by attrition, Pompey allowed himself to be chivied by his officers into eventually accepting Caesar's invitation to battle. Caesar's veteran legions defeated the Pompeians, despite being outnumbered. Caesar pardoned every enemy who requested it, including

Chart 2 Key Events of the Second Roman Civil War, 49–44 BCE

Event Name	Date	Region/ Locale	Key Commanders (Pompeians first)	Combatant numbers*	Victor
Senate declares senatus consultum ultimum for preservation of Republic	Jan. 7, 49	Rome	Cato, Metellus Scipio, Lentulus, Pompey	—	—
Crossing the Rubicon	Jan. 10, 49	Gaul/Italy border	Caesar	1 legion	—
Capture of Ariminum	Jan. 49	Italy	Caesar		Caesar
Capture of Ancona	Jan. 49		Caesar	3 cohorts	Caesar
Pompeians evacuate	Jan. 17, 49	Rome	Pompey		Caesar
Siege of Corfinium	Feb. 49	Central Italy	L. Domitius Ahenobarbus vs. Caesar	30 cohorts vs. 2 legions	Caesar
Pompeians evacuate	March 49	Southern Italy	Pompey	—	Pompeians
Capture of Sardinia	Spring 49	Sardinia	G. Scribonius Curio	2 legions, auxilia	Caesar
Capture of Sicily	April 49	Sicily	M. Cato (younger) vs. Curio	— vs. 3 legions, auxilia	Caesar
Spanish Campaign	June– Aug. 49	Spain	L. Afranius, M. Petreius, M. Varro vs. Caesar	7 legions, auxilia vs. 6 legions, auxilia	Caesar

Event Name	Date	Region/ Locale	Key Commanders (Pompeians first)	Combatant numbers*	Victor
Siege of Massilia	April– Sep. 49	Southern Gaul	L. Domitius Ahenobarbus vs. G. Trebonius, D. Brutus	8,000 vs. 3 legions	Caesar
Battle of Ilerda	Aug. 49	Spain	L. Afranius, M. Petreius vs. Caesar	5 legions, auxilia vs. 6 legions, auxilia	Caesar
Africa Campaign	Summer 49	Near Utica	P. Attius Varus, King Juba vs. Curio	2 legions, auxilia vs. 2 legions, auxilia	Pompeians
Illyricum Campaign	Summer 49	Illyricum	— vs. L. Antonius	— vs. 15 cohorts	Pompeians
Siege at Dyrrachium	Jan.–July 48	Western Greece	Pompey, M. Calpurnius Bibulus, Libo vs. Caesar, Calvinus, Antony (after April 11)	9 full legions, auxilia vs. 11 weak legions, auxilia	—
Battle of Dyrrachium	July 10, 48	Greece	Pompey vs. Caesar, Antony	9 full legions, 5,000 light auxilia, 7,000 cavalry vs. 11 half-legions, 500 cavalry	Pompeians
Battle of Pharsalus	August 9, 48	Thessaly, Greece	Pompey vs. Caesar	110 cohorts, 7,000 cavalry vs. 80 cohorts, 1,000 cavalry	Caesar

(Continued)

Chart 2 Key Events of the Second Roman Civil War, 49–44 BCE (*Continued*)

Event Name	Date	Region/ Locale	Key Commanders (Pompeians first)	Combatant numbers*	Victor
Alexandrian War	Sept. 48– Feb. 47	Egypt	Ptolemy XIII vs. Caesar, Cleopatra, Mithradates of Pergamum	20,000 men vs. 3 half-legions, 800 cavalry, auxilia	Caesar
Battle of Nicopolis	Fall 48	Armenia	Pharnaces of Bosporus vs. Gn. Domitius Calvinus	20,000 vs. 3 or 4 partial legions, auxilia	Pharnaces
Battle of Zela	Aug. 2, 47	Pontus	Pharnaces of Bosporus vs. Caesar	20,000 vs. 3 weak legions, 2 cohorts of veterans, auxilia	Caesar
Africa Campaign	Dec. 47– Apr. 46	Africa	Scipio, Cato, Juba, Labienus, Petreius vs. Caesar	10 legions, 4 auxilia legions, auxilia, 120 elephants vs. 6 legions, auxilia	—
Battle near Ruspina	Jan. 46	Africa	Labienus, Petreius vs. Caesar	11,200 cavalry, auxilia vs. 30 cohorts, 400 cavalry, 150 archers	Pompeians
Battle of Thapsus	April 6, 46	Africa	Scipio, Juba, Labienus vs. Caesar	10+ legions, auxilia vs. 8 legions, auxilia	Caesar

Event Name	Date	Region/Locale	Key Commanders (Pompeians first)	Combatant numbers*	Victor
Spanish Campaign	Nov. 46–Sept. 45	Spain	Labienus, Gn. Pompey (younger), Sex. Pompey vs. Caesar	13 legions, auxilia vs. 8 legions, 8,000 cavalry	Caesar
Battle of Munda	March 17, 45	Spain	Labienus, Gn. Pompey (younger), Sex. Pompey vs. Caesar	13 legions, 12,000 auxilia vs. 8 legions, 8000 cavalry	Caesar

* Legion size unknown; theoretically 5,000–6,200 men at full strength; 10 cohorts = 1 legion. Roman sources often do not report numbers for both sides.

Sources: A. K. Goldsworthy, *Caesar: Life of a Colossus* (New Haven, CT: Yale University Press, 2006); A. K. Goldsworthy, *Caesar's Civil Wars, 49–44 BC* (Oxford, UK: Osprey, 2002).

Brutus and Cicero. Some opposition leaders withdrew to North Africa as Pompey sailed to Egypt, where he expected assistance but was murdered by the king.

Caesar made Antony his master of horse to hold Rome while he followed Pompey to Egypt. Finding a source of grain and wealth, Caesar involved himself in Ptolemaic politics by supporting Cleopatra VII as queen. He fought a small war in Alexandria to break a siege and secure Cleopatra's throne in 47. Then he moved north and won a victory at Zela in Anatolia against Pharnaces and dispatched the message to Rome "I came, I saw, I conquered." Returning to Rome in September, Caesar was elected consul for 46, secured order, and resolved a mutiny among his veteran legions before sailing to North Africa.

His campaign against the Pompeian opposition dragged on but culminated in the Battle of Thapsus in April 46. Caesar won even though his soldiers violated orders and attacked before the signal. This battle ended the war in Africa, as the remaining cities not captured surrendered to Caesar without further fighting. Even this battle was not the end of the civil war, however, as several opposition leaders escaped to Spain. These leaders included Pompey's surviving sons and Titus Labienus, a talented commander who had served Caesar in the Gallic Wars, and they raised a large force of 13 legions. Caesar, having been appointed dictator and making Lepidus his master of horse in Rome, moved against Spain in late 46. After some maneuvering, Caesar laid siege to the key city of Munda. Following a difficult battle in the spring of 45, he won an immense victory in which the enemy lost more than 30,000 men. Pompey's elder son, Magnus, was captured and executed, but the younger son, Sextus, was the only Pompeian leader to escape. Caesar celebrated a triumph over Spain in 45, the effective end of the civil war.

The victory in this civil war made it possible for Caesar to address many of what he saw as the problems that Rome faced, but in the process he dominated the Roman Republic. His assassination and then Civil War III followed soon afterward. In a sense, the result of Civil War II was continued turmoil.

Caesar's victory in the civil war was remarkable and never a foregone conclusion. He took many chances against a committed opposition, and it could all have unraveled at numerous points. Caesar was a smart, talented commander, but it is important to recognize that his reputation is heavily colored by his own *Commentaries* of the war, supplemented by one of his officers. In these works Caesar took pains to emphasize his personal role in winning while justifying his actions and downplaying his personal role in instigating the war. This source has heavily influenced accounts, ancient and modern, of the civil wars.

Lee L. Brice

See also: Aemilius Lepidus, Marcus; Antonius, Marcus; Cleopatra VII; Gallic Wars; Julius Caesar, Gaius; Junius Brutus, Marcus; Licinius Crassus, Marcus; Mutiny; Pharsalus, Battle of; Pompeius Magnus, Gnaeus; Pompeius Magnus, Sextus; Senate; Triumvirate, First

References

Breed, B., C. Damon, and A. Rossi, eds. *Citizens of Discord: Rome and Its Civil Wars.* Oxford: Oxford University Press, 2010.

Caesar. *War Commentaries of Caesar.* Translated by Rex Warner. New York: New American Library, 1960.

Goldsworthy, A. *Caesar: Life of a Colossus.* New Haven, CT: Yale University Press, 2006.

Griffin, M., ed. *A Companion to Julius Caesar.* Oxford, UK: Wiley-Blackwell, 2009.

Seager, R. *Pompey the Great.* Oxford, UK: Blackwell, 2002.

Civil War III

The assassination of Caesar in March 44 BCE may not have resulted in immediate combat, but it was the trigger for the third and final civil war of the Roman Republic. When the assassins were forced out of Rome by public anger, some went to their assigned province and began fighting with the governors who had been assigned there by Caesar. Brutus and Cassius each began gathering supporters and raising armies in the east. No one in Rome could have predicted that the state would survive the turmoil.

Octavian arrived in Rome in April 44 and was named in the will as Caesar's adopted son and heir. Octavian cultivated the support of Cicero and the Senate as a foil to Antony. By October the competition between Antony and Octavian grew too heated, so both men began raising armies of their own, primarily among Caesar's veterans, by promising immense bonuses in return for support in getting revenge on the assassins. Antony as consul also had legions waiting for him in Brundisium. He led them north toward his assigned province, Cisalpine Gaul, but near Rome two legions mutinied and joined Octavian. Soon afterward the Senate declared Antony an outlaw and granted Octavian formal power and authority to assist the new consuls against him, even as Antony laid siege to one of the assassins, Decimus Brutus, at Mutina. Octavian joined the consuls in the successful attack on Antony at Mutina in April 43. Antony lost heavily and had to withdraw into Gaul. Lepidus and several other former Caesarian commanders joined him. Both consuls had died at Mutina, so Octavian successfully incited his legions to march on Rome and demand their bonuses and a consulship for him. Although he was supposed to support Decimus Brutus, Octavian stalled and negotiated with Antony and Lepidus.

In November 43 the three men met at Bononia and agreed to form the Second Triumvirate to run the state and get revenge on the assassins. In return for their soldiers' support, they promised additional bonuses and free land on discharge. They also proscribed their enemies, including Cicero, to eliminate opposition and raise cash to pay the soldiers. Antony and Octavian led a combined army against Brutus and Cassius, meeting in Macedonia at Philippi in October 42. The triumvirs won, and the assassins committed suicide.

Afterward Octavian settled the veterans in Italy and dealt with the turmoil that resulted, while Antony went east to raise more money to pay the soldiers' bonuses. The following year Antony started a relationship with Cleopatra VII. While he was in Egypt, his brother stirred up opposition to Octavian that culminated in the so-called Perusine War, which ended with Octavian's successful siege of Perusia. Antony returned to Brundisium in 40. It looked like there would be war between Octavian and Antony, but the soldiers on both sides intervened and forced the triumvirs to make peace. Lepidus was sent to Africa to rule there in a diminished capacity, but not out of office.

The following year Octavian had trouble with Sextus Pompey, who was leading a strong naval force on Sicily. Eventually Sextus' raids and blockade became so serious that in 39 the triumvirs had to recognize his authority and grant him special powers. Beginning in 38, Octavian, alleging broken agreements, campaigned against Sextus unsuccessfully for two years until Agrippa organized the building of several new fleets and the training of crews in 37. In 36 Octavian launched a combined naval campaign and invasion of Sicily by his forces and supported by Lepidus. Agrippa defeated Sextus decisively at Naulochus, and Lepidus accepted the surrender of Messana in Sicily. Lepidus miscalculated the way power worked when he took sole credit for the victory. Over the next

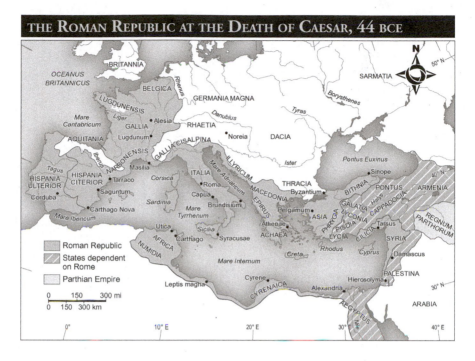

THE ROMAN REPUBLIC AT THE DEATH OF CAESAR, 44 BCE

several days his entire army defected to Octavian. When Lepidus apologized, Octavian simply deposed him from power but did not kill him. Octavian's troops then mutinied, but he was able to resolve the situation by discharging many veterans. In the same year Antony suffered a humiliating defeat in Parthia, despite the financial backing of Cleopatra. The events of 36 left Octavian in strong, undisputed control of Rome and the west.

Although most authors write of the remainder of this civil war as if the outcome was inevitable, it is important to remember that it was not. Antony was still popular in Rome and had a better military reputation than Octavian, despite the events in 36. Octavian spent the next three years campaigning in Illyria to improve his military reputation and strengthen his legions. In 32 after Antony made a series of bad political decisions connected with Cleopatra, the Senate and the Roman people supported war against Egypt.

In September 31 the two sides met at Actium, where Octavian and Agrippa had bottled up Antony's fleet and army. In the naval breakout, Antony and Cleopatra escaped but lost most of their fleet. Their army surrendered without fighting. The following year after settling his veterans in Italy, Octavian invaded Egypt. Antony committed suicide, and after negotiations began, Cleopatra committed suicide or was assassinated to make it

Chart 3 Key Events of the Third Roman Civil War, 44–30 BCE

Event Name	Date	Region/ Locale	Key Commanders	Combatant numbers*	Victor
Assassination of Caesar	Mar. 15, 44	Rome	Cassius, Brutus vs. Caesar	—	Assassins
Raising legions	Fall 44	Campania	Octavian	2–3 legions	—
Soldiers mutiny and change sides	Nov. 44	Brundisium and Rome	Antony	2 legions	Octavian
Seizure of Macedonia	Dec. 44	Macedonia	G. Antonius vs. M. Junius Brutus	—	Brutus
Seizure of Syria	Jan. 43	Syria	G. Cassius vs. P. Cornelius Dolabella	6 legions vs. 2 legions	Cassius
Battle at Forum Gallorum	Apr. 14, 43	North Italy	M. Antony vs. G. Vibius Pansa, Aulus Hirtius	2 legions, 1 praetorian cohort, auxilia vs. 6 legions, 1 praetorian cohort, auxilia	Hirtius, Octavian
Battle of Mutina	Apr. 21, 43	North Italy	Antony, L. Antonius vs. Hirtius, Octavian, D. Brutus	2 legions vs. 6–8 legions	Octavian
Bononia Pact	Nov. 43	North Italy	Antony, M. Aemilius Lepidus and Octavian	—	Triumvirs
Capture of Sicily	Winter 43–42	Sicily	Sex. Pompeius	—	Pompeius

Event Name	Date	Region/Locale	Key Commanders	Combatant numbers*	Victor
First Battle of Philippi	Oct. 2 or 3, 42	Macedonia	Antony, Octavian vs. Cassius, Brutus	19 legions, 33,000? cavalry vs. 17 legions, 12,000 cavalry, 5000 archers	Triumvirs
Second Battle of Philippi	Oct. 23, 42	Macedonia	Antony, Octavian vs. Brutus	17–18 legions, cavalry vs. 15 legions, cavalry	Triumvirs
Perusine Revolt	41–Feb. 40	Italy	L. Antonius, Fulvia vs. Octavian	8 legions vs. 12 legions	Octavian
Parthian Invasion	Jan.–Feb. 40	Syria	Q. Labienus, Pacorus of Parthia vs. L. Decidius Saxa	? cavalry, ?cataphracts vs. 2 legions, auxilia	Parthia
Capture of Sardinia	mid-40	Sardinia	Sex. Pompeius vs. ?	4 legions vs. ?	Pompeius
Death of Calenus in Gaul	mid-40	Gaul	Octavian received Gaul and legions	11 legions	—
Pact of Brundisium	Oct. 40	Italy	M. Antony and Octavian	—	Triumvirs
Pact of Misenum	Spring 39	Italy	Antony, Octavian and Sex. Pompeius	—	—
Reconquest of Macedon	39	Macedonia	Asinius Pollio v. Illyrian Parthini	11 legions vs. ?	Pollio

(*Continued*)

Chart 3 Key Events of the Third Roman Civil War, 44–30 BCE (Continued)

Event Name	Date	Region/Locale	Key Commanders	Combatant numbers*	Victor
Reconquest of the East	39–38	Cilicia, Syria	P. Ventidius Bassus, Antony vs. Labienus, Phranipates, Pacorus, Antiochus of Comagene, Antigonus	11 legions, cavalry, slingers vs. cavalry, cataphract	Antony
Battle of Cilician Gates	39	Cilicia	Ventidius vs. Labienus	2? legions, cavalry, slingers vs. 2 legions, cavalry, cataphract	Ventidius
Battle of Amanus Pass	39	Syria	Ventidius vs. Phranipates	4+ legions, cavalry, slingers vs. horse archers, cataphract	Ventidius
Battle of Gindarus	38	Syria	Ventidius vs. Pacorus	4+ legions, cavalry, slingers vs. horse archers, cataphracts	Ventidius
Revolts in Gaul	38	Gaul	M. Vipsanius Agrippa vs. Aquitanii, Ubii	4+ legions, auxilia vs.?	Agrippa
Siege of Jerusalem	38–July 37	Judaea	Herod, Sosius vs. Antigonus	4+ legions, auxilia vs.?	Sosius (Antony)
Battle of Cumae	Summer 38	Italy	Calvisius, Menodorus vs. Demochares, Menecrates	fleet vs. fleet	Sextus
Skirmish off Scyllaeum	Late 38	Italy	Octavian vs. Sextus (and weather)	fleet vs. fleet	Sextus

Event Name	Date	Region/Locale	Key Commanders	Combatant numbers*	Victor
Tarentum Pact	Spring 37	Italy	Antony and Octavian	—	Triumvirs
Conquest of Armenia	37	Armenia	Canidius Crassus vs. Artavasdes II	? vs. ?	Crassus
Parthian War	June–Oct. 36	Armenia, Media	Antony vs. Monaeses, Phraates IV of Parthia, Artavasdes I of Media	16 legions, 20,000+ cavalry, 30,000 auxilia vs. 50,000 horse archers, cavalry, cataphract,	Parthia
Battle of Mylae	Aug. 36	Off Sicily	Agrippa vs. Papia	fleet vs. fleet	Agrippa
Battle of Taormina	Aug. 36	Off Sicily	Octavian vs. Sextus	fleet vs. fleet	Sextus
Battle of Naulochus	Sept. 3, 36	Off Sicily	Agrippa vs. Sextus	300 ships vs. 300? ships	Agrippa
Capture of Messana	Sept. 36	Sicily	Octavian, Agrippa, Lepidus vs. Sextus, Plinius	25+ legions, auxilia, fleet vs. 8+ legions, auxilia	Octavian
Armenian War	34–33	Armenia	Antony, vs. Artavasdes II	16 legions, cavalry, auxilia vs. ?cavalry	Antony
Illyrian-Dalmatian War	35–33	Dalmatia, Illyria, Pannonia	Octavian, Agrippa, Statilius Taurus, etc. vs. Liburni, Iapudes, Delmatae	10+ legions?	Octavian

(Continued)

Chart 3 Key Events of the Third Roman Civil War, 44–30 BCE *(Continued)*

Event Name	Date	Region/ Locale	Key Commanders	Combatant numbers*	Victor
Actian Campaign	Jan.–Sept. 31	Greece	Octavian, Agrippa vs. Antony, Cleopatra VII	80,000 legionaries, cavalry, auxilia, 400 ships vs. 63,000 legionaries, 12,000 cavalry, auxilia, 400– 500 ships	Octavian
Battle of Actium	Sept. 2, 31	Greece	Octavian, Agrippa vs. Antony, Cleopatra VII	8 legions and 5 cohorts (on ship), auxilia, 250–300 ships vs. 8 legions (on ship), auxilia, 230 ships	Octavian
Egyptian Campaign	Spring– Summer 30	Egypt	Octavian vs. Antony, Cleopatra VII	10? legions vs. 10,000 soldiers, auxilia	Octavian
Capture of Alexandria	July 31, 30	Egypt	Octavian vs. Antony, Cleopatra VII	10? legions vs. —	Octavian

* Legion size unknown, theoretically 5,000–6,200 men at full strength; 10 cohorts = a legion. Roman sources often do not always report numbers for both sides.

Source: Josiah Osgood, *Caesar's Legacy: Civil War and the Emergence of the Roman Empire* (Cambridge: Cambridge University Press, 2006).

look like she had died by her own hand. Egypt became the property of Octavian, and he was able to use the wealth he acquired to pay off his promises to his troops and his creditors.

The last battle was in 31, but the civil war did not end until 30, with Octavian as the last triumvir standing. The result of this last civil war was the end of the Republic when in 27 Octavian announced the "restoration of the Republic," and the Roman Empire began formally.

Lee L. Brice

See also: Actium, Battle of; Aemilius Lepidus, Marcus; Antonius, Marcus; Cassius Longinus, Gaius; Cleopatra VII; Fleet, Roman; Julius Caesar, Gaius; Julius Caesar Octavianus, Gaius; Junius Brutus, Marcus; Mutiny; Philippi, Battle of; Pompeius Magnus, Sextus; Senate; Triumvirate, Second; Vipsanius Agrippa, Marcus

References

Breed, Brian, Cynthia Damon, and Andreola Rossi, eds. *Citizens of Discord: Rome and Its Civil Wars.* Oxford: Oxford University Press, 2010.

Brice, Lee L. "Disciplining Octavian: An Aspect of Roman Military Culture during the Triumviral Wars 44–30 BCE." In *Warfare and Culture in World History,* edited by Wayne Lee, 35–60. New York: New York University Press, 2011.

MacKay, Christopher. *The Breakdown of the Roman Republic: From Oligarchy to Empire.* Cambridge: Cambridge University Press, 2009.

Osgood, Josiah. *Caesar's Legacy: Civil War and the Emergence of the Roman Empire.* Cambridge: Cambridge University Press, 2006.

Southern, Patricia. *Mark Antony.* Charleston, SC: Tempus, 1998.

Cleopatra VII

Cleopatra was born to Ptolemy XII and Cleopatra VI in 69 BCE. Although born in Egypt, she was the descendant of a Macedonian dynasty dating back to the late fourth century. When Ptolemy XII died in 51, Cleopatra VII and her brother, Ptolemy XIII, became the rulers of Egypt. Upholding Ptolemaic custom, Cleopatra and her brother married; however, they soon had a falling out. As a result, Cleopatra was driven from Alexandria in 48. Cleopatra's relevance to Roman military history is tied to the two civil wars that closed out the Roman Republic and coincided with her rule in Egypt.

Idealized bust of Cleopatra VII, last Ptolemaic monarch of Egypt, carved after her death. She associated with G. Julius Caesar and Marcus Antonius, but she committed suicide rather than surrender to Octavian in 30 BCE. (Sandro Vannini/Corbis)

Caesar, in pursuit of Pompey, arrived in Egypt in 48 with one legion. Cleopatra and Caesar formed a relationship that benefited each of them. The negative, seductress reputation attached to Cleopatra is a leftover of later Roman propaganda. Caesar gained access to wealth and grain for his soldiers, and Cleopatra acquired a powerful military patron. They maneuvered to put Cleopatra on the throne, fighting and winning a small war against Ptolemy XIII in 47 to do so. Evidence that Cleopatra directed any of the campaign is lacking, but as a Hellenistic queen she certainly could have done so, and her mercenaries were helpful to Caesar's forces as were her allies.

In 42 following the Battle of Philippi, the Second Triumvirate needed wealth to pay its soldiers, so Antony went east to raise money. In 41 he summoned Cleopatra along with other regional leaders to meet him in Tarsus. Afterward Antony forged a relationship with her that began similarly to Caesar's—he needed wealth and grain, while she needed a Roman military patron to remain independent. The complicated nature of their personal relationship is largely irrelevant to military history.

Militarily, Cleopatra provided logistical support for Antony's failed Parthian war of 36 and his annexation of Armenia in 34. Her relationship with Antony, who was legally married to Octavia until 32, fueled a fierce propaganda campaign by Octavian as tensions rose between the triumvirs. When the Senate declared war in 31, it was against Cleopatra and Egypt, not Antony.

In preparation for the war, Cleopatra provided Antony with logistical support, infantry, a fleet, and wealth. She went with him to Greece, but it is unclear the extent to which she directed the campaign, although she had every right to have done so as queen of Egypt and commander of her own forces. It is difficult to separate her actual military role from Roman propaganda. Agrippa and Octavian were able to outmaneuver Antony and Cleopatra, eventually blockading them at Actium. The Battle of Actium was a breakout attempt in which Cleopatra and Antony escaped in their large ships but with heavy losses. They did not offer any substantial resistance afterward.

In 30, with Octavian already in possession of most of Egypt and about to enter Alexandria, Antony committed suicide. After some negotiation, Cleopatra also died, either by her own hand or made to look as if she commited suicide. Octavian made Egypt his own personal property and used the wealth that he acquired to pay off his immense debts, including his soldiers' bounties. Cleopatra was the last Ptolemaic monarch. She had been a shrewd politician in her relations with Rome until she (and Antony) underestimated Octavian. Her wealth contributed much to Roman military activity in the years 48–29.

Joyce Salisbury and Lee L. Brice

See also: Actium, Battle of; Antonius, Marcus; Civil War II; Civil War III; Julius Caesar, Gaius; Julius Caesar Octavianus, Gaius; Parthian Empire; Philippi, Battle of; Pompeius Magnus, Gnaeus; Ptolemaic Dynasty; Triumvirate, Second; Vipsanius Agrippa, Marcus

References

MacKay, Christopher. *The Breakdown of the Roman Republic: From Oligarchy to Empire.* Cambridge: Cambridge University Press, 2009.

Osgood, Josiah. *Caesar's Legacy: Civil War and the Emergence of the Roman Empire.* Cambridge: Cambridge University Press, 2006.

Roller, Duane. *Cleopatra: A Biography.* Oxford: Oxford University Press, 2010.

Walker, Susan, and Peter Higgs. *Cleopatra of Egypt: From History to Myth.* Princeton, NJ: Princeton University Press, 2001.

Cohort Legion. *See* Legion, Cohort

Comitia Centuriata

The Comitia Centuriata was Rome's traditional military assembly, but by the fourth century BCE it had evolved into a popular assembly. Military responsibilities of the assembly included electing magistrates with the power of imperium (consuls and praetors), declaring war and ratifying peace, and passing laws.

The assembly was originally organized to reflect the division of Roman legions into centuries of cavalry, infantry, and support staff. Despite changes in its size, the way it voted continued to reflect dominance by the wealthy, as was the case in the military. Citizens were placed into 1 of 193 voting centuries in five levels of wealth. The wealthiest citizens were in the cavalry centuries, and then there were the engineer centuries, the infantry centuries ranked by age and wealth into five classes. Then there were the musician centuries and finally everyone who fell below the minimum wealth qualification for military service, proletarians, in 1 century. Within the top four levels, half the centuries had older men and half had younger men.

Voting was by century and originally was not secret. The way the centuries were arranged meant that the wealthier and older voters had more centuries and that each century had fewer men in it, so those men held voting power greater than the percentage of society they composed. Voting started near the top of the wealthy centuries and proceeded in descending order of status. Since voting stopped as soon as a majority of centuries (97) agreed, the wealthy and the old dominated the voting. Since voting might stop as soon as a majority was reached, this meant that the proletarians often might not have voted. This pattern was not originally seen as unfair, because the poor could not serve in the military. However, as the functions of the assembly grew to include laws and because the poor eventually served in the military, it was increasingly an assembly that enforced elite interests.

The Comitia Centuriata voted on laws, proposals, candidates, and treaties put to it by consuls or praetors but could not amend them. The Senate traditionally advised the consuls and praetors on proposals. Sulla passed a law requiring that all laws be passed only in the Comitia Centuriata and that any law or proposal put to the assembly be approved by the Senate, but these laws were repealed a few years after Sulla's death. The tribal assembly was the foil to the Comitia Centuriata since tribunes could bring popular proposals there, but it had no military functions. The military assembly remained active to the end of the Roman Republic.

Lee L. Brice

See also: Cornelius Sulla Felix, Lucius; Proletarians; Senate

References

Erdkamp, P., ed. *A Companion to the Roman Army.* Oxford, UK: Wiley-Blackwell, 2011.

Lintott, A. *The Constitution of the Roman Republic.* Oxford: Oxford University Press, 1999.

Nicolet, Claude. *The World of the Citizen in Republican Rome.* Translated by P. S. Falla. Berkeley: University of California Press, 1980.

Commanders, Legionary. *See* Legionary Commanders

Cornelius Cinna, Lucius

Lucius Cornelius Cinna was born to a patrician family and grew up with all the advantages of Roman aristocracy. He served successfully in the Social War and was elected consul for 87 BCE.

As consul, Cinna made a promise to suppress any attempts to repeal the reforms instituted before Sulla went east against Mithradates VI. After being expelled from Rome for breaking his promise, Cinna raised an army in Italy and marched on Rome with Gaius Marius, thus continuing Civil War I, which was started by Sulla. Together they took Rome, killing a number of Sulla's supporters.

Cinna retained the office of consul in 85 and 84 while attempting to enact reforms. When Sulla announced in 84 that he was returning to Rome, Cinna raised an army to oppose him. During training, the men—perhaps realizing that they would fight Sulla's experienced legions—mutinied and killed Cinna. Sulla's victorious return and reforms overshadowed all of Cinna's efforts.

Lee L. Brice

See also: Civil War I; Cornelius Sulla Felix, Lucius; Marius, Gaius; Mithradates VI; Mutiny; Social War

References

Lovano, M. *The Age of Cinna: Crucible of Late Republican Rome.* Stuttgart: Steiner, 2002.

Rosenstein, N., and R. Morstein-Marx, eds. *A Companion to the Roman Republic.* Oxford, UK: Blackwell, 2010.

Cornelius Scipio Aemilianus Africanus, Publius

Publius Cornelius <u>Scipio Aemilianus</u> Africanus (the Younger) was born in Rome circa 185 BCE, the son of Lucius Aemilius Paullus. Pursuing a typical political career, Scipio Aemilianus started in the military by serving under his father at Pydna. Because Paullus had four sons, he gave up one who was adopted as son and heir by Publius Scipio, son of Scipio Africanus. Since it was an adoption, the young man retained part of his former family name. The name Africanus was not added until after his victory in 146. He is sometimes called Scipio Africanus the Younger to distinguish him from his grandfather.

Scipio Aemilianus served as military tribune in Spain and in the first years of the Third Punic War, where he found the army in Africa poorly disciplined. In 147 the people elected him consul despite his being too young to hold a praetorship, much like his grandfather. The Senate, under popular pressure, gave him command in Africa. There he restored order to the army and captured Carthage after a siege, sacking and razing it and selling the captives into slavery. This victory earned him a triumph and the official name Africanus.

Scipio Aemilianus' next important military activity was another siege, this time in Spain. The war there had not gone well for Rome, so the people elected him consul for 134 and sent him to the command in Spain. Before departing he had difficulty finding sufficient men to serve in his army, so he enlisted his clients and poor volunteers as an emergency measure. Once in Spain he laid siege to Numantia, taking it in 133. He won a second triumph for this victory and took the unofficial additional name Numantinus.

Scipio Aemilianus seems to have been a good commander, at least at sieges, and was extremely ambitious, but he lacked the opportunities (and perhaps the talent) that his grandfather had enjoyed, even if they shared the same name. Scipio Aemilianus' reputation in Roman history (ancient and modern) largely depends on his close relationship with the historian Polybius, whom he considered his mentor. It is important to keep this relationship in mind when reading ancient accounts of Scipio Aemilianus' career.

Lee L. Brice

See also: Aemilius Paullus, Lucius; Carthage; Cornelius Scipio Africanus, Publius; Polybius; Punic Wars; Punic Wars, Consequences of the; Spanish Wars; Tribunes, Military

References

Astin, A. E. *Scipio Aemilianus*. Oxford: Oxford University Press, 1967.

Hoyos, Dexter, ed. *A Companion to the Punic Wars*. Oxford, UK: Wiley-Blackwell, 2011.

Polybius. *Histories*. Translated by R. Waterfield and B. McGing. Oxford: Oxford University Press, 2010.

Cornelius Scipio Africanus, Publius

Publius Cornelius Scipio Africanus was born in Rome circa 236 BCE. The adnomen "Africanus" was not added until after his victory in 202. He is sometimes called Scipio Africanus the Elder to distinguish him from his grandson. Pursuing a typical political career, he started in the military during the Second Punic War. Scipio was a military tribune in the Battle of Cannae and earned recognition for bravery in rallying the survivors.

The people conferred on the popular Scipio command of Spain in 210, despite his being too young to hold a praetorship. Scipio reorganized Roman forces and brilliantly outmaneuvered three Carthaginian armies in Spain. In 209 he took the strategically important city of New Carthage by unorthodox tactics. He defeated Hannibal's brother, Hasdrubal Barca, in 208 at Baecula by aggressive tactics. After Hasdrubal departed Spain that same year to deliver supplies to Hannibal, Scipio did not pursue him, choosing instead to remain in Spain and consolidate his earlier gains. Then, with only 48,000 men, he defeated the remaining two Carthaginian armies of around 70,000 men under Mago Barca and Hasdrubal Gisco in the Battle of Ilipa in 206. This battle firmly established Roman rule over all of Spain.

Scipio then returned to Italy. He was elected consul in 205 and then was ordered to Sicily to conquer Carthaginian allies. Once this had been accomplished and despite doubts on the part of some senators, Scipio began operations against Carthage in 204. Landing in Africa with 35,000 men, he besieged Utica in 204 but was unable to take it and retired to a camp that he established on the coast. He then campaigned against Carthaginian commander Hasdrubal Gisco and Carthage's ally Syphax of the Maseasulli, defeating both in the Battle of the Great Plains in 203. Carthage ordered the return of Hannibal from Italy in 203, and he raised a new army and made preparations to meet Scipio. With the failure of peace negotiations, the two leading commanders of

Bust of a Roman commander, thought to be P. Cornelius Scipio Africanus. He fought during the Second Punic War, defeating Hannibal at Zama in 203 BCE. (DEA/G. Dagli Orti/De Agostini/Getty Images)

each side met at Zama. Greatly assisted by Masinissa's Numidian cavalry, Scipio triumphed over his opponent in the spring of 202, and Carthage was forced to sue for peace.

Returning to Rome, Scipio celebrated a triumph in 200 and took the ad-nomen "Africanus." Later in the 190s he campaigned with his brother Lucius against Antiochus III, expelling him from Greece. They invaded Asia, but Scipio fell ill and had no role in the battle at Magnesia in 190. Scipio, who had a reputation for being sick much of his life, died in 184. He was certainly a good commander, but since most of the evidence about him comes from Polybius, a client and member of the family's inner circle, it is difficult to be sure Scipio deserved all the praise he has received.

Spencer C. Tucker

See also: Cannae, Battle of; Hannibal; Punic Wars; Seleucid Dynasty; Zama, Battle of

References

Goldsworthy, Adrian. *The Punic Wars.* London: Cassell, 2000.

Hoyos, Dexter, ed. *A Companion to the Punic Wars.* Oxford, UK: Wiley-Blackwell, 2011.

Lazenby, J. F. *Hannibal's War: A Military History of the Second Punic War.* Norman: University of Oklahoma Press, 1998.

Scullard, Howard H. *Scipio Africanus: Soldier and Politician.* London: Thames and Hudson, 1970.

Cornelius Sulla Felix, Lucius

Lucius Cornelius <u>Sulla</u> Felix was born in 138 BCE into an undistinguished patrician family. The name Felix (which means "lucky") was added later once he had become dictator. He served under Marius in the Jugurthine War. Sulla made his reputation by arranging Jugurtha's capture in 105, incurring Marius' jealousy. Sulla served under Marius in 104–103. During the Social War, Sulla distinguished himself in the siege of Pompeii and was elected consul for 88.

As consul, Sulla was supposed to take command in the war against Mithradates IV, king of Pontus. When a tribune arranged for Marius instead of Sulla to receive the command, Sulla complained to his soldiers, who voted (but not most of his officers) to join him in marching on Rome to regain the potentially lucrative command. On taking Rome and thus starting a civil war, his supporters hunted down and killed the tribune, and Marius fled to Africa. Sulla enacted some reforms and arranged for Cinna to be consul for 87.

Soon after Sulla had departed with his army for the east, however, Cinna and Marius marched on Rome, seized power, and outlawed Sulla and his supporters. Sulla, in Greece, robbed cities and sanctuaries to pay his soldiers and then defeated Mithradates' larger army at Chaeronea in 86 and at Orchomenus in 85. Forcing Mithradates to peace terms in Anatolia, Sulla billeted his troops in Greek cities in Ionia and extorted cash from the cities.

Returning to Italy in 83, Sulla was joined by Crassus and Pompey, among others. Sulla won a series of battles

Lucius Cornelius Sulla was a successful Roman military commander who forced Mithradates VI out of Greece and fought in the first Roman Civil War against Marius. This bust is a later copy of an original. (Allan T. Kohl/Art Images for College Teaching)

while fighting his way to Rome and then took the city after a fierce battle at the Colline Gate in 82. When Sulla took power in Rome, he executed and banned many enemies; sent Pompey to mop up opposition in Sicily, Africa, and Spain; took the adnomen "Felix"; and had himself appointed dictator for the preservation of the Republic. In this post Sulla enacted a number of military reforms, including limits on the duration of overseas commands; tightened treason laws; and required governors to get senatorial permission to start wars and to leave their assigned province with an army. He also settled his veterans on land seized in Italy.

Sulla abdicated in 80 and died in 78. He wrote memoirs that later historians employed, although Sulla's memoirs have not survived. He was successful, but his decision to march on Rome initiated the first civil war and set a precedent for commanders employing their armies against the state.

Spencer C. Tucker

See also: Civil War I; Cornelius Cinna, Lucius; Jugurthine War; Licinius Crassus, Marcus; Marius, Gaius; Mithradates VI; Pompeius Magnus, Gnaeus; Social War

References

Badian, Ernst. *Lucius Sulla: The Deadly Reformer.* Sydney, Australia: Sydney University Press, 1970.

Keaveney, Arthur. *The Army in the Roman Revolution.* London: Routledge, 2007.

Keaveney, Arthur. *Sulla: The Last Republican.* 2nd ed. London: Routledge, 2005.

Crassus, Marcus Licinius. *See* Licinius Crassus, Marcus

Cynoscephalae, Battle of

Flamininus had been sent to Macedon in 198 BCE and had spent much of his time marshaling allies and trying to bring Philip V, king of Macedon, to battle. Both leaders had about 25,000 men including soldiers and cavalry, although Flamininus also had elephants. After much maneuvering west of Pherae in Thessaly the following spring, both armies camped within several miles of each other on either side of a ridge. Both sides were apparently unaware that their prey was so close.

On the morning of the battle, Philip wished to start moving before dawn as he attempted to move north, but there was a dense fog or mist, so he sent out light troops to reconnoiter the terrain. On top of the ridge between the armies they ran into Roman light infantry engaged in the same mission. The Macedonians called for support, and their cavalry came to push back the Romans. In response, Flamininus committed his Greek cavalry, still unaware that Philip's entire army was nearby. The Roman force with cavalry support held their own against the Macedonians and stopped giving ground.

As the mist cleared and messages arrived, Philip, seeing his men on the ridge hard-pressed, engaged his mercenaries. Philip's Thracian and Illyrian mercenaries arrived on top of the ridge and pushed the Romans back. Philip made his way to the ridgetop with his *peltasts,* committing them into battle line on his right as he called up his phalanx. The problem he had was that the heavy infantrymen were scattered, since he had sent men off to forage. As a result they marched to battle piecemeal, and Philip engaged them at the ridgetop on his left as he had sufficient numbers to do so. Simultaneously Flamininus committed a legion to the combat, and the combination began to push the light troops and mercenaries back.

Once Philip had a sufficient phalanx formation, he engaged them even as more units were climbing the slope. They began to push down the slope against the legion, making great headway as the Romans slowly backed down the slope. Flamininus then sent his second legion, with elephants in front, into battle on his right. This force exploited gaps in the Macedonian left that were opening as the phalanx pushed downhill before properly forming up. The result was that the Romans stopped the Macedonian left with great slaughter and turned it back even as more units were arriving to engage. Philip, on the Macedonian right and unaware that the battle was turning, continued to push downslope. A military tribune seized a chance and led 20 maniples uphill around the Macedonian right flank and fell on the rear of the left flank, which broke and fled. The Roman force pursued with great slaughter.

The result of the battle was the end of the Second Macedonian War. The battle's importance also stems from it being the first engagement between a phalanx and legions for which historians have good sources.

Lee L. Brice

See also: Greece; Macedonian Wars; Quinctius Flamininus, Titus

References

Eckstein, Arthur. *Rome Enters the Greek East: From Anarchy to Hierarchy in the Hellenistic Mediterranean, 230–170 BC.* Oxford, UK: Wiley-Blackwell, 2008.

Hammond, N. G. L. "The Campaign and the Battle of Cynoscephalae in 197 B.C." *Journal of Hellenic Studies* 108 (1988): 60–82.

Polybius. *Histories.* Translated by R. Waterfield and B. McGing. Oxford: Oxford University Press, 2010.

D

Decimation

Decimation, or *fustuarium,* was the ultimate penalty for a military unit that exhibited indiscipline. The name comes from the notion of killing every 10th man, but in reality the ratio was up to the commander, and we know of instances when it was less. According to Roman law, any infraction of regular discipline could be subject to capital punishment. When a unit such as a cohort, maniple, or century broke in battle, refused to march, mutinied, or otherwise displayed serious indiscipline, a commander could inflict capital punishment.

According to Polybius, the way that decimation worked was that a commander would surround the guilty unit with a larger part of the legion from which it came. The guilty unit would then either be separated into groups of up to a 10th or kept together if it was a smaller unit. Every soldier in the unit would then draw lots (sortition) to see who would be executed. The men who drew the lots were then executed by their comrades in the guilty unit. According to Polybius, the execution was carried out with clubs, but there were cases when the men used swords. Regardless, the remainder of the guilty unit received barley rations and may have been subject to additional penalties.

The reason for carrying out the executions in this manner was not just as a deterrent. Collective punishment maximized the impact on the unit without sacrificing too many men. Additionally, by executing their comrades, the survivors had an opportunity to discharge their guilt for the unit's offense. The oath to obey that soldiers took was a religious one, so indiscipline was a religious as well as military crime. The decimation was thus a ritual punishment.

During the Republic this punishment was occasionally used, though there seems to have been resurgence in its use during the triumvirate. Octavian and one of his officers used it during the civil wars. As a punishment, decimation did not always work. Antony used it in Brundisium in 44 before marching to Gaul, only subjecting 30 men to the penalty, but then the rest of the guilty legion defected to Octavian when they neared Rome.

Lee L. Brice

See also: Antonius, Marcus; Discipline; Julius Caesar Octavianus, Gaius

References

Brice, Lee L. "Disciplining Octavian: An Aspect of Roman Military Culture during the Triumviral Wars 44–30 BCE." In *Warfare and Culture in World History,* edited by Wayne Lee, 35–60. New York: New York University Press, 2011.

Keppie, L. J. F. *The Making of the Roman Army: From Republic to Empire.* Updated ed. Norman: University of Oklahoma Press, 1998.

Polybius. *Histories.* Translated by R. Waterfield and B. McGing. Oxford: Oxford University Press, 2010.

Decorations, Military. *See* Military Decorations

Discipline

The Roman military has a reputation for brutal discipline, but it is important to recognize that military discipline is more complex than adherence to orders or punishment of infractions; it is a means of control that included physical, mental, and social components reinforced with positive as well as negative sanctions. The military purpose of discipline was victory. Success was achieved by keeping men in the battle line long enough to win, having them follow orders in the heat of battle, and maintaining peace and order at all times.

Soldiers' introduction to military discipline occurred at enlistment, when they took the military oath promising to obey all their commanders' orders for the duration of the war. During training, discipline was further ingrained as recruits learned their place in line, how to fight, and the expectations to which they were subject. Reinforcement of this physical and mental discipline was ongoing throughout service in drills, duties, and combat. In their units, soldiers were also subject to forms of social discipline, as their comrades and officers expected them to do their duty and support each other. Discipline should be thought of as a matrix of control.

There were penalties for indiscipline. According to Roman law, any infraction of regular discipline could be subject to capital punishment. When individuals or a unit such as a cohort, maniple, or century displayed indiscipline, a commander could inflict capital punishment, such as decimation. Desertion was a capital crime too. There were lesser penalties, such as having to bivouac outside the legionary fortifications, standing guard duty for extended periods, flogging, barley instead of wheat to eat, and reduced pay or rations. Commanders had great flexibility in imposing penalties; there do not seem to have been specific regulations connecting infractions and particular punishments, so most infractions may not have received death penalties. Once the penalties were carried out, it was common for indisciplined soldiers and units to receive a chance to prove that they could recover their reputation in battle and other assignments.

Discipline was not just punishment. Roman commanders had a variety of ways to honor and reward individuals and units that distinguished themselves. Polybius reports that during fighting, commanding officers should be on horses so they can see which soldiers merit reward as well as punishment. The most basic reward was to excuse men (*immunes*) from tedious daily duties, but increasing rations or pay was possible for a unit or an individual. Promotion to a higher rank was also a possible reward. There was also a wide variety of unit and individual decorations that could be awarded, all of which carried with them recognition by comrades and society.

A mental and social component of Roman discipline that was too often ignored was status. In a status-conscious society that valued military success as much as Rome, rewards and penalties were extremely important. Every penalty carried with it a loss, just as every reward increased the recipient's status. Minor penalties and rewards might only reverberate in the unit or legion, but the greater the honor or penalty, the more likely it was to be known in the broader community and would impact the soldier's life after leaving the military. The evidence for status is lopsided, of course, since Roman authors record numerous instances of military awards resulting in success outside the military but seldom report an instance of punishment having a negative impact.

Roman discipline was more complicated and flexible than its reputation for brutality conveys. As noted previously, commanders had great flexibility in assigning penalties and rewards. There is also much evidence that soldiers could speak frankly to their commanders so long as this did not undermine discipline. Discipline was not so rigid that men could not find opportunities for individual valor. Officers seem to have occasionally encouraged individual displays of heroics when it was necessary to overcome a difficult objective. Legionary discipline was not always a perfect combination of its various aspects, but taken as whole it was an important component of Rome's overall military success.

Lee L. Brice

See also: Centurions; Decimation; Military Decorations; Military Oath; Mutiny; Polybius; Stipendium; Training

References

Brice, Lee L. "Disciplining Octavian: An Aspect of Roman Military Culture during the Triumviral Wars, 44–30 BCE." In *Warfare and Culture in World History,* edited by Wayne Lee, 35–60. New York: New York University Press, 2011.

Brice, Lee L. "Second Chance for Valor: Restoration of Order after Mutinies and Indiscipline in the Roman Military." In *Aspects of Ancient Institutions and Geography,* edited by L. L. Brice and D. Sloötjes, 23–34. Leiden: Brill, 2014.

Goldsworthy, A. *The Army at War, 100 B.C.–A.D. 200.* Oxford, UK: Clarendon, 1996.

Lendon, J. E. *Soldiers and Ghosts: A History of Battle in Classical Antiquity.* New Haven, CT: Yale University Press, 2006.

Phang, S. E. *Roman Military Service: Ideologies of Discipline in the Late Republic and Early Empire.* Cambridge: Cambridge University Press, 2008.

E

Elephants, War

Elephants had been used in Africa and in the East for centuries before the Roman military first encountered them in 280 BCE during the Pyrrhic Wars. Elephants were effective when used properly. They were intimidating by nature for infantry, horses could not tolerate their smell, and they were effective as weapons and fighting platforms. Additionally, the presence of elephants projected the wealth and status of the leader using them.

The two types of elephants that the Romans encountered were the Indian elephant and the African forest elephant. The Indian elephant had been semidomesticated for centuries before Hellenistic kings and commanders started using them against each other in the eastern Mediterranean. Indian elephants were tall and strong, capable of carrying a platform or turret on their backs from which soldiers or archers could fight. African forest elephants were smaller and much more amenable to taming than the larger African savanna elephants. Forest elephants did not usually support a platform during battle, being trained to carry two riders and employed as weapons. Carthage used these elephants especially during the Punic Wars. Numidians trained their cavalry to cope with the elephants' smell.

Initially the Romans did not stand up to either species of elephants. Eventually Roman commanders found the elephants' vulnerabilities, especially their tendency to stampede into their own troops if sufficiently harassed. The Roman commanders started to train specialized units to harass the elephants with missile fire or hamstring them with their swords. At Zama in 203, Scipio had his men leave gaps in the line to let the elephants pass through.

Romans used elephants in several battles, including at Cynoscephalae in 197 and Numantia in 133. At Magnesia, the Romans had African elephants but succeeded in stampeding Antiochus' Indian elephants into his own phalanx. Caesar had elephants at Thapsus, the last time that a Roman commander employed them during the Republic. Most commanders found elephants to be more trouble than they were worth.

Lee L. Brice

See also: Cornelius Scipio Africanus, Publius; Cynoscephalae, Battle of; Greece; Magnesia, Battle of; Pyrrhic Wars; Zama, Battle of

References

Charles, M. B. "African Forest Elephants and Turrets in the Ancient World." *Phoenix* 62(3–4) (2008): 338–362.

Glover, R. F. "The Tactical Handling of the Elephant." *Greece and Rome* 17(49) (1948): 1–11.

Etruscan Wars

Unlike later Roman conflicts for which we have more sources, the Etruscan Wars do not survive well in the ancient sources. Numerous difficulties arise in assembling their course. These wars occurred so early in Roman history that extensive elements of the early narratives are shrouded in mythology and should be heavily discounted. Livy is our best surviving source for this early period, but he wrote four centuries after the events and drew on sources that were recorded at least two centuries after the events they described. Also, his account does not become more detailed until the last phase of the Etruscan conflict, and then it breaks off abruptly with events in 293. The problems in all of our sources are such that no continuous narrative of the Etruscan Wars can be reconstructed. It is, however, possible to discern at places the general course of the wars.

The Etruscan Wars began with Rome's three wars against the city of Veii, beginning in 483 BCE. Veii was a successful Etruscan city nine miles north of Rome. Both cities were of similar size and strength and had been in competition for years. It is not clear from our sources which side struck first, but the warfare was annual, and the raiding by both sides continued alongside regular campaigns. There was a Roman battle victory in 480, but the Veiians were still able to invade and set up a camp in Roman territory on the Janiculum Hill. In response, the Fabian clan of Romans set up a fort in Veiian territory on the Cremera River. Veii destroyed this fort in 477. Finally in 474, the two sides signed a 40-year truce.

As it happened, the truce coincided with the Battle of Cumae off central Italy. The Greek tyrant Hiero I of Syracuse, allied with Aristodemus of Cumae, defeated a large Etruscan fleet in the bay of Naples. Rome played no role in the engagement, but the naval battle resulted in the end of Etruscan hegemony in central Italy and left a power vacuum into which Rome would eventually turn its energies.

The second war with Veii began in 437 when the Veiian leader Lars Tolumnius had Roman ambassadors murdered. In the ensuing warfare, Tolumnius died in single combat. In 436 or 435, Rome attacked and began to siege the Veiian city of Fidenae. Roman soldiers tunneled into the city's citadel, capturing it. Remarkably, no other Etruscan city sent aid to Fidenae or Veii, so they had to sign a 30-year truce in 435. The final conflict with Veii began when Rome attacked it directly after the Veiians refused to pay an indemnity for the prior conflict. Rome laid siege to Veii. Livy's report that the siege lasted 10 years and ended the same way as the siege of Fidenae are too poetic to be true. There may have been a siege, and the city did fall in circa 396 and was absorbed into Roman territory. The end of this conflict was merely the end of the first phase in the Etruscan Wars.

There was a brief war (358–351) between Rome and the Etruscan city of Tarquinii, which was later supported by the Etruscan communities of Falerii and Caere. Tarquinii soldiers raided Roman territory, and when they refused to pay reparations, the war began. As with so many Roman wars in this period, the quality of the leadership and combat was erratic, so the war dragged on. Rome won a major victory in 353, forcing Caere to sign a truce, and two years later after much pillaging, Tarquinii and Falerii signed truces also, ending the war. As with the prior conflict, most of the Etruscan communities did not send aid, though this pattern is not surprising given that the Etruscans did not maintain a federal or imperial system.

The final phase of the Etruscan Wars began in 311 when Etruscan cities, probably Volsinii, Perusia, Cortona, Arretium, and Clusium, banded together and attacked the Roman colony at Sutrium, in formerly Etruscan territory. What triggered the attack is not recorded, but it may have been connected with Roman warfare with the Samnites and Gauls. Rome responded aggressively, forcing Perusia, Cortona, and Arretium to sign treaties in 311 and forcing Volsinii to sign a treaty in 308. Even after bringing these cities to make peace, the Romans continued fighting in Etruria annually as the Samnites tried to forge a broader alliance to distract or crush

Rome. This phase of the war turned more aggressive after the Battle of Sentinum against a Samnite coalition in 295. Roman commanders moved against the Etruscan cities that had allied with the Samnites, and more vigorous annual, or nearly so, campaigns into Etruria continued.

After 293 Livy's narrative is lost for most of the third century, so there are only occasional notices. In 284 a Roman army was defeated by Gauls with Etruscan allies near Arretium, but in 283 Rome defeated a similar force at Lake Vadimon. By 280, the Etruscan communities of Vulci, Volsinii, Rusellae, Vetulonia, Populonia, Volaterrae, and Tarquinii had been forced to become allies of Rome. Caere's conquest in 273 was the effective end of the Etruscan Wars. A last gasp occurred when Falerii revolted in 241, but the city was was razed and its population relocated as an example to other allies. Rome finally had unchallenged dominance of Etruria.

The Etruscan Wars read as if the outcome was a foregone conclusion, but it is important to recall that Rome lost numerous battles, and for a time early in the wars, part of its territory was occupied. During the later phase of the wars, Rome was distracted with wars in central Italy but still managed to bring this series of conflicts to a conclusion.

Lee L. Brice

See also: Etruscan Wars, Causes of the; Etruscan Wars, Consequences of the; Livy; Rome; Samnite Wars; Syracuse

References

Bradley, Guy. *Early Rome to 290 B.C.: The Beginnings of the City and the Rise of the Republic.* Edinburgh, UK: Edinburgh University Press, 2012.

Cornell, T. J. *The Beginnings of Rome: Italy and Rome from the Bronze Age to the Punic Wars (1000–264 BC).* London: Routledge, 1995.

Erdkamp, P., ed. *A Companion to the Roman Army.* Oxford, UK: Wiley-Blackwell, 2011.

Livy. *History of Rome.* 14 vols. Translated by B. O. Foster. Loeb Classical Library. Cambridge, MA: Harvard University Press, 1919.

Etruscan Wars, Causes of the

Unlike later Roman conflicts for which we have more sources, the Etruscan Wars do not survive well in the ancient sources, so there are number of difficulties in assembling the causes of the wars. These wars occurred so early in Roman history that some of the circumstances that led to conflict are shrouded in mythology. Livy is our best surviving source for this early period, but he wrote four centuries after the events and drew on sources that were recorded centuries after the events they described. Also, his account does not become more detailed until the last phase of the Etruscan conflict, but the Samnite Wars dominate that part of the narrative, and then it breaks off abruptly with events in 293. Despite these problems, it is still possible to discern the more general causes of the Etruscan Wars. The description here focuses on the historical rather than the semimythic conflicts that predate the Roman Republic.

According to one tradition, when the last king, Tarquinius Superbus, was overthrown, he appealed for assistance to the Etruscan cities of Veii, Caere, and Tarquinii. These cities raised an army but were defeated. The tradition records that Tarquin sought the assistance of the king of the Etruscan city of Clusium, Lars Porsenna, but Porsenna, who initially assisted Tarquin, was eventually moved by Roman bravery. The entire tradition is such a mix of legend, confusion, and fact that most of the details have been rejected. The Tarquinii family was overthrown and ejected, but evidence for an Etruscan war is overblown. Clusium may have attacked and even occupied Rome, but it was not the beginning of a larger war. We can be sure that this was not the beginning of the Etruscan Wars.

Although raiding for booty, some of which was undertaken against Etruscan territory, was a common cause of warfare in the pre-Republican period, the actual Etruscan Wars were more complicated. The wars began with Rome's three wars against the city of Veii, beginning in 483 BCE. Veii was a successful Etruscan city nine miles north of Rome. The war seems to have begun over competition for trade and communication routes. Rome was at a major river ford, so north-south traffic west of the Appenines could cross the Tiber there, but Veii controlled another ford upstream at Fidenae. Similarly, neither city had unrestricted control of the banks of the Tiber out to the sea, a necessary condition for controlling river trade. It is not clear from our sources which side struck first or why, but it probably was tied to an effort to secure territorial control. The cause of the first Veiian war is lost, but the second war began when Roman ambassadors to Veii were murdered. The last war began in 406 when the Veiians refused to pay an indemnity for the prior conflict, so Rome made a preemptive attack on them directly. The end of this conflict in 396 was merely the end of the first phase in the Etruscan Wars.

There was a brief war (358–351) between Rome and the Etruscan city of Tarquinii, which was later supported by Falerii and Caere. According to Livy, the cause of this war was a raid by Tarquinii soldiers into Roman territory. As noted previously, raiding for economic gain was a common cause of conflict; Roman settlers north of the Tiber must have been tempting targets. The fighting ended with a 40-year truce that does not seem to have been broken by either side.

The next sustained phase of the Etruscan Wars began in 311 when Etruscan cities, probably Volsinii, Perusia, Cortona, Arretium, and Clusium, attacked the Roman colony at Sutrium, in formerly Etruscan territory. The event that triggered the attack is not recorded, but it may have been connected with Roman warfare in central Italy. Even after bringing these cities to make peace, the Romans continued fighting in Etruria annually. This phase of the war turned more aggressive after the Battle of Sentinum, in which Rome defeated a Samnite coalition in 295. Roman leaders, angry that some Etruscans had allied with the Samnites and anxious to make sure that it stopped, moved vigorously against the cities that had joined the Samnites. After an army of Gauls and perhaps some Etruscan allies defeated a Roman army in 284, the Romans struck back the following year, crushing the Gauls and their Etruscan allies at Lake Vadimon. Caere tried to hold out but in 273 also capitulated, ending the Etruscan Wars.

Lee L. Brice

See also: Etruscan Wars; Etruscan Wars, Consequences of the; Livy; Rome; Samnite Wars

References

Bradley, Guy. *Early Rome to 290 B.C.: The Beginnings of the City and the Rise of the Republic*. Edinburgh, UK: Edinburgh University Press, 2012.

Cornell, T. J. *The Beginnings of Rome: Italy and Rome from the Bronze Age to the Punic Wars (1000–264 BC)*. London: Routledge, 1995.

Erdkamp, P., ed. *A Companion to the Roman Army*. Oxford, UK: Wiley-Blackwell, 2011.

Livy. *History of Rome*. 14 vols. Translated by B. O. Foster. Loeb Classical Library. Cambridge, MA: Harvard University Press, 1919.

Rosenstein, N., and R. Morstein-Marx, eds. *A Companion to the Roman Republic*. Oxford, UK: Blackwell, 2010.

Etruscan Wars, Consequences of the

Trying to reconstruct the course of the Etruscan Wars that began in 483 BCE may be problematic due to our poor sources, but appreciating the consequences of the conflict is not difficult at all. Livy, our best surviving source for this early period, constructs his narrative in such a way as to allow his readers to see foreshadowing and early emergence of later innovations and problems, political and military.

The Etruscan Wars ended in 273 when Caere capitulated and was forced to become subordinate to Rome. Most of the immediate consequences of the war were predictable for both sides. Forced to become Roman allies, the Etruscans lost control of their foreign relations. They also had to provide soldiers for Rome's wars but had no vote or influence in Rome's deliberations about war and peace. Most of the Etruscan cities did not receive citizenship benefits, and there was no explicit promise that they would. After Falerii revolted, Rome made an example of it by razing the city to the ground and relocating the populace to a new colony that would still be an ally.

As bad as these measures were, these cities did enjoy some benefits from alliance. Roman alliance meant peace in the sense that other allies could not declare war on them, and they received Roman protection. These cities did not have to pay Rome regular taxes once they became allies. They also enjoyed a level of autonomy in their internal affairs. Rome tended to support elite families in these cities. When the elite families of Volsinii appealed to Rome in 264 because they had been ejected from power, Rome sacked the city, making provision for the elite families and some other survivors to resettle a new colony.

The other immediate impacts during the war were much more widespread, even if impossible to quantify. In addition to the numerous battle deaths on both sides, an unknown number of men, women, and children died violently off the battlefield during the war. A number of cities, including Veii, Fidenae, and Privernum, had been entirely destroyed or depopulated. Agricultural production had suffered from the raiding and pillaging in parts of Etruria and central Italy, causing additional economic, social, and medical problems. All of this meant an overall decline in the population that was spread unevenly in Rome and Etruria but affected all economic levels, free and slave. The loss was great, but within 10 years after making peace, many cities had rebounded.

Despite these losses, Rome benefited immensely in the long term from the war. Starting with the elimination of Veii and the seizure of its territory in 396, Rome added a great deal of territory to its public holdings. Rome also established a number of colonies that had the economic benefit of removing some of the poor from the city by giving them land elsewhere but also spreading Roman commercial interests and control over resources. Rome also gained control over Etruria, thus freeing up resources for employment to the south and adding to Rome's pool of allied manpower reserves. This was the first war in which Rome fielded an army that included as many or more allied troops as legionaries. Rome applied the military, commercial, and colonial practices that evolved to win the Etruscan Wars to later conflicts in central and southern Italy. These wars contributed immensely to Rome's later success.

Another consequence of these wars was internal political change in Rome. In his narrative, Livy connects the wars with a number of points in Rome's political conflict called the Struggle of the Orders. During the wars, the Plebeians used crises to assert their demands. Thus, tribunes of the Plebeians were able to assert independent authority, the first Plebeian consul was elected, and the first Plebeian dictator was named. The Etruscan Wars were not internal conflicts in Rome, but they contributed to internal political change.

While the wars spread destruction and turmoil, over the long term they were an immense boon to Rome. They laid much of the groundwork for later Roman military and economic success. The Etruscan allies were sufficiently satisfied with the arrangement that when Hannibal invaded Italy in 218, they contributed men to Rome's armies and remained loyal. When the Social War erupted, Rome's allies participated but accepted the offers of citizenship and peace early. Shrouded in legend and lost sources, the Etruscan Wars were an important episode in Roman military history.

Lee L. Brice

See also: Etruscan Wars; Etruscan Wars, Causes of the; Hannibal; Livy; Rome; Social War

References

Bradley, Guy. *Early Rome to 290 B.C.: The Beginnings of the City and the Rise of the Republic.* Edinburgh, UK: Edinburgh University Press, 2012.

Cornell, T. J. *The Beginnings of Rome: Italy and Rome from the Bronze Age to the Punic Wars (1000–264 BC).* London: Routledge, 1995.

Erdkamp, P., ed. *A Companion to the Roman Army.* Oxford, UK: Wiley-Blackwell, 2011.

Livy. *History of Rome.* 14 vols. Translated by B. O. Foster. Loeb Classical Library. Cambridge, MA: Harvard University Press, 1919.

Rosenstein, N., and R. Morstein-Marx, eds. *A Companion to the Roman Republic.* Oxford, UK: Blackwell, 2010.

Evocati

Veterans reenlisted for a wide variety of reasons. Veterans who reenlisted at the invitation of their commanders after serving their full required term of 6 years were called *evocati* (sing. *evocatus*) because they were called back. Most of our evidence for them comes from the late Roman Republic and the Roman Empire, but they are attested in the late third century BCE. One such case might be that of Spurius Ligustinus, who served 22 years during the early second century and was called back and promoted repeatedly.

Some *evocati* became centurions and other lower-level officers or were asked to take roles in legionary administration, but most seem to have remained in the ranks, possibly organized as separate units within the legion under their own *evocati* officers.

These veterans were extremely valuable as experienced anchors in a legion. During the civil wars at the end of the Republic, we know of entire legions made up mostly or entirely from these called-back veterans. These men had been critical to Pompey's political success, and he relied on these *evocati* to fill out his ranks with capable men. Similarly, the triumvirs also drew upon them heavily.

Lee L. Brice

See also: Civil War II; Civil War III; Pompeius Magnus, Gnaeus; Triumvirate, Second

References

Brice, Lee L. "Discharging Pullo and Vorenus: Veterans in *Rome*." In *Rome Season Two: Trial & Triumph,* edited by Monica Cyrino. Edinburgh, UK: Edinburgh University Press, 2014.

Keppie, L. J. F. *The Making of the Roman Army: From Republic to Empire.* Updated ed. Norman: University of Oklahoma Press, 1998.

F

Fabius Maximus Verrucosus, Quintus

Quintus <u>Fabius</u> Maximus Verrucosus was born into a prominent Roman family sometime around 266 BCE. His early career was typical of Roman elites, but unusually, he served as consul repeatedly, in 233, 228, 215, 214, and 209, and was appointed dictator for six months twice, in 221 and 217. He is sometimes known also by the pejorative name Cunctator ("Delayer") because of his strategy in 217–216.

Fabius is best known for his role in campaigning against Hannibal in the Second Punic War. Hannibal crossed the Alps in 218 and won victories over Roman armies at Trebia in 218 and Lake Trasimene in 217. Fabius was appointed dictator for a six-month term as Hannibal pushed down the east coast of Italy.

Recognizing Hannibal's skill, Fabius chose to avoid a decisive battle in the plains in which Hannibal could use his superior cavalry. Rather, Fabius pursued a strategy of harassing Hannibal, hindering his supplies, and wearing him down in a war of attrition. Castigated in Rome for this approach, Romans accused Fabius of cowardice and called him derisively Cunctator. Finally in 216 when Fabius' term ended, the Romans replaced him with two consuls, Paullus and Varro, who were ordered to combine their forces and engage Hannibal. The result was the disaster at Cannae in 216.

Although numerous southern Italian cities defected to Hannibal following the disaster of Cannae, Rome reverted to Fabius' strategy and continued to fight. Afterward Rome's commanders avoided open battle in Italy with Hannibal. The attrition strategy was especially effective because

Hannibal had to protect his new allies. Constantly harassing Hannibal's supply lines to Carthage and making provisioning of his forces difficult gradually weakened him.

Elected consul for 209, Fabius retook the city of Tarentum in southern Italy, which had revolted against Rome. He opposed Scipio's plan to invade Africa but died in 203. Fabius gave his name to a strategy, the Fabian strategy.

Spencer C. Tucker

See also: Cannae, Battle of; Hannibal; Punic Wars

References

Goldsworthy, A. *The Punic Wars*. London: Cassell, 2000.

Hoyos, Dexter, ed. *A Companion to the Punic Wars*. Oxford, UK: Wiley-Blackwell, 2011.

Lazenby, J. F. *Hannibal's War: A Military History of the Second Punic War*. Norman: University of Oklahoma Press, 1998.

Flamininus, Titus Quinctius. *See* Quinctius Flamininus, Titus

Fleet, Roman

Rome did not bother with a fleet until the First Punic War, which began in 264 BCE, because it had not previously needed a navy. Since the war was in Sicily, Rome needed a fleet and thus used captured Carthaginian ships as its model navy and trained crews from scratch. The standard Roman ships became the triremes, quadriremes, and quinquiremes, the same ships as Carthage. These ships required more rowers but could carry more soldiers and cargo.

The Romans were inexperienced, so they made up for it by inventing the *corax*, a movable boarding bridge attached to the Roman deck with a large, sharp spike on top. The large spike kept the enemy from ramming or escaping, and then Roman soldiers marched across the bridge and fought as if they were on land. The problem was that the bridge made the Roman ships top-heavy and dangerous in rough seas, so Rome eventually discontinued its use. Rome lost many fleets during the war and even had to enlist

The trireme was the primary warship used by Carthage, Greece, and Rome during the Roman Republic. Larger versions would come to dominate naval warfare, but the trireme remained in service through Actium. This image is the modern reconstruction, the *Olympias*. (Lee L. Brice)

freed slaves as rowers. Despite the losses, the fleet won some key victories and transported men, thus contributing to eventual victory.

During the Second Punic War, the fleet not only moved men but also effectively controlled the seas around Italy and cut off Hannibal from naval supply. The fleet played similar roles in all later conflicts. By 67 when pirates had become a problem, Pompey showed his talent with a fleet by defeating them in six months. In addition to the usual uses, Caesar used his fleet in 49 to assist in the siege of Massilia in southern Gaul. Control of the seas was critical in the later civil wars, so both sides had fleets.

During the final civil war, fleets were again critical to the course of the war. The assassins used them to try to keep Antony and Octavian out of Greece in 42. Sextus Pompey used his fleet to control Sicily, blockade Italy, and force the triumvirs to concede authority. Agrippa emerged as the superior naval commander, organizing Octavian's fleet buildup and victories at Mylae and Naulochus in 36 and finally winning again at Actium in 31, a battle that was decided entirely at sea, for which he received a naval crown.

Roman naval battles continued to be decided by a combination of ramming and fighting from the deck. During much of the Republic, commanders put legionaries on ships rather than keep specialized marines for the fighting, as they would during the Roman Empire. Agrippa invented a new kind of grapnel hook that could be fired from a *ballista* and then drawn in close for engagement. Rowers did not enjoy the status of legionaries, but they were critical to Roman successes. In addition to rowing, they could be light troops when called upon after a ship beached.

A key reason that the navy received less attention from Roman authors is that command of the legions was flashier and the bulk of naval personnel were the rowers, most of whom came from the poor and noncitizens.

Lee L. Brice

See also: Actium, Battle of; Antonius, Marcus; Civil War II; Civil War III; Julius Caesar, Gaius; Julius Caesar Octavianus, Gaius; Military Decorations; Piracy; Pompeius Magnus, Gnaeus; Pompeius Magnus, Sextus; Punic Wars; Punic Wars, Consequences of the; Slaves and Camp Followers; Vipsanius Agrippa, Marcus

References

Morrison, J. S. *Greek and Roman Oared Warships.* Oxford, UK: Oxbow, 1996.

Murray, William. *The Age of Titans: The Rise and Fall of Great Hellenistic Navies.* Oxford: Oxford University Press, 2012.

Forts

Roman legions on campaign in enemy territory were expected to build wooden fortifications every night to guard against the enemy. During the early Roman Republic, legions developed a system of building marching forts that were always set up the same way every time so that regardless of the available daylight, arriving units knew exactly where their tents were, or if there was a call to arms at night, every man knew his post.

Polybius records in great detail how the fort was laid out with four gates and two roads that met at the commander's headquarters (*praetorium*). Each maniple, and later each cohort, had an assigned place inside. Every aspect of the Roman fort, including the space between the walls and the paths between units, had a specific purpose. The marching fort was built of wooden stakes with a ditch, all on a site chosen in advance and supervised by military tribunes. Allies and legionaries participated in the construction. The forts were not intended to provide absolute protection or survive siege, because Roman military doctrine called for leaving camp and fighting in the open.

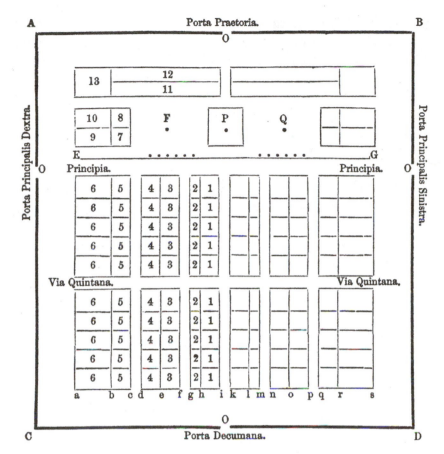

Plan of a Roman army camp (after a description by the historian Polybius, second century BC), another example of an orderly community of the pre-modern world. Some of the features shown include (P) the general's tent (tents #7-10) the general's staff, and (F) the public market. The rows of tents numbered 1-6 housed, respectively, the cavalry, the infantry of the third, second, and first lines of battle, the allied cavalry, and the allied infantry. (Ramsay, William. A Manual of Roman Antiquities, 1851)

Building forts also provided training for soldiers in teamwork and following orders and in siege preparation. Rome used similar forts for longer occupations and sieges but might build those out of stone instead of wood. Aemilianus, for example, trained his men for the rigorous campaigns against Numantia by having them build and dismantle forts daily. Eventually his men built a stone wall and wooden towers and forts for six miles around the city. Caesar's men were expert fort builders by the end of the Gallic Wars. The regular layout remained part of forts for centuries beyond the Republic.

Forts were for more than just defense. They were also a method of marking territory. Each night the Roman fort was an expression of control over a patch of enemy territory. As the legions moved through a region, they left behind the marks of where the fortification had been, demonstrating to all their control, strength, and aggression.

Lee L. Brice

See also: Cornelius Scipio Aemilianus Africanus, Publius; Discipline; Gallic Wars; Julius Caesar, Gaius; Siege; Training; Tribunes, Military

References

Goldsworthy, A. K. *The Roman Army at War, 100 B.C.–A.D. 200.* Oxford, UK: Clarendon, 1996.

Keppie, L. J. F. *The Making of the Roman Army: From Republic to Empire.* Updated ed. Norman: University of Oklahoma Press, 1998.

Fustuarium. *See* Decimation

G

Gallic Wars

Caesar left for his provinces of Cisalpine Gaul and Transalpine Gaul in 58 immediately after his consulship and soon found an opportunity to deploy his three legions. The Helvetii, forced to migrate due to pressure from Germanic tribes, requested permission to cross Roman territory. Caesar refused and, after recruiting and training two new legions in Cisalpine Gaul, destroyed the Rhône River bridge. The Helvetii tried to force a crossing of the Rhône and then turned north, where Caesar defeated them as they tried to cross the Saone River. Both groups continued north, fighting again at Bibracte. They lost again and by terms of surrender returned to their original lands and became Roman allies.

Soon afterward Caesar encountered the Germanic Suebi, against whom the Sequani, Aedui, and a number of other tribes requested Roman support. After unsuccessful negotiations, the Suebi invaded. While Caesar was eager to fight, many of his officers and soldiers did not want to fight so soon after defeating the Helvetii. When Caesar's army occupied Vesontio the soldiers mutinied, but Caesar resolved it quickly. They then defeated the Suebi and drove them back across the Rhine.

The following spring, Caesar enlisted two more legions from Cisalpine Gaul. He campaigned among the Belgae in northern Gaul. These tribes, especially the Nervii, responded by using irregular warfare to avoid pitched battle. The Roman army adapted and won a decisive victory at the Sambre River. The Aduatuci were then defeated after a siege.

Despite these successes, matters in Gaul were less settled after two years than anticipated. Several tribes, including the Veneti of northwestern

Chart 4 Key Events of Caesar's Gallic Campaign, 58–51 BCE

Event Name	Date	Caesar's Key Officers**	Roman Numbers***	Opposition Leaders**	Gallic Tribes or Numbers**
Caesar takes command	58	Titus Atius Labienus	4 legions	—	—
Helvetii leave home	March 58	—	—	—	Helvetii 239,000
Helvetii try Rhône crossing	58	Labienus	1 legion, auxilia	Nammeius, Verucloetis	Helvetii
Battle of Arar (Saône)	58	—	3 legions, auxilia	—	Tigurine
Battle of Bibracte	June 58	Labienus	6 legions, auxilia	—	Helvetii, Boii, Tulingi
Vesontio Campaign	Sept. 58	Publius Licinius Crassus, Labienus	6 legions, auxilia	Ariovistus	Harudes, Triboci, Marcomanni, Nemetes, Vangiones, Seducci, Suebi
Skirmish at Aisne Ford	57	—	auxilia = cavalry, light troops, archers, and slingers	—	Belgae
Battle of Sambre	57	Labienus	8 legions, auxilia	Boduognatus	Nervii, Veromandui, Atrebates
Siege of Aduatici	57	—	8 legions, auxilia	—	Aduatuci
Campaign vs. Veneti	56	Decimus Brutus	4 legions, fleet	—	Veneti
Campaign in Normandy	56	Q. Titurius Sabinus	1 legion?, auxilia	Viridovix	Calvados, Eure

Event Name	Date	Caesar's Key Officers**	Roman Numbers***	Opposition Leaders**	Gallic Tribes or Numbers**
Campaign in Aquitania	56	P. Crassus	12 cohorts, auxilia	Adcantuannus	Sotiates, Vocates, Tarusates
Campaign vs. Veneti allies north*	56	Sabinus	2+ legions	—	Morini
Germanic Campaign	55	—	8 legions, auxilia	—	Usipetes, Tencteri
Invasion of Britain	55	—	2 legions, auxilia cavalry	—	Britons
Invasion of Britain	54	Q. Atrius, G. Trebonius	5 legions, auxilia	Cassivellaunus	Britons
Ambush at Atuatuca*	Winter 54	L. Aurunculeius Cotta, Sabinus	15 cohorts, auxilia	Ambiorix, Catuvolcus	Eburones
Gallic Revolt	Winter 54	Q. Tullius Cicero	1 legion, auxilia	Ambiorix	Eburones, Atuatuci, Nervii
Gallic Revolt	Winter 54–53	Labienus	1–3 legions, auxilia	Indutiomarus,	Treveri,
Caesar's relief	Winter 54	G. Fabius, G. Trebonius	2 legions, auxilia	Ambiorix	Nervii, 60,000 men
Chastising Gaul	53	Labienus	10 legions, auxilia	Ambiorix, Catuvolcus	Nervii, Menapii, Treverii, Eburones, Atuatici
Raid over Cevennes	Winter 52	Decimus Brutus	cohorts, auxilia	—	Arverni

(Continued)

Chart 4 Key Events of Caesar's Gallic Campaign, 58–51 BCE (Continued)

Event Name	Date	Caesar's Key Officers**	Roman Numbers***	Opposition Leaders**	Gallic Tribes or Numbers**
Siege of Vellaunodunum	Winter 52	—	8 legions, auxilia	—	Senones
Sack of Cenabum	Winter 52	—	8 legions, auxilia	—	Carnutes?
Siege of Noviodunum	Winter 52	—	8 legions, auxilia	Vercengetorix	Bituriges
Siege of Avaricum	Spring 52	—	8 legions, auxilia	Vercingetorix	Bituriges, 40,000
Siege of Gergovia*	52	Fabius	6 legions, auxilia	Vercingetorix, Lucterius	Arverni
Battle of Lutetia	52	Labienus	4 legions, auxilia	Camulogenus	Parisii
Siege of Alesia	52	Labienus, Reginus, Caninius, Trebonius, Antony	10 legions, auxilia	Vercingetorix, Commius, Eporedorix, Viridomarus, Vercassivellaunus	80,000+ inside; 100,000 –250,000+ relief force
Defeat of Bellovaci	51	Labienus	4 legions, auxilia	Correus, Commius	Bellovaci
Andean Revolt	51	Caninius, Fabius	4.5 legion, auxilia	Dumnacus,	Andes
Siege of Uxellodunum	51	Caninius, Fabius, Q. Calenus	4–6 legions	Drappes, Lucterius	
Organization of Gaul	50	—	—	—	—

* Roman defeat.
** If known.
*** Legion size = 5,000–6,200; number of auxilia usually unknown. All names and numbers are from Caesar's Commentaries.
Source: Caesar, *War Commentaries of Caesar*, translated by Rex Warner (New York: New American Library, 1960).

Gaul and the Aquitani of southwestern Gaul, revolted in 56 and were forced to make peace after separate campaigns. That same year Caesar invaded Britain. He claimed that he needed to chastise the tribes of Britain who had given support to the rebellious Gauls. Caesar's desire to conquer a region not previously visited by Romans and to conquer new and unknown peoples was at least as significant a motivation. The first invasion did not go as well as hoped, and the forces were fortunate to have been able to get back to Gaul safely.

More unrest began in the spring of 55, this time from the Germanic Usipeti and Tencteri tribes, whose soldiers crossed the Rhine under pressure from the Suebi. After a treacherous attack during negotiations, Caesar refused the leaders' apology and attacked their camp without warning. The next month he led his army across the Rhine over a bridge built for this purpose in less than 10 days. This bridging was a direct response to the Germanic tribes, who had asserted that Roman power did not extend across the river. Caesar destroyed the bridge after crossing back to Gaul, proving that the bridge was built to impress the Germanic tribes.

In 54 Caesar again invaded Britain. He asserted the same reason as previously but clearly wanted to complete a conquest. Roman operations were more successful the second time, conquering territory south of the Thames but achieving no permanent occupation. Caesar, however, withdrew to Gaul for the winter because of potential trouble. Bad harvests that fall made it necessary to garrison the legions separately, making them more vulnerable, but Caesar did not lower the amount of grain requisitioned from the Gallic tribes. The pressure that this caused in addition to already existing resentment of Rome increased resistance.

The Eburones, in northeastern Gaul, were the first to attack Roman forces that winter. After attacking a detachment from the 15 cohorts under Sabinus and Cotta, the assault quickly moved to the camp, but the Gauls withdrew after a cavalry skirmish. Their leader, Ambiorix, tricked the commanders into believing that they had safe passage, but while on the march the entire column was surrounded and annihilated. The Nervii attempted the same strategy against Quintus Cicero, but he fortified camp and delivered a message to Caesar, who personally led a Roman relief force. Caesar then consolidated Roman forces into three camps instead of five and spent the winter with the army.

For the campaigns of 53, Caesar enlisted 2 more legions and was lent 1 legion by Pompey. Caesar now had 10 legions. He expected the trouble to increase with spring and sought revenge on Ambiorix and other Gauls

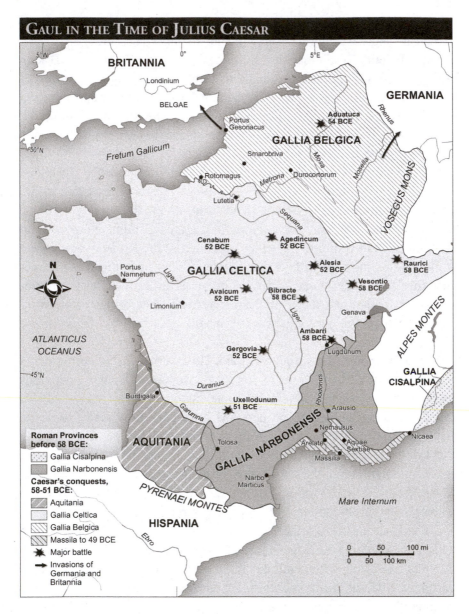

GAUL IN THE TIME OF JULIUS CAESAR

BRITANNIA

Londinium

GERMANIA

BELGAE

Portus
Gesoriacus

Aduatuca
54 BCE

GALLIA BELGICA

Rhenus

Smarobriva

Mosa

Mosella

Rotomagus

Metrona

Durocortorum

Fretum Gallicum

VOSEGUS MONS

Lutetia

Sequana

Cenabum
52 BCE

Agedincum
52 BCE

Alesia
52 BCE

Raurici
58 BCE

Portus
Namnetum

Liger

GALLIA CELTICA

Vesontio
58 BCE

Avaicum
52 BCE

Bibracte
58 BCE

Limonium

Liger

Genava

ATLANTICUS
OCEANUS

Ambarri
58 BCE

ALPES MONTES

Lugdunum

Gergovia
52 BCE

GALLIA
CISALPINA

Burdigala

Duranius

Uxellodunum
51 BCE

Rhodonus

Arausio

Garumna

AQUITANIA

Tolosa

GALLIA NARBONENSIS

Nemausus

Arelate

Aquae
Sextiae

Nicaea

Massilia

Mare Internum

Narbo
Marticus

PYRENAEI MONTES

HISPANIA

Ebro

Roman Provinces before 58 BCE:
Gallia Cisalpina
Gallia Narbonensis
Caesar's conquests, 58-51 BCE:
Aquitania
Gallia Celtica
Gallia Belgica
Massila to 49 BCE
Major battle
Invasions of Germania and Britannia

0   50   100 mi
0   50 100 km

who had attacked Roman troops. The army spent most of the campaigning season in Germany. Ambiorix eluded capture, and the Gauls and Germans resorted to guerrilla warfare while the Romans placed greater pressure on their resources.

The operations of that campaign season only increased Gallic resentment so that many Gallic tribes united in 52, led by Vercingetorix. He was a talented strategist, but the Gauls were too weak to oppose the Roman army directly, so they focused on a strategy of attrition.

The first major encounter after this decision was at Avaricum. Despite strong initial resistance during the siege, the Gauls were unable to sustain their efforts and were slaughtered as they fled to Vercingetorix's camp nearby. Caesar then proceeded to Gergovia, the major town of the Arverni. Although the Romans managed to take the Gallic camps surrounding the town, they advanced too far and were finally driven back and abandoned the town.

The defeat inspired the Aedui and other Gallic tribes to break from Caesar. Vercingetorix continued his strategy and fortified Alesia, which was already well positioned. Caesar situated his army near the town and began a circumvallation siege. Vercingetorix sent out cavalry to bring support and relieve the food stocks before the Roman wall was complete, forcing Caesar to prepare a 14-mile counterwall and increase foraging. The Gauls assembled a large army and coordinated their external attacks with Vercingetorix inside Alesia. The Romans drove back several attacks, but the Gauls pressed weak parts of the counterwall. In a huge battle against the attackers on both sides of the Roman walls, the Romans were victorious. Afterward Vercingetorix surrendered. This would be the last serious resistance of the war. Rome celebrated a 20-day thanksgiving upon hearing of the victory.

The last actions that mattered were the siege of Uxellodunum and the subduing of the Atrebates, who had joined Vercingetorix's revolt. Those campaigns completed Caesar's Gallic War.

Finally, Caesar's own *Commentaries* on these wars are the key source. Vivid, detailed in places, and clear, they were written mostly by Caesar to report his achievements, justify them to the citizens of Rome, and gloss over many negative issues while heightening his genius and personal role. As a source, they should be used with appropriate historical skepticism.

Rosemary Moore

See also: Allies, Roman; Julius Caesar, Gaius; Siege; Stipendium; Triumvirate, First

References

Caesar. *War Commentaries of Caesar.* Translated by Rex Warner. New York: New American Library, 1960.

Erdkamp, P., ed. *A Companion to the Roman Army.* Oxford, UK: Wiley-Blackwell, 2011.

Goldsworthy, A. *Caesar: Life of a Colossus.* New Haven, CT: Yale University Press, 2006.

Griffin, Marian, ed. *A Companion to Julius Caesar.* Oxford, UK: Wiley-Blackwell, 2009.

Lendon, J. E. *Soldiers and Ghosts: A History of Battle in Classical Antiquity.* New Haven, CT: Yale University Press, 2006.

Nardo, Don. *Caesar's Conquest of Gaul.* San Diego, CA: Lucent, 1996.

Gracchus, Gaius. *See* Sempronius Gracchus, Gaius

Gracchus, Tiberius. *See* Sempronius Gracchus, Tiberius

Greece

Direct connections between Greece and the Roman military began in earnest after 202 BCE and continued until the Battle of Actium in 31. The changing nature of Roman imperialism can be seen in the wars that Rome fought in Greece.

Roman involvement in Greece began before the Second Punic War when Rome fought several campaigns in Illyria in support of Italian interests and made alliances with several Greek coastal cities. Then Rome sent an army against Philip V of Macedon in 215 because he had allied with Hannibal. During this First Macedonian War, Rome became an ally of the Aetolian League, a confederation of cities in western Greece, and with Pergamum, a Hellenistic kingdom in Asia Minor. The war eventually finished in 205, having changed the situation in Greece little.

Rome returned to Greece in 200 to fight the Second Macedonian War after Pergamum and the Aetolians requested aid. Flamininus arrived in 198, and after much maneuvering in Thessaly in north Greece he met Philip in battle at Cynoscephalae the following year, defeating him and forcing peace. Philip withdrew from Greece, and Flamininus declared the "freedom of the Greeks" and withdrew.

The Aetolians were not satisfied with the settlement, so they made an alliance with Antiochus III, king of the Seleucid Empire. The Aetolians and some other Greek cities that were unhappy with Rome invited him to invade and settle things. Rome responded by invading Greece and acquired

On a plain near the Greek town of Chaeronea Sulla fought and defeated the army of Mithradates VI in 86. (Lee L. Brice)

the support of the Achaean League, a confederation of cities in the Peloponnese (and enemy of the Aetolians) after defeating Antiochus in 191 at Thermopylae and forcing him to withdraw. The Aetolian League was not disbanded but was forced to become an ally of Rome. In the aftermath Rome again withdrew, and the league slowly dissolved.

Perseus, successor of Philip as king of Macedon, sought to recover his kingdom's glory, so he agitated Greece against Roman interests and sent an army south. Pergamum requested aid against Perseus, so Rome declared war and sent an army. After Paullus arrived in 168, he forced Perseus out of Greece and defeated him utterly at Pydna the same year, again with Achaean support. After the victory, infighting in the Achaean League resulted in Polybius being among 1,000 Greeks sent to Rome as hostages.

When a pretender to the throne raised a revolt in former Macedonia, Rome intervened in 148, crushing it and making it the province of Macedonia by 146. Simultaneously with the Roman victory, internal conflict in the Achaean League erupted into renewed fighting called the Achaean War. The local Roman commander, Mummius, responded to the fighting by sacking and razing Corinth in 146 and taking many works of art back to Rome. Rome brought much of Greece under its control as the province of Achaia, although it would not become a formally organized province until 46.

Roman merchants active in Greece developed an interest in the Aegean. They made the ancient sacred island of Delos into a commercial center. In 166 Rome took control of Delos away from Rhodes and gave it to Athens. In the aftermath Delos prospered and became the center of the slave trade, but Rhodes suffered and ceased patrolling against pirates. Mithradates' commander sacked Delos in 88, and pirates sacked it in 69, after which its importance faded.

Mithradates VI of Pontus invaded Greece in 88, welcomed by some Greek cities including Athens. In 87 Rome sent Sulla, who sacked or extorted several Greek cities, including Athens and Delphi, before defeating Mithradates in central Greece at Chaeronea and Orchomenos in 86 and forcing him to withdraw back to Asia.

During the civil war, Caesar chased Pompey to Greece in 48, but after the tide turned at Dyracchium, he found himself pursued to Pharsalus in Thessaly, not far from where the Battle of Cynoscephalae had been fought. After the battle both sides moved on, but Greece was a site of civil war combat again in 42. Antony and Octavian defeated Brutus and Cassius in 42 at Philippi in Macedonia. Then in 31, Octavian defeated Antony and Cleopatra VII at Actium in western Greece. Afterward, Greece remained a peaceful province.

Lee L. Brice

See also: Actium, Battle of; Aemilius Paullus, Lucius; Civil War II; Civil War III; Cornelius Sulla Felix, Lucius; Macedonian Wars; Mithradates VI; Pharsalus, Battle of; Philippi, Battle of; Piracy; Polybius; Punic Wars, Consequences of the; Quinctius Flamininus, Titus; Seleucid Dynasty

References

Eckstein, Arthur. *Rome Enters the Greek East: From Anarchy to Hierarchy in the Hellenistic Mediterranean, 230–170 BC.* Oxford, UK: Wiley-Blackwell, 2008.

Hoyos, Dexter, ed. *A Companion to Roman Imperialism.* Leiden: Brill, 2012.

Polybius. *Histories.* Translated by R. Waterfield and B. McGing. Oxford: Oxford University Press, 2010.

H

Hannibal

Hannibal Barca was born in 247 BCE, probably in Carthage. He was the son of the commander Hamilcar Barca, who expanded Carthaginian territory in North Africa and in Spain. Hannibal's father took him to Spain and raised him to be a skillful military leader.

In 221 Hannibal took command of Carthaginian forces in Spain and subdued the northern part of the peninsula. In 219 he attacked Saguntum, despite Roman warnings, and captured it after nine months.

Hannibal then took the war to Italy in 218, apparently believing that if he was successful there the Roman allies would switch sides, causing the collapse of Roman power. Setting out with as many as 50,000 men, 9,000 horses, and some elephants, he crossed the Pyrenees, traveled through southern Gaul, and crossed the Alps in the autumn.

Hannibal won repeated victories over Roman armies sent out to meet him, famously at the Trebia River (218) and Lake Trasimene (217). He practiced a policy of releasing Italians and keeping Roman prisoners. Fabius Maximus was the first Roman commander to figure out an effective strategy against him: attrition. After a change in Roman command, Hannibal won his most famous victory at Cannae in 216, during which through superior tactics and masterly control of his own forces he destroyed two Roman armies.

A number of Greek cities in southern Italy then joined Hannibal, but not as many cities as he had hoped. This situation presented him with a dilemma—either expend manpower in the protection of the cities that

This idealistic Roman bust is of the Carthaginian commander Hannibal, who initiated the Second Punic War in 218 BCE by marching on Italy. Although considered the best Carthaginian commander, he lost the war in 203 when he was defeated at Zama. (Bettmann/Corbis)

had switched sides or take the Roman strongholds. He captured Tarentum in 212 but then lost it in 209. Romans refused battle with Hannibal except under the most favorable circumstances, harassing his supply lines and laying siege to his allies where they could. During this time Hannibal received few reinforcements from Carthage. His brother, Hasdrubal, attempted to join Hannibal from Spain with reinforcements but was slain in northern Italy in 207, cutting Hannibal's last hope for help from Spain.

Hannibal campaigned in Italy for 16 years until the Carthaginian leadership recalled him to Africa in 202, when Carthage itself came under attack by Scipio. Defeated decisively at Zama in 202, Hannibal advocated peace. Eventually forced to flee Carthage, he found refuge with King Prusias of Bithynia. Hannibal, aware that he would be turned over to Rome, committed suicide there in 183.

All our accounts of Hannibal are by hostile Roman sources, so it is good to treat ancient sources with reasonable historical skepticism. Roman authors had a vested interest in making Hannibal look great, the better to heighten their own victory. Hannibal was a good commander up to a point but remains overrated, given his overall career.

Spencer C. Tucker and Lee L. Brice

See also: Cannae, Battle of; Cornelius Scipio Africanus, Publius; Fabius Maximus Verrucosus, Quintus; Punic Wars; Punic Wars, Causes of the; Punic Wars, Consequences of the; Zama, Battle of

References

Cornell, Tim, Boris Rankov, and Philip Sabin, eds. *The Second Punic War: A Reappraisal.* London: Institute for Classical Studies, 1996.

Daly, G. *Cannae: The Experience of Battle in the Second Punic War.* London: Routledge, 2001.

Goldsworthy, A. *The Punic Wars.* London: Cassell, 2000.

Hoyos, Dexter, ed. *A Companion to the Punic Wars.* Oxford, UK: Wiley-Blackwell, 2011.

Lazenby, J. F. *Hannibal's War: A Military History of the Second Punic War.* Norman: University of Oklahoma Press, 1998.

I

Imperium

Imperium was the ultimate power held by Roman magistrates. It was essentially the power of life and death, vested by the community. Magistrates with imperium could lead armies and judge cases of capital punishment on behalf of Rome.

Magistrates who held imperium included, in descending order of authority, dictators, masters of horse, consuls, praetors, proconsuls, and propraetors. Lictors accompanied magistrates with imperium. The holder's authority determined the number of lictors. In the event that two imperium holders disagreed, the man with more authority always outranked; if they had equal authority, they cancelled each other out.

There were few limits on imperium. Most magistrates only served a limited time, and they were subject to prosecution after office if they had violated the law. Proconsuls and propraetors received imperium usually for a year at a time and limited to their assigned province; however, when Pompey fought pirates in 67, his imperium was for three years.

Grants of greater imperium (*imperium maius*) allowed the magistrate to outrank any magistrate they encountered during their assignment. Private individuals could be granted imperium (*privatus cum imperio*) in exceptional circumstances, as were Pompey and Octavian. The Senate usually handled these circumstances, but there were several cases when laws passed in the assemblies granted these powers.

Lee L. Brice

See also: Julius Caesar Octavianus, Gaius; Legionary Commanders; Pompeius Magnus, Gnaeus

References

Lintott, A. *The Constitution of the Roman Republic.* Oxford: Oxford University Press, 1999.

Nicolet, Claude. *The World of the Citizen in Republican Rome.* Translated by P. S. Falla. Berkeley: University of California Press, 1980.

Italic War. *See* Social War

J

Jugurthine War

The Jugurthine War began in 112 BCE when Jugurtha, an heir to the kingdom of Numidia in North Africa, captured and murdered the other last surviving heir, killing a number of Italian merchants in the process. The initial campaigns went badly for Rome and led to popular accusations of corruption against a number of senators. In addition to corruption and incompetent Roman commanders, Jugurtha had fought with Rome in Spain, so he was familiar with how the legions fought and had the advantage of a guerrilla war.

Caecilius Metellus led the war in 109–108. Although he won some battles, he could not end the war. Marius, Metellus' second-in-command, used his commander's failure as a campaigning posture to run as consul for 107 and promised to end the war quickly. After election he accepted army volunteers, even from among the proletarians.

Marius too won some victories but had difficulty concluding the war. Finally, in 105 Marius' quaestor, Sulla, convinced one of Jugurtha's allies, Bocchus, to hand the enemy over to Rome. Jugurtha was captured and later executed. Rome gave the Numidian kingdom to Bocchus and a suitable ruler rather than annex it. Marius' veterans received land in North Africa in 103. Sulla took great pride in capturing Jugurtha, and it was this issue that caused friction between Sulla and Marius.

Lee L. Brice

See also: Cornelius Sulla Felix, Lucius; Marius, Gaius; Proletarians

References

Boatright, Mary, Daniel Gargola, Noel Lenski, and Richard Talbert. *The Romans: From Village to Empire.* 2nd ed. Oxford: Oxford University Press, 2012.

Erdkamp, P., ed. *A Companion to the Roman Army.* Oxford, UK: Wiley-Blackwell, 2011.

MacKay, C. *The Breakdown of the Roman Republic: From Oligarchy to Empire.* Cambridge: Cambridge University Press, 2009.

Julius Caesar, Gaius

Gaius Julius Caesar was born in 100 BCE into a patrician Roman family that traced its roots back to Venus. He was connected to Marius by marriage but survived Sulla's proscriptions. Caesar went into politics as soon as he was able and had a remarkable career. His important military activity began when he served as a praetor in Spain in 61, where he won a military victory sufficient for a triumph. Returning to Rome in 60 where he faced opposition from the Senate, he declined the triumph and joined with Crassus and Pompey in a secret cabal (the First Triumvirate) to oppose the optimates in the Roman Senate. This coalition was successful in securing Caesar the consulship for 59.

As consul, Caesar was able to get passage of laws giving Pompey's veterans land and legalizing Pompey's reorganization of the eastern provinces. After his term Caesar became governor of Illyricum and both provinces of Gaul for five years, an unprecedented set of appointments. The triumvirate later secured extension of this governorship another five years to the end of 50, allowing Caesar to focus on the war and remain immune from prosecution.

Using the pretext of broken treaties, Caesar fought the Gallic Wars that secured most of Gaul for Rome. During the wars he employed innovative tactics and used his cavalry to good advantage. The culmination of the campaign was the siege in 52 of Alesia, the stronghold of Gallic leader Vercingetorix. Caesar's victory broke Gallic resistance. During the conquest of Gaul, Caesar's army grew from 2 to 13 legions, mostly raised and trained by him. He provided all of these troops with opportunities to profit via war booty and doubled soldiers' pay (*stipendia*) during the war to 900 sesterces. Caesar enriched himself immensely during the war, using the funds for many purposes, including paying his supporters and bribing opponents. Also during these campaigns, officers who would later become important acquired military experience.

It is difficult to be too certain about many campaign details, because our only source is Caesar's *Commentaries* on the wars. These were written to appeal to the mass of citizens back in Rome, and he highlighted his own genius as well as the justification and success of the wars.

The triumvirate ended when Crassus died during his Parthian campaign in 53. Caesar's daughter, Julia, who had married Pompey to secure the triumvirate, died the previous year, severing the other connection. In 52–50 amid increasing civil unrest, the Senate repeatedly asked Pompey to take control of Rome as sole consul. Pompey was now pressed by a conservative group of senators to break with Caesar, whom they feared.

Caesar wanted permission from the Senate to run for consul again for 49 without having to leave his province, an act that would immediately end his immunity from prosecution. After numerous attempts to compromise failed and claiming that his dignity was under attack, Caesar crossed the Rubicon River in January 49 with one legion, thus leaving his province without permission. Pompey led the side of the optimate opposition in Civil War II.

Caesar quickly secured Rome and then Italy as Pompey and the senatorial opposition withdrew to the east, where Pompey had many supporters. Caesar pursued him but not until a rapid expedition to secure Spain. Their armies met in 48 at Pharsalus in northern Greece, where Caesar defeated Pompey. Pompey escaped to Egypt, where he was murdered by the king of Egypt. Caesar practiced a policy of clemency in which he would pardon Roman elites who surrendered if they promised not to fight further; as a result, he pardoned numerous senators after the battle.

Caesar then campaigned in Egypt, where he met Cleopatra. Their relationship was one in which each had much to gain by the other's participation, since Caesar needed wealth and food for his armies, while Cleopatra needed security and the throne, both of which she gained. Caesar fought campaigns in Asia Minor in 47 and in North Africa in 46 and then finished the war by defeating Pompey's sons in Spain in 45. Throughout these campaigns Caesar had a number of highly competent officers, including Mark Antony and Marcus Aemilius Lepidus. As with the Gallic Wars, one prime source for the civil wars is Caesar's *Commentaries,* which were finished by a close friend. In these the authors emphasize Caesar's personal genius and his justification of the war.

G. Julius Caesar was an able commander and politician who conquered Gaul and then initiated the Second Civil War in 49 BCE. A charismatic figure, popular author, and master of propaganda, he dominated Rome during this period and was assassinated in 44. (Corel)

In 46 Caesar had secured appointment by the Senate as dictator for 10 years. Although the formality of elections continued, Caesar in fact held power. Antony and Lepidus each served as Caesar's master of the horse or second-in-command at different times. In February 44 his dictatorship was extended for life. What Caesar intended is unclear, although he was not an emperor. He seems to have wanted the kingship, but the public apparently opposed this step. He did enact numerous reforms, the most important of which from a military perspective was his attempt to settle his veterans on land purchased for the purpose. He also doubled military pay at some point during his wars. At his death Caesar was planning a campaign against Parthia to avenge Crassus' death.

Not all Romans approved of Caesar's political acts, accusing him of tyranny. Conspirators assassinated him on March 15, 44. In his will he adopted Gaius Octavianus as his son and heir. The result was a renewed round of civil war.

Caesar's own *Commentaries* on both his major wars and the general way in which his reputation was used in propaganda over the following century make it difficult to tease out much with certainty about the man. He was not an emperor, but no one could have predicted that the result of his death would lead eventually to the emergence of the Roman Empire.

Spencer C. Tucker and Lee L. Brice

See also: Aemilius Lepidus, Marcus; Antonius, Marcus; Civil War II; Cleopatra VII; Cornelius Sulla Felix, Lucius; Gallic Wars; Julius Caesar

Octavianus, Gaius; Licinius Crassus, Marcus; Marius, Gaius; Mutiny; Parthian Empire; Pharsalus, Battle of; Pompeius Magnus, Gnaeus; Senate; Stipendium; Training; Triumph; Triumvirate, First

References

Caesar. *War Commentaries of Caesar.* Translated by Rex Warner. New York: New American Library, 1960.

Erdkamp, P., ed. *A Companion to the Roman Army.* Oxford, UK: Wiley-Blackwell, 2011.

Gelzer, M. *Caesar: Politician and Statesman.* Translated by P. Needham. Cambridge, MA: Harvard University Press, 1968.

Goldsworthy, A. *Caesar: Life of a Colossus.* New Haven, CT: Yale University Press, 2006.

Griffin, Marian, ed. *A Companion to Julius Caesar.* Oxford, UK: Wiley-Blackwell, 2009.

Syme, R. *The Roman Revolution.* Oxford: Oxford University Press, 1938.

Tritle, Lawrence A., and J. Brian Campbell, eds. *The Oxford Handbook of Classical Military History.* Oxford: Oxford University Press, 2012.

Julius Caesar Octavianus, Gaius

Born into an old but undistinguished Roman family in 63 BCE, Gaius Octavianus was a great-nephew of Caesar. Octavian accompanied Caesar to Spain in 46 and afterward was sent by him to Greece for military training. After Caesar's murder, Octavian was named in the will as heir and adopted son. Octavian thus became Gaius Julius Caesar Octavianus. Historians generally use Octavian to distinguish him from his adopted father. Octavian would not acquire the name Augustus until 27.

Returning to Rome in April 44, Octavian befriended Cicero and used senatorial connections and his father's reputation to win support. After clashing with Antony in the summer of 44, Octavian raised a private army from among Caesar's veterans by promising them enormous bounties. The clash with Antony resulted in him leaving Rome and Octavian receiving imperium from the Senate in return for supporting the consuls against Antony. Their combined force defeated Antony at Mutina in April 43.

Octavian used the victory to gain more authority and funds from the Senate by inciting his soldiers to march on Rome. He was then supposed to pursue Antony, but in November 43 at Bononia, Octavian joined with

Antony and Lepidus to create a formalized triumvirate, ostensibly to restore the Roman Republic but also avenge Caesar's murder. The triumvirs proscribed enemies and seized their property to pay their own soldiers.

Octavian moved into Greece with Antony in 42 against Brutus and Cassius, the leading assassins. The triumvirs won the Battle of Philippi decisively, although Octavian emerged with a poor military reputation after abandoning his camp in the first engagement of the battle. Afterward Octavian returned to Italy to settle veterans, while Antony went east to raise money with which to pay the troops.

During 41, Octavian gradually settled the soldiers and dealt with conflicts between the veterans and dispossessed landowners. The short Perusine War occurred when Antony's wife and brother, Fulvia and Lucius, provoked conflict with Octavian over his troop settlement efforts and raised an army against him. That conflict ended with the siege and sack of Perusia in late 41 without causing an open break with Antony, probably because Octavian spared Fulvia and Lucius. When Antony returned to Brundisium in 40, Octavian marched to blockade him and prepared for war, but the troops on both sides forced the triumvirs to make peace, which they formalized by Antony marrying Octavian's sister Octavia.

Sextus Pompey captured Sicily and blockaded Italy, leading Octavian to campaign against him, but in 39 Octavian and Antony had to accept Sextus' control of Sicily under treaty and gave him some powers. Alleging a broken treaty, Octavian campaigned unsuccessfully against Sextus in 38–37. Agrippa organized a new fleet and training and then won naval victories against Sextus at Mylae and Naulochus, ending his threat. In the aftermath, Octavian deposed Lepidus from the triumvirate. The soldiers mutinied afterward, however, and forced Octavian to meet their demands for discharge and settlement. Having restored peace in the west, Octavian needed to strengthen his legions' hardiness and improve his military standing, so he campaigned in Illyria in 34–32, securing a stronger military reputation through battlefield leadership.

Octavian quarreled with Antony over the latter's treatment of his sister Octavia and his marriage to Cleopatra VII. After an extended propaganda campaign and public missteps by Antony, in 32 Octavian secured a public oath of loyalty in the west and a declaration of war against Cleopatra. After most of a year spent maneuvering in western Greece, Octavian and Agrippa were able to blockade the forces of Antony and Cleopatra near Actium. In early September 31, Octavian defeated Antony and Cleopatra at sea in the Battle of Actium. Although their leader escaped with Cleopatra, Antony's land forces negotiated to surrender without a fight. Octavian then demobilized much of the combined armies and prepared to march on Egypt. Meeting minor opposition, he invaded the following year, capturing Alexandria. Antony committed suicide, and Cleopatra took her life or was assassinated to make it look as if she had. Octavian then took Egypt as Roman territory and used its wealth to pay off his numerous debts.

The victory at Actium secured Octavian's primacy, but no one could be certain until his victory in Egypt. Although he faced no further challengers, the Roman Empire would not formally begin until 27 when Octavian proclaimed the Republic restored and in return received the name Augustus.

Lee L. Brice

See also: Actium, Battle of; Aemilius Lepidus, Marcus; Antonius, Marcus; Cassius Longinus, Gaius; Civil War II; Civil War III; Cleopatra VII; Discipline; Imperium; Julius Caesar, Gaius; Junius Brutus, Marcus; Philippi, Battle of; Pompeius Magnus, Sextus; Triumvirate, Second; Vipsanius Agrippa, Marcus

References

Brice, Lee L. "Disciplining Octavian: An Aspect of Roman Military Culture during the Triumviral Wars, 44–30 BCE." In *Warfare and Culture in World History,* edited by Wayne Lee, 35–60. New York: New York University Press, 2011.

Cooley, Allison, trans. and ed. *Res Gestae Divi Augustae.* Cambridge: Cambridge University Press, 2009.

Eck, Werner. *The Age of Augustus.* 2nd ed. Oxford, UK: Wiley-Blackwell, 2007.

Galinsky, Karl. *Augustus: Introduction to the Life of an Emperor.* Cambridge: Cambridge University Press, 2012.

Osgood, Josiah. *Caesar's Legacy: Civil War and the Emergence of the Roman Empire.* Cambridge: Cambridge University Press, 2006.

Junius Brutus, Marcus

Marcus Junius Brutus, son of Marcus Junius Brutus and Servilia, was born in 85 BCE. Brutus' political career began in 58 as assistant to Cato the Younger, then governor of Cyprus. Brutus' military career was limited as he slowly climbed the political ladder and achieved typical experience.

Brutus joined the Pompeian forces when civil war broke out in 49, despite having been an enemy of Pompey because the latter had murdered his father. After Caesar defeated Pompey at Pharsalus in 48, Brutus promptly apologized to Caesar and received a pardon, joining Caesar's associates. Brutus was governor of Cisalpine Gaul in 46 and praetor in 44.

After Caesar became dictator for life in February 44, Brutus joined a conspiracy plotting to assassinate him. Brutus quickly became one of its leaders along with Gaius Cassius Longinus. The plot resulted in Caesar's murder on March 15, 44, in Rome.

Mark Antony, consul at the time and a former lieutenant of Caesar, arranged a pardon for the assassins but inflamed public anger, forcing Brutus and the other conspirators to leave Rome. Brutus and Cassius went first to the province of Macedonia, which Brutus was assigned to govern. They immediately began raising funds and an army among the eastern provinces. Over the next two years they raised a large army and took control of many of the eastern Roman provinces. Planning to return to Italy, they moved west and into Greece in 42.

Against Brutus and Cassius, the Second Triumvirate had formed in 43 with the primary goal of getting revenge on the assassins. Antony and Octavian brought their combined army into Greece and slowly moved against Brutus and Cassius. At Philippi in northern Greece, the two sides met in October. Although Brutus won the first engagement, against Octavian's forces, Cassius lost to Antony and took his own life. Soon afterward Brutus' men forced him into a battle against the triumvir's forces, and he lost decisively, after which he committed suicide.

Brutus' military career may not justify his place in history, but his role in the assassination of Caesar guaranteed Brutus' lasting memory.

Lee L. Brice

See also: Aemilius Lepidus, Marcus; Antonius, Marcus; Cassius Longinus, Gaius; Civil War II; Civil War III; Julius Caesar, Gaius; Philippi, Battle of; Pompeius Magnus, Gnaeus; Triumvirate, Second

References

Clarke, M. L. *The Noblest Roman: Marcus Brutus and His Reputation*. Ithaca, NY: Cornell University Press, 1981.

Rosenstein, N., and R. Morstein-Marx, eds. *A Companion to the Roman Republic*. Oxford, UK: Wiley-Blackwell, 2010.

L

Latin Wars

Rome may originally have been just another city-state in Latium, but by the late sixth century Rome had established military hegemony over the Latin cities. How this dominance was achieved is lost in the mythology of early Rome. What is certain is that Rome was dominant, but the other cities remained fully independent. The Latin cities took advantage of uncertainty in Rome after the defeat of Lars Porsenna at Aricia in 504 BCE to form an anti-Roman alliance and break away from Roman influence. This first of the Latin Wars climaxed in the Battle of Lake Regillus in 499 or 496. The war did not end until 493 with the Treaty of Spurius Cassius.

The treaty created a strong defensive military alliance in which Rome exercised leadership and the member cities were made independent. The alliance permitted a strong defense of Latium against the raids of neighboring tribes. The treaty was renewed in 486 and again in 358, the latter improving Rome's position in relation to its Latin allies.

Not all Latin cities were participants in the alliance that historians have sometimes called the Latin League. Rome seized Tusculum and made it Roman territory in 381. Tibur and Praeneste fought Rome beginning in the fourth century when Roman interest in expansion began to demonstrate a genuine threat to the cities. Both cities fought on their own and allied themselves with the indigenous Volsci against Rome. Praeneste was defeated in 380. Tibur fought Rome semicontinuously during 361–354. The relationship seemed to be deteriorating gradually as the Latins worried about losing independence and the threat from raiding tribes was less of a threat, since nearby indigenous enemies—Sabines, Hernici, and Aequi—had been defeated.

The Latin cities revolted against Rome in 341 in what came to be known as the Latin Wars. The revolt was driven by fear of losing their independence. They allied with the Volsci and other indigenous groups Aurunci, Sidicini, and Campani to the south. The result was exactly what the cities had sought to avoid. Rome won a series of victories against the rebels and by 338 imposed a new settlement. Some territories became parts of the Roman state with full citizenship, while other communities became allies with varying levels of rights but no independent external relations, even with other Latin cities. Several cities, including Tibur and Praeneste, remained independent allies but surrendered some territory to Rome as public land for colonization. A number of cities south of Latium as far away as Campania were forced to become allies and received partial citizenship.

As a result of the Latin Wars, Rome had added much allied and partial citizen territory. This expansion led to more Roman public land and a new wave of colonization. Increased manpower reserves were another result of the wars. This expansion was certainly the result of creeping aggressive imperialism, the effects of which would reverberate for a century. Rome may not have participated in the 474 Battle of Cumae, but this expansion was certainly a long-term result of that naval engagement.

Lee L. Brice

See also: Allies, Roman; Rome

References

Bradley, Guy. *Early Rome to 290 B.C.: The Beginnings of the City and the Rise of the Republic.* Edinburgh, UK: Edinburgh University Press, 2013.

Cornell, T. J. *The Beginnings of Rome: Italy and Rome from the Bronze Age to the Punic Wars (1000–264 BC).* London: Routledge, 1995.

Legion, Cohort

Marius enacted a number of military reforms in the late second century BCE that may have included the serious reorganization of the legion into 10 cohorts instead of maniples. Sources do not report that he made the change to cohorts all at once. Polybius reports the limited use of cohorts in the early second century, and in Caesar's *Commentaries* we still find some actions taken by maniples, so it seems most likely that the reform was more incremental. On the other hand, the introduction of the eagle as the primary standard would have made more sense in a cohort legion, where the distinctions between the three lines were eliminated. The process that Marius formally initiated changed the legion dramatically.

Cohorts as primary tactical units had been experimented with before, but Marius seems to have moved toward regularizing its use. The new legion was organized into 10 cohorts, each including 3 maniples made up of 2 centuries of 80 men each. Each cohort thus included 480 men but the same number of officers. The three-line arrangement remained as each new cohort included maniples that had originally been *hastati, principes,* and *triarii.* Now the *triarii* and *velites* were armed the same as the first two lines, and the *velites* were folded into the regular legion. One source credits Marius with increasing the legion to 6,200 men, in part by doubling the first cohort, but it is not clear that Marius regularized such a change. Such expansion may have been an emergency measure, just as 5,000 men in a manipular legion had been during the late third century. Cavalry and skirmishers were more commonly *auxilia* troops by this time.

The standardization of equipment and organization was in part a product of taking poor volunteers and the state providing everyone's equipment, but it also served tactical needs. An advantage of going to cohorts was that communication was easier because the commander only needed to send

Roman relief from from Cumae, Italy, depicting legionaries wearing typical early Republican armor. (DEA/A. Dagli Orti/De Agostini/Getty Images)

orders to 10 centurions (the lead centurion in each cohort) instead of the 30 in the manipular legion. A standard arrangement of cohorts in battle may have been in three lines, but sources are inconsistent in reporting these details. In any case, the cohort legion remained the norm for the next four centuries.

Lee L. Brice

See also: Arms and Armor, Roman; Centurions; Julius Caesar, Gaius; Legion, Manipular/Polybian; Legionary Commanders; Marius, Gaius

References

Erdkamp, P., ed. *A Companion to the Roman Army.* Oxford, UK: Wiley-Blackwell, 2011.

Pollard, N., and J. Berry. *The Complete Roman Legions.* London: Thames and Hudson, 2012.

Potter, D. "The Roman Army and Navy." In *The Cambridge Companion to the Roman Republic,* edited by H. I. Flower, 66–88. Cambridge: Cambridge University Press, 2004.

Sabin, Philip, Hans Van Wees, and Michael Whitby, eds. *The Cambridge History of Greek and Roman Warfare,* Vol. 1. Cambridge: Cambridge University Press, 2007.

Tritle, Lawrence A., and J. Brian Campbell, eds. *The Oxford Handbook of Classical Military History.* Oxford: Oxford University Press, 2012.

Legion, Manipular/Polybian

Legions were probably first constituted in the sixth century BCE, when they fought more like Greek hoplites. How they were organized in this early period remains uncertain, but by the late fourth century they were organized into maniples. Polybius, writing in the mid-second century, provides the earliest and best description of how they were organized, so some historians call the legion he described Polybian.

A legion included about 4,200–5,000 men organized into 30 maniples, arranged in three lines of 10 each. The front line was the *hastati.* The *hastati* included soldiers up to their mid-20s in age, armed with two *pila* and *gladius.* The second line, *principes,* included men in their late 20s and their 30s, armed the same as the *hastati.* The *triarii,* in the third line, were the older experienced men armed with a thrusting spear and *gladius.* In addition, there were up to 1,200 *velites* or skirmishers, young men each armed with javelins, a *gladius,* and a small shield.

Each line included 10 maniples made up of two centuries each. The maniples in the front two lines included 120 men each, while the third line had 60 men in each maniple. The century was an administrative rather than a tactical unit, so the maniple was the smallest combat unit. Two centurions assisted by two *optiones* led each maniple. Each maniple had two standard-bearers to help keep the troops in line. Supporting the legion were 300 cavalry.

Standard arrangement in a two-legion army was to station the legions side by side with allies on the flanks. Cavalry or allied troops would protect exposed flanks. The skirmishers lined up in front of the legion. Normally, the three lines would form up by leaving gaps between each maniple so the men in front could pull back if necessary. Once skirmishing was done, the *velites* would move through the gaps to line up with the *triarii,* and then the first two lines closed up the gaps. The three lines marched toward the foe, throwing *pila* before engaging. Details on how the early legion engaged enemies are often not recorded by Roman historians.

Lee L. Brice

See also: Arms and Armor, Roman; Cavalry; Centurions; Legion, Cohort; Legionary Commanders; Polybius; Standards

References

Erdkamp, P., ed. *A Companion to the Roman Army.* Oxford, UK: Wiley-Blackwell, 2011.

Pollard, N., and J. Berry. *The Complete Roman Legions.* London: Thames and Hudson, 2012.

Tritle, Lawrence A., and J. Brian Campbell, ed. *The Oxford Handbook of Classical Military History.* Oxford: Oxford University Press, 2012.

Zhmodikov, A. "Roman Republican Heavy Infantrymen in Battle (IV–II Centuries B.C.)." *Historia* 49 (1999): 67–78.

Legionary Commanders

Not just anyone could command a legion. Only officers with the power of imperium could command legions in battle. Originally, commanders included consuls and praetors. In emergencies, Rome added the dictator and master of the horse for a six-month term. Military tribunes also commanded legions but only as day-to-day administration, not typically in combat or tactically unless the commander had died in battle and not been replaced.

During the third century BCE, the Senate encountered unexpected needs for more officers with imperium as larger wars broke out, and then there were provinces. Rather than create even more praetors, the Senate decided to create the power to appoint former consuls and praetors to extended or prorogued magistracies as proconsuls and propraetors. These promagistrates held imperium, but it was limited to their appointment and did not extend outside their province. They could select military tribunes to assist with managing their legions but only in the confines of their appointment.

During the late third or early second century, Rome needed more officers, so commanders began to select subordinates—legates—who would accompany them on assignment and assist in commanding the legions. These legates were nominated by the commander and approved by the Senate. The Senate would have favored men with command experience who had at least been praetors. Legates held imperium as if they were propraetors, but their power was always subordinate to their commander and limited to his appointed duties, so they had to follow his orders. However, the commander had wide latitude in delegating duties, so legates could direct legions or bases far afield and exercise initiative consistent with their orders. They were entirely responsible to their commander, who enjoyed the fame for their victories and the shame of their defeats.

Legates could serve with military tribunes or take up the same duties too, in addition to combat leadership. Military tribunes were expected to take up combat command of their legions in the event of an emergency, such as death of the commander. Because of the youth of many tribunes, it was expected that a commander would have legates rather than tribunes lead if he needed extra combat officers.

During the first century, legates became more common. They were critical to Pompey's and Caesar's campaigns as well as in the civil wars. These subordinate leaders were a result of Rome's wars of expansion. The higher elected magistracies remained the dominant legionary commanders, but in terms of numbers there were numerous legates.

Lee L. Brice

See also: Civil War II; Civil War III; Imperium; Julius Caesar, Gaius; Pompeius Magnus, Gnaeus; Senate; Tribunes, Military

References

Erdkamp, P., ed. *A Companion to the Roman Army*. Oxford, UK: Wiley-Blackwell, 2011.

Keppie, L. J. F. *The Making of the Roman Army: From Republic to Empire*. Updated ed. Norman: University of Oklahoma Press, 1998.

Sabin, Philip, Hans Van Wees, and Michael Whitby, eds. *The Cambridge History of Greek and Roman Warfare*. 2 vols. Cambridge: Cambridge University Press, 2007.

Tritle, Lawrence A., and J. Brian Campbell, eds. *The Oxford Handbook of Classical Military History*. Oxford: Oxford University Press, 2012.

Length of Service. *See* Stipendium

Lepidus, Marcus Aemilius. *See* Aemilius Lepidus, Marcus

Licinius Crassus, Marcus

Marcus Licinius Crassus was born circa 115 BCE to a patrician family. Because his father, a commander, died in combat during Civil War I, Crassus left Rome in 87. He joined Sulla in 83 and raised a legion at his own expense. Crassus fought alongside Sulla in Italy and played a critical role in the final struggle for Rome at the Colline Gate.

Crassus' next military command was not until 72, when he became commander against the slave rebellion led by Spartacus. In 71 Crassus finally ended the slave war and was elected consul for 70.

In 60, Crassus teamed up with Pompey and Caesar to form a cabal known as the First Triumvirate, an informal union that succeeded in getting Caesar elected consul for 59. Pompey's military success in the east and Caesar's victories in Gaul demonstrated that status and prestige depended on military success more than anything else, so as consul in 55, again with the help of the triumvirate, Crassus arranged that after office he would be governor of Syria for five years, giving him plenty of opportunities for glory.

As governor in 54, Crassus prepared for war and seized an opportunity for a military campaign against the Parthians. At the time, Parthia was not a threat to the Romans. Crassus' invasion was unnecessary. His campaign in 54 went well and captured territory, but he had to return to raise money and supplies for an additional push. During the second invasion he quickly wound up in trouble, unprepared for the desert tactics and outdone by a superior Parthian commander. Crassus and his son lost their lives as well as much of Crassus' army over several days near Carrhae in 53. Crassus' death was the final blow to the First Triumvirate, ending any pretense that it could still work. The legionary standards lost in the defeat would not be recovered until 19.

Lee L. Brice

See also: Cassius Longinus, Gaius; Civil War I; Cornelius Sulla Felix, Lucius; Julius Caesar, Gaius; Parthian Empire; Pompeius Magnus, Gnaeus; Spartacus Slave War; Triumvirate, First

References

Erdkamp, P., ed. *A Companion to the Roman Army.* Oxford, UK: Wiley-Blackwell, 2011.

Rosenstein, N., and R. Morstein-Marx, eds. *A Companion to the Roman Republic.* Oxford, UK: Wiley-Blackwell, 2010.

Ward, A. M. *Marcus Crassus and the Late Roman Republic.* Columbia: University of Missouri Press, 1977.

Licinius Lucullus, Lucius

Lucius Licinius Lucullus was born circa 108. Little is known of his early career before he served Sulla during the Social War and then as quaestor in 88. Lucullus was the only one of Sulla's officers supporting his march on Rome and remained tied to Sulla during the Mithradatic War, directing Sulla's fleet and even arranging for Mithradates to escape. Lucullus supported Sulla throughout Civil War I and the aftermath.

Consul in 74, Lucullus arranged to get command in the renewed war against Mithradates VI. Lucullus was initially successful, chasing Mithradates into Armenia. Lucullus invaded Armenia, capturing the capital, but this nearly brought Parthia into the conflict. Continued campaigning in Armenia led to an army mutiny. By 68 there was popular pressure to recall him, and in 67 Pompey replaced him.

Once in Rome, Lucullus had to wait four years to celebrate a triumph. He led Senate opposition to Pompey and Caesar that resulted in the First Triumvirate in 60 and retired afterward.

Lee L. Brice

See also: Cornelius Sulla Felix, Lucius; Julius Caesar, Gaius; Mithradates VI; Mutiny; Pompeius Magnus, Gnaeus; Social War; Triumph; Triumvirate, First

Reference

Rosenstein, N., and R. Morstein-Marx, eds. *A Companion to the Roman Republic.* Oxford, UK: Blackwell, 2010.

Livy

Titus Livius, or Livy as he has come to be known, was born in 59 BCE in Patavium in northern Italy. He was from an elite citizen family but did not go into politics, seeking instead typical hobbies of the elite, including oration and writing. Livy was in Rome during part of Augustus' reign and seems to have known the emperor well, perhaps acting as tutor to members of the family.

Livy wrote a number of works but is best known for his history of Rome titled *Books from the Founding of the City* (*Ab Urbe Condita Libri*). The entire work originally included 142 books, but only a fraction (books 1–10 and 21–45) and some summaries survive.

Livy's work is important to military historians because the pieces that do survive are either our only source for some periods or provide a comparison for other historians such as Polybius, or both. So even where Livy makes errors, he is still valuable for the information he does provide. His lack of military experience and his reliance on literary works are the chief drawbacks in his work.

Livy's history, written and released in parts between 27 BCE and 16 CE and a bit later, is also important for providing a sense of contemporary perceptions of the Roman military and its history. Traditional morality, military prowess, and stability are all emphasized in his narrative. His work is full of references to traditional discipline and procedures as well as exempla of moral behavior and great deeds by officers and soldiers. This presentation of the past accorded well with Augustus' own propaganda and reform initiatives. While their moral philosophies may have coincided, it is not entirely clear that Livy wrote at Augustus' request or direction.

Lee L. Brice

See also: Julius Caesar Octavianus, Gaius; Polybius

References

Feldherr, A., ed. *Cambridge Companion to the Roman Historians*. Cambridge: Cambridge University Press, 2009.

Livy. *History of Rome*. 14 vols. Translated by B. O. Foster. Loeb Classical Library. Cambridge, MA: Harvard University Press, 1919.

Marincola, John, ed. *A Companion to Greek and Roman Historiography*. Oxford, UK: Wiley-Blackwell, 2007.

Lucullus. *See* Licinius Lucullus, Lucius

M

Macedonian Wars

Roman engagement with Macedon may have started because Philip V, king of Macedon, feared that Rome was encroaching on his interests. Rome fought two so-called Illyrian wars in the 220s and 219 BCE in support of Italian interests and made alliances with several Illyrian peoples and Greek coastal cities. Philip seems to have been sufficiently alarmed at Roman encroachment in Illyria that in 215 he signed a treaty of alliance with Hannibal. As a result, Rome declared war in 214 and sent a punitive expedition. The First Macedonian War accomplished little except to result in Rome acquiring alliances with the Aetolian League of Greece and the Anatolian kingdom of Pergamum. The war ended in 205 with a peace treaty.

Rome returned to Greece in 200 to fight the Second Macedonian War after Pergamum and the Aetolians requested aid. Romans were in a belligerent mood, ready to seek revenge against Hannibal's former allies. Initially the Roman commander could not force Philip into a pitched battle, but Flamininus arrived in 198. After much maneuvering in Thessaly in northern Greece, he met Philip in battle at Cynoscephalae in 197, defeating him and forcing a peace settlement. Philip withdrew from Greece, surrendered his fleet, and signed a treaty of alliance with Rome. Rome then withdrew and did not annex the territory.

Perseus, successor of Philip as king of Macedon, sought to recover his kingdom's glory. Perseus restored his kingdom's connections with various Greek cities and islands and quickly came to exercise much influence in Greek affairs. Despite having assisted Rome as an ally against Antiochus III and the Aetolians, Perseus became a foil to Roman influence. He even

The Macedonian Wars were a series of conflicts that began in 214 BCE and lasted until 146 with the sack of Corinth in Greece. Mummius razed the city to the ground, but Julius Caesar re-founded it as a Roman colony in 46 BCE. (Lee L. Brice)

sent an army south, settling disputes and winning many friends. Pergamum again sought aid, inflating the threat that Perseus posed to Roman interests. Rome declared the Third Macedonian War in 171 and sent an army. The Romans were outmaneuvered for the first several years until Paullus arrived in 168. He restored discipline and quickly forced Perseus north, out of Greece, defeating him at Pydna the same year with the support of the Achaean League from the Peloponnese. After the victory, Rome again refused to annex Macedon. Instead, they eliminated the royal dynasty in 167 and broke the kingdom into four republics allied with Rome. Perseus marched in Paullus' triumph and died in captivity.

When a pretender to the throne, Andriscus, raised a revolt in Macedonia, Rome intervened in 148, declaring the Fourth Macedonian War. Quintus Caecilius Metellus defeated Andriscus and crushed Macedonian opposition by 146. His victory contributed to the outbreak of the Achaean revolt in the same year. Rome made the former kingdom into the province of Macedonia in 146. Achaea was added to the province soon afterward. Polybius is our best source for the wars and relations between 200 and 146.

Lee L. Brice

See also: Aemilius Paullus, Lucius; Greece; Polybius; Punic Wars, Consequences of the; Quinctius Flamininus, Titus; Triumph

References

Eckstein, Arthur. *Rome Enters the Greek East: From Anarchy to Hierarchy in the Hellenistic Mediterranean, 230–170 BC.* Oxford, UK: Wiley-Blackwell, 2008.

Erdkamp, P., ed. *A Companion to the Roman Army.* Oxford, UK: Wiley-Blackwell, 2011.

Hoyos, Dexter, ed. *A Companion to Roman Imperialism.* Leiden: Brill, 2012.

Polybius. *Histories.* Translated by R. Waterfield and B. McGing. Oxford: Oxford University Press, 2010.

Magnesia, Battle of

Antiochus III, king of the Seleucid Empire, had invaded Greece in 192 BCE, but he was defeated by Rome at Thermopylae in 191 and had to withdraw. A Roman force under the command of Lucius Scipio, brother of Scipio Africanus who was present, crossed into Asia in 190. Linking up with the army led by their ally, Eumenes II of Pergamum, they gathered their forces and moved against Antiochus before Rome sent the new consul out so that the battle occurred in January 189.

Antiochus had plenty of time to find and prepare a strong position. He occupied an entrenched position near Magnesium ad Sipylum along the route to his regional capital at Sardis and the coastal cities to the south. The site was open and flat, perfect for his phalanx, cavalry, and chariots. He was well informed of Roman movements and could not be caught by surprise or outflanked. He had a force that was up to 50,000–70,000 strong, including numerous allies. He was stronger in cavalry, fielding more than 12,500, including 6,000 armored *cataphracts* in addition to mounted archers and scythed chariots.

Arranging his forces in Macedonian fashion with the phalanx in the center supported by hoplites on either side, Antiochus also placed cavalry and 3,000 *cataphracts* next to the hoplites on each side and light armed troops and horse archers on the farthest flanks. He also left gaps between the phalanx units to accommodate two Indian elephants while keeping 16 in reserve on each flank. The chariots and *peltasts* were in front of his battle line.

The Romans advanced with a force of 30,000–50,000 men including only 3,000 cavalry, according to ancient sources. The Roman infantry force included three or four legions and allies arranged in the usual three lines, with legions in the center and allies on the wings. Lucius Scipio anchored his left flank against the river and placed nearly all his and the Pergamene cavalry on the right flank. He assigned four cavalry units and volunteer infantry to guard the camp and held 16 African jungle elephants in reserve.

Sources for the battle conflict, so it is difficult to be certain about many details, but some aspects are clear. The battle began with a charge by scythed chariots, but they were defeated by archers and slingers. The chariots caused some chaos in Antiochus' forces on his left as they withdrew. Antiochus' cavalry on his right, under his direct command, tore through the Roman left, scattering the allied soldiers and then charging for Scipio's camp, which they failed to take. Simultaneously, Eumenes' defeated the Seleucid left, including the *cataphracts,* and pushed toward the Seleucid center. The legions advanced, throwing their *pila* and causing more confusion. At some point in the confusion Antiochus' elephants stampeded, causing his phalanx formation to break and flee as much from the elephants as from Eumenes' assault on their flank. The remaining Seleucid army fled the field in disarray with heavy losses, leaving their unprotected camp to be pillaged by the Roman army.

After failing to take the Roman camp, Antiochus escaped the obvious defeat. He was forced to make peace at Apamea and pay a huge indemnity. Rome did not annex any territory and quickly withdrew, leaving Pergamum as the biggest winner from this war.

Lee L. Brice

See also: Cavalry; Cornelius Scipio Africanus, Publius; Elephants, War; Greece; Macedonian Wars; Seleucid Dynasty

References

Eckstein, Arthur. *Rome Enters the Greek East: From Anarchy to Hierarchy in the Hellenistic Mediterranean, 230–170 BC.* Oxford, UK: Wiley-Blackwell, 2008.

Grainger, John D. *The Roman War of Antiochos the Great: Mnemosyne, Bibliotheca Classica Batava Supplementum.* Leiden: Brill.

Ma, John. *Antiochus III and the Cities of Western Asia Minor.* Oxford: Oxford University Press, 2000.

Manipular Legion. *See* Legion, Manipular/Polybian

Marius, Gaius

Gaius <u>Marius</u> was born circa 157 BCE of a plebeian family. He pursued a political career with success. Marius served in the Spanish Wars and then after a term as praetor became governor in Further Spain in 114. He served as legate during the Jugurthine War but was elected consul for 107, promising to end the war. It is with his election as consul that Marius' impact on Rome and the military emerge.

Once elected consul, Marius found that the Senate had not authorized sufficient funds for him to enroll the army that he needed, so he called for volunteers from those whose wealth was less than the minimum qualification for

Bust of Gaius Marius, Roman commander who won the Jugurthine War and defeated the Germanic tribes in 102–101 BCE. He later fought Sulla's supporters in the First Civil War in 88–86 BCE. (DeAgostini/Getty Images)

military service—proletarians (*proletarii*). Marius could afford to do so because of Gaius Gracchus' law that the state had to provide arms and armor of all soldiers. As volunteers they could receive no pay from the state, but there would be opportunities for enrichment. The call was successful, and Marius raised an army. He campaigned with slow success, but the war only ended when his quaestor, Sulla, negotiated to have Jugurtha betrayed to Rome. Marius held a grudge against Sulla for taking credit.

While Marius was in Africa mopping up the war, he was elected consul for 104 despite his absence because the Romans had suffered significant defeats from Germanic tribes migrating through northern Italy. Finding the crisis alarming, he set about reforming the army for the war. He was reelected for 103 and 102 to continue the training and move against the tribes.

Marius' reforms may have included improving the organization, equipment, and training of the legions. He developed earlier experiments in the cohort as the principal legionary unit instead of the smaller maniple, though the extent of his use of it is unclear. Marius is credited with increasing the size of the legion to 6,200 men, but it is not clear if he was actually responsible for that change. Roman authors credited Marius with also introducing a new spear with a shaft that would fail on impact with stone so that the enemy could not use it, and he gave the legions the eagle as their common standard. As for training, he introduced a number of methods that were also used in training gladiators, including the wooden sparring post. Marius also trained his soldiers to carry more of their own gear and supplies on long marches, an old method that had been abandoned.

Marius continued to rely on poor volunteers to supplement his ranks. Since they had nothing to lose they served long careers, and for them the military became a career instead of a civic duty. Marius' veterans had not been promised any reward, but Marius arranged in 103 for them to receive free land in North Africa. This settlement set a new precedent for volunteers, the implications of which may have been lost on Marius. Such settlements did not become typical, however, until later.

Marius used this force to annihilate the Teutones at Aquae Sextiae in 102, and after being elected consul again for 101, he helped defeat the Cimbri at Vercellae in 101. He celebrated a second triumph for these and was elected consul for 100. Although he had arranged for his veterans from the Jugurthine War to receive land, he was not able to do so for the veterans of the wars in the north. Frustrated, he left Rome and went on several embassies, including to Mithradates VI.

Marius returned to Italy on the eve of the Social War and performed well in that crisis, although he was not made supreme commander. When in 88 his former quaestor, Sulla, was elected consul and assigned the potentially rich command against Mithradates VI of Pontus, Marius' supporter, the tribune Sulpicius, reversed the command assignment by a popular law. Sulla was so enraged at this subversion of his command that he marched his six legions on Rome. Rufus was slain, and Marius fled to Africa, where his veterans had been settled.

After Sulla had departed for the east, Cinna invited Marius to join him in marching on Rome in 87. Marius raised an army from among his veterans and supporters. He conquered Italy and seized power, executing a large number of political opponents and establishing himself in power. Marius died in Rome in 86 several days after having been elected consul. A capable, ambitious general, he was an important military reformer and innovator.

Spencer C. Tucker and Lee L. Brice

See also: Arms and Armor, Roman; Civil War I; Cornelius Cinna, Lucius; Cornelius Sulla Felix, Lucius; Jugurthine War; Legion, Cohort; Mithradates VI; Proletarians; Social War; Standards; Training

References

Erdkamp, P., ed. *A Companion to the Roman Army.* Oxford, UK: Wiley-Blackwell, 2011.

Evans, Richard J. *Gaius Marius: A Political Biography.* Pretoria: University of South Africa Press, 1994.

Keaveney, Arthur. *The Army in the Roman Revolution.* New York: Routledge, 2007.

Potter, D. "The Roman Army and Navy." In *The Cambridge Companion to the Roman Republic,* edited by H. I. Flower, 66–88. Cambridge: Cambridge University Press, 2004.

Marsic War. *See* Social War

Military Decorations

Awards were an important component of military discipline. Recognition for outstanding service or extraordinary individual achievement could take a variety of forms. The most basic reward was to excuse individuals or units from tedious daily duties, a designation called *immunes,* but increasing rations or pay was also possible for a unit or an individual. Promotion to a higher rank was also a possible reward.

In addition to these basic but important rewards, there were specific ornaments and decorations to win. Units also could win wreaths and other symbols of valor. They would display these achievements on their standard. Sometimes units in the later Roman Republic received from their commander special titles to honor them, such as Legion IV "of Mars," Legion V "the Larks," and Legion VI "the Ironclad."

Particular acts could earn a soldier precious metal symbols such as *philae* (plates), *phalerae* (discs), *armillae* (armbands), *torques* (collars), a silver spear, or even a miniature standard. Except for the spear and standard, these could be worn on the uniform or on the person to exhibit the honor,

Roman military discipline included positive incentives and rewards such as honors and decorations. These are *torques* and *armillae* recorded on a tombstone. That the soldier wanted to be remembered for them shows how important they were to him. (DeAgostini/Getty Images)

and the latter could be displayed at a soldier's home. Special valor could be rewarded with a crown, an extraordinary honor bestowed for various deeds. These deeds included winning single combat, having naval success, saving the life of a citizen, or being the first person to climb an enemy wall. Agrippa, for example, won a naval crown for his victory at Naulochus. Award of these honors seems to have been haphazard early on but evolved into a complicated system depending on the deed and the rank of the winner by the end of the Republic.

There were some honors that were unique to commanders and had to be awarded by their soldiers or the Senate. After a successful battle or campaign, soldiers could acclaim their commander an imperator. This acclamation was an honorary designation only. A commander who was serving as legate under another commander could win crowns. In the case of Agrippa, he was serving under Octavian, who decided to award the crown to him. Finally, the ultimate honor was a triumph. The triumph was an immense military parade. The ovation was a lesser form of the parade. Only the Senate could approve these honors.

All of these awards brought the recipient an increase in status, both in the military and outside it. Some junior officers such as Scipio and Marius used military decoration to stimulate their political career. Increased rations and pay as well as promotion probably had a noticeable effect on a soldier's well-being, too. The extent to which soldiers valued these rewards is visible on tombstones of veterans that invariably list or illustrate such rewards.

Lee L. Brice

See also: Discipline; Legionary Commanders; Polybius; Standards; Vipsanius Agrippa, Marcus

References

Keppie, L. J. F. *The Making of the Roman Army: From Republic to Empire.* Updated ed. Norman: University of Oklahoma Press, 1998.

Maxfield, V. *Military Decorations of the Roman Army.* Berkeley: University of California Press, 1981.

Military Oath

A mental component of military discipline was the oath, or *sacramentum*. When the oath was instituted remains unknown, but it was in place by the time of the Second Punic War in 218 BCE. When men were called up for service, they took the oath. The full text of the *sacramentum* is unknown, but references in literary sources suggest that it carried religious and legal sanctions for the maintenance of order—obedience to commands, discipline, and military law. Violation of the oath was originally a religious crime resulting in the offender being called "accursed," but over time as violation became less religiously significant, it still held the offender liable to punishment under military law.

Originally, recruits swore to serve the commander (and thus the state) obediently for the duration of the current campaign. When wars became so numerous that men served continuously for years, the new recruits swore to serve the commander for as long as necessary (up to 16 years maximum during emergencies). In these cases they renewed the oath whenever a new commander arrived. After Marius' reforms, when the connection between legions and commanders became more personal, the oath to serve the commander also took on a more individual flavor but seems to have retained much of its original purpose.

The oath thus bound soldiers closely to their army for the duration of their service. The swearing of the oath to the commander and its renewal when a new commander took over shows that during the Roman Republic, the *sacramentum* was not a vague oath of loyalty to the state but instead was a specific bond of obedience to the commander. While the personal nature of the oath was necessary in order to enforce military requirements, it eventually had the unintended consequence of contributing to instability. Individual commanders were able to take political and economic advantage of their military strength, in part because of the personal connection between soldier and commander embodied in the oath.

There was clearly more to the oath than personal connections—it was an important component in the matrix of discipline. The oath was sufficiently ingrained that there were instances when a reminder of its sanctions played a role in restoring stability. Caesar's reference to the oath during a mutiny in 47 was what contemporaries thought brought his legions back into order. Such instances demonstrate the potential disciplinary authority of the oath, but they were uncommon. In these cases, the oath was sufficient to restore order because of the lack of incentive for soldiers to act further once the commander had shown that he would not loosen authority. There were many instances when the oath alone failed to retain the soldiers' loyalty.

The purpose of the oath was to maintain military order. The *sacramentum* was effective in part because it was grounded in the religious and hierarchical nature of Roman society and functioned as one element among several with the combined purpose of maintaining military discipline.

Lee L. Brice

See also: Discipline; Julius Caesar, Gaius; Mutiny

References

Brice, Lee L. "Disciplining Octavian: An Aspect of Roman Military Culture during the Triumviral Wars, 44–30 BCE." In *Warfare and Culture in World History,* edited by Wayne Lee, 35–60. New York: New York University Press, 2011.

Keaveney, Arthur. *The Army in the Roman Revolution.* London: Routledge, 2007.

Phang, S. E. *Roman Military Service: Ideologies of Discipline in the Late Republic and Early Empire.* Cambridge: Cambridge University Press, 2008.

Military Pay. *See* Stipendium

Military Tribunes. *See* Tribunes, Military

Mithradates VI

Mithradates (or Mithridates) was born circa 131 BCE in northern Anatolia, the eldest son of Mithradates V Euergetes, the king of Pontus. After his father was assassinated in 120, his mother ruled as regent but favored her younger son until 113, when Mithradates assassinated his mother and brother to take sole control as Mithradates VI Eupator. He then conquered the Crimea and the northern coast of the Black Sea, using the wealth and the army that these provided to push the limits of his kingdom west and south, encroaching on other domains where he could.

After Roman embassies by Marius and Sulla, in 90 Mithradates invaded the western Anatolian kingdom of Bithynia and annexed Cappadocia while Rome was busy with the Social War. Mithradates may even have provided some monetary support to the Italians who were revolting. Rome sent in legions from the province of Asia, and Mithradates withdrew. But after Roman commanders encouraged the king of Bithynia to invade Pontus,

Mithradates VI was King of Pontus who invaded Greece in 88 BCE, but was defeated by Sulla in 87 at Chaeronea and again on the plain of Orchomenos, after which Mithradates' army withdrew from Greece. (Lee L. Brice)

Mithradates was able to make the war look like Roman aggression. The result was the First Mithradatic War in which Mithradates' cavalry defeated the army of Bithynia and his army defeated three Roman commanders in turn. In 88 he capitalized on anti-Roman feelings by secretly conspiring to have all Romans and Italians in the province of Asia murdered in one day (the so-called Asian Vespers), a plot that came close to success and ensured a strong Roman reaction. After being welcomed into western Anatolia as a liberator, Mithradates invaded Greece, receiving support from Athens.

Rome responded by sending Sulla in 87. He sieged, sacked, or extorted a number of Greek cities, including Athens and Delphi, on his way to central Greece, where in 86 he defeated Mithradates' larger army decisively at Chaeronea and Orchomenos. Sulla offered peace terms, but Mithradates declined until pressed by the legions under Fimbria in 85. Then he agreed to pay 3,000 talents gold, gave Rome 80 ships, withdrew from all conquests, and became an ally of Rome. Mithradates and Sulla both bought time to deal with matters back home. The Second Mithradatic War began in 83 as soon as Sulla departed for Italy and consisted of some opportunistic raids by the Sullan commander Murena, who was angry that Sulla had made the peace. This war was ended by Sulla's command in 81.

When the last king of Bithynia bequeathed his kingdom to Rome in 75, Mithradates began building resources for renewed war. He made an alliance with the Roman renegade in Spain, Sertorius, in 74, when Rome appointed Lucullus to command in Anatolia. Mithradates invaded Bithynia late that year or the next, precipitating the Third Mithradatic War. Lucullus responded vigorously, forcing Mithradates to depart his kingdom for the safety of his son-in-law's protection in Armenia. Lucullus invaded Armenia, but his continued unsuccessful campaigning there led to an army mutiny, and by 68 Mithradates had managed to return to Pontus and raise the kingdom against Rome once again.

Popular pressure in Rome led to Pompey replacing Lucullus in 66. Pompey quickly defeated Mithradates several times in Pontus, forcing him to flee north to Crimea. Pompey did not chase him and spent the next several years settling affairs in Anatolia to ensure that Mithradates could not take advantage of a power vacuum when Rome withdrew. After a revolt by his own son, Mithradates committed suicide in 63 rather than risk falling into the hands of Rome.

Mithradates was certainly a capable enemy of Rome and a master of propaganda, though it hardly seems fair to call him the deadliest—Hannibal caused far more havoc. Mithradates' murder of Italians in Asia in 88 was shocking but was not genocide, as some have labeled it. Observations that

Sulla could have put an end to Mithradates are inviting but must remain counterfactual speculation.

Lee L. Brice

See also: Cornelius Sulla Felix, Lucius; Greece; Licinius Lucullus, Lucius; Pompeius Magnus, Gnaeus; Sertorius, Quintus; Social War

References

Harris, W. V. *War and Imperialism in Republican Rome, 327–70 B.C.* Oxford: Oxford University Press, 1985.

Hoyos, Dexter, ed. *A Companion to Roman Imperialism.* Leiden: Brill, 2012.

Mayor, Adrienne. *The Poison King: Life and Legend of Mithradates, Rome's Deadliest Enemy.* Princeton, NJ: Princeton University Press, 2011.

McGing, B. "Subjection and Resistance: To the Death of Mithradates." In *A Companion to the Hellenistic World,* edited by A. Erskine, 71–89. Oxford, UK: Blackwell, 2005.

Mutiny

Any army that requires discipline to maintain order and ensure its effectiveness in combat will be open to indiscipline or military unrest. Mutiny is merely one type of military unrest and was not the most common variety. It was also not the most dangerous type of military unrest, but because of its notoriety and the attention that sources devote to incidents, it merits attention. Mutiny is defined as collective, violent (actual or threatened) opposition to established, regular military authority. Not every ancient army was sufficiently regularized with established regulations and penalties for a term such as "mutiny" to apply, but Roman military discipline was sufficiently regular that the term can be applied to numerous incidents in Roman military history.

Because soldiers were trained to fight, could often be armed, and were accustomed to working together, they represented a much greater threat when they engaged in collective unrest than did typical crowds of nonsoldiers. In addition to its potential for violence, mutiny damaged military order in the units where it occurred and could even undermine discipline among military units that did not even participate; therefore, it was a great threat to military stability. However, the nature of political leadership and army command during the Roman Republic meant that mutiny was not a direct threat to the stability of the state. Soldiers mutinied against their officers, not against Rome itself.

Roman authors usually blamed mutinies on soldiers' idleness and/or the "madness" of soldiers. Some authors blamed ambitious officers for instigating mutinies. Republican-era mutinies were not limited to the regular soldiers. Centurions and even tribunes became involved in most mutinies, including against Cinna, Caesar, and Octavian. It is not surprising that centurions did so, since they were promoted from the ranks and were closely connected to the soldiers. While there were cases of commanders inciting indiscipline, such as Octavian's behavior after the Battle of Mutina when he instigated his soldiers to march on the Senate, most mutinies were not the result of political manipulation. There seem to have been more mutinies during civil wars, which is a function of the fact that we have more surviving sources for these periods and thus have a more complete picture of what occurred.

Every Roman commander who fought long enough encountered a mutiny. Scipio Aemilianus, Sulla, Pompey, Caesar, Antony, and Octavian all had to deal with mutinies, some of which were serious. Aemilianus faced a mutiny during his Numantia Campaign. Caesar had to resolve a mutiny at Vesontio during the Gallic Wars and several times during Civil War II, but most important, before Caesar could go after the Pompeian resistance in Africa in 47, he had to settle a mutiny among his legions in Campania by discharging several legions. Antony lost two legions to mutiny in late 44 when he competed with Octavian for control of Rome. Octavian had to settle two of the largest mutinies that ever occurred in Roman forces after his victories at Naulochus and Actium. He was able to resolve both by separating the ringleaders from the rest of the force. None of these mutinies resulted in open revolt.

Most mutinies led to no more than a commander having to meet some grievances, such as immediate discharge, but in the case of Cinna and several other leaders, mutiny resulted in a commander's death.

The Roman military had no policy that officers were required to follow in resolving mutiny. Officers learned by experience, so if they had not seen how a mutiny might be resolved they were at a disadvantage. Any violation of discipline was punishable by death, but it was not practical to execute everyone in a mutinous legion. Also, during the civil wars, officers could not afford to alienate their troops and often had to meet their demands, not punish ringleaders, or both. Cinna may have neglected this point when his men initially mutinied in 84. Sulla and Pompey each ignored mutinous behavior at critical times, and the incidents resolved on their own once they had run their course. Caesar and Octavian had to meet the mutinous soldiers' demands for discharge. When possible, commanders isolated the ringleaders, and the rest of the legion would usually return to order quickly, though more vigilance was needed for a while afterward. Ringleaders might be executed wholesale or decimated, as Antony did at Brundisium in 44. Octavian attempted to limit centurions and tribunes from participating by increasing their pay and benefits to the point of creating a social and economic gulf between the ranks.

The fact that Roman soldiers mutinied does not detract from Rome's reputation as a military success, nor does it detract from the deserved fame of generals such as Caesar and Pompey. The resolution of such incidents and the restoration of order was what distinguished good commanders. The fact that no mutiny grew out of control or led on its own to revolution is a good indication of the effectiveness of Roman responses.

Lee L. Brice

See also: Antonius, Marcus; Centurions; Civil War I; Civil War II; Civil War III; Cornelius Cinna, Lucius; Cornelius Scipio Aemilianus Africanus, Publius; Cornelius Sulla Felix, Lucius; Discipline; Julius Caesar, Gaius; Julius Caesar Octavianus, Gaius; Military Oath; Pompeius Magnus, Gnaeus; Tribunes, Military

References

Brice, Lee L. "Disciplining Octavian: An Aspect of Roman Military Culture during the Triumviral Wars, 44–30 BCE." In *Warfare and Culture in World History,* edited by Wayne Lee, 35–60. New York: New York University Press, 2011.

Brice, Lee L. *Holding a Wolf by the Ears: Mutiny and Military Unrest in the Roman Army, 90 BCE–70 CE.* Baltimore: Johns Hopkins Press, forthcoming 2015.

Brice, Lee L. "Second Chance for Valor: Restoration of Order after Mutinies and Indiscipline in the Roman Military." In *Aspects of Ancient Institutions and Geography,* edited by L. L. Brice and D. Slootjes, 23–34. Leiden: Brill, 2014.

Keaveney, Arthur. *The Army in the Roman Revolution.* London: Routledge, 2007.

Tritle, Lawrence A., and J. Brian Campbell, eds. *The Oxford Handbook of Classical Military History.* Oxford: Oxford University Press, 2012.

O

Octavian. *See* Julius Caesar Octavianus, Gaius

P

Parthian Empire

After Alexander the Great died, the Seleucid Empire ruled many of the territories formerly held by Persia and Alexander. In 245 BCE during a period of Seleucid instability, the nomadic Parni invaded the satrapy of Parthia. The Seleucids were unable to expel them and were forced to accept their leaders as subject kings. During the second century, the Seleucid kingdom gradually declined so that by 120 the Parthian king Mithradates I had captured Babylon and soon afterward drove the Seleucids from power.

Then began a period of warfare with Rome, one that would last beyond the end of the Roman Republic. Lucullus nearly started a war with Parthia while fighting Mithradates VI in Anatolia. Pompey may have encountered Parthians when he annexed Syria in 64. As governor of Syria in 54, Crassus took advantage of internal disarray to invade Parthia twice. He lost his life in the second campaign fighting the Parthians at Carrhae in 53. Caesar was preparing for a Parthian war when he was assassinated. In 40–39 Parthian forces raided into Syria with great effect and even held territory until forced out by Ventidius and then Antony's invasion in 37. That invasion went badly, nearly costing Antony his life. By 30, Rome had made peace with Parthia.

Parthian military success was dependent in large part on its horse-based army. Parthia used infantry, but it was often perceived as ineffective and unimportant. The king did not, however, maintain a standing army because of its expense. Drawing upon Persian precedents, the king called for his nobility to provide units for the army from their vast territories. This mobilization took

The Parthian Empire became a powerful eastern empire that included Mesopotamia and the Iranian plain. They repeatedly clashed with Roman commanders during the first century BCE as both sides struggled for dominance in the east. (Lola Aykutoglu/ Dreamstime.com)

time to gather strength, so Parthia could be slow to react. Once the army was gathered, the king could sometimes have discipline troubles with his officers, since he could not always discipline the nobility as he might choose.

The key to Parthia's success against Rome was its cavalry. The Parthians' horses were bred to the environment and performed well in it. There were heavy cavalry, with lances and armored riders and horses called *cataphract* to act as a type of shock force. These were extremely effective in exploiting gaps or running down light cavalry, but they could not charge into organized heavy infantry. They would sometimes charge and then pull back to intimidate infantry and force them closer together as easier targets for the archers.

Supplementing these were light cavalry horse archers employing composite bows. Their normal tactic was to ride up and fire, but if pressed they were to feign retreat in order to draw out parts of the enemy force. The riders would suddenly wheel around and fire into pursuers. If the enemy was heavy infantry, the horse archers would try to pull part of the force into a position where the *cataphract* could ride them down. The combination of hit-and-run tactics could be extremely effective, such as at Carrhae.

The cavalry required good logistical support before and after battles to carry the armor and feed the horses as well as the riders. Horses required much more water and fodder than their riders, a constant drain on campaigning. Arrows also had to be supplied in large numbers to keep up a steady barrage. When all the parts came together, as they did at Carrhae in 53, the Parthian cavalry was a powerful opponent.

Because they left no written histories, much of the information about the Parthians is derived from archaeological work, numismatics, and Roman literary sources. The Parthians were a successful opponent for Rome and were key to Roman campaigns in the east.

Tom Sizgorich and Lee L. Brice

See also: Antonius, Marcus; Julius Caesar, Gaius; Licinius Crassus, Marcus; Licinius Lucullus, Lucius; Pompeius Magnus, Gnaeus

References

Hoyos, Dexter, ed. *A Companion to Roman Imperialism.* Leiden: Brill, 2012.

Pollard, N. *Soldiers, Cities, and Civilians in Roman Syria.* Ann Arbor: University of Michigan Press, 2000.

Sabin, Philip, Hans Van Wees, and Michael Whitby, eds. *The Cambridge History of Greek and Roman Warfare.* 2 vols. Cambridge: Cambridge University Press, 2007.

Sage, Michael M. *The Republican Roman Army: A Sourcebook.* London: Routledge, 2008.

Paullus. *See* Aemilius Paullus, Lucius

Pharsalus, Battle of

The Battle of Pharsalus, fought in 48 BCE, was the culmination of the initial phase of the civil war that began in 49. Caesar had taken Italy, and Pompey withdrew to Greece. After a swift campaign in Gaul and Spain, Caesar pursued Pompey to Greece.

In January 48 after assembling sufficient shipping for half of his army, Caesar sailed across the Adriatic to Dyrrachium, where Pompey was building his forces, and started a siege. Antony arrived with reinforcements, but Pompey sallied from Dyrrachium and drove Caesar away. Pompey then pursued Caesar northeast into Thessaly, while another Pompeian army secured Macedonia. Caesar hoped that by threatening to attack this latter force he could draw Pompey into an attack. Pompey, who now had Caesar heavily outnumbered and could wear him down, was reluctant to risk a pitched battle.

Pompey and Caesar met at Pharsalus in Thessaly in August 48. Both armies were camped next to the Epineus River a few miles from each other. Each day the armies deployed, only to return to camp. Caesar gradually moved his forces closer to Pompey, hoping to entice him into an attack. Pompey's men and officers became impatient and eventually clamored so much for Pompey to accept battle that he felt he could not resist even though he had a considerable logistical advantage. Pompey had some 45,000 infantry and 7,000 cavalry, while Caesar commanded only 22,000 infantry and 1,000 cavalry. Caesar's left flank rested on the bank of the Enipeus River, but his right flank was the weak point because his cavalry was outnumbered. Caesar formed his troops in three lines but held back six cohorts of about 2,000 men in a fourth line to cover his right rear. He extended the intervals between his cohorts to match the frontage of Pompey's line. Caesar's third line was a reserve to the other two.

Pompey held his men at the ready in a compact mass to break Caesar's charge. Caesar therefore ordered an attack on Pompey's stationary force. Caesar's men rushed forward, javelins leveled. When they saw that Pompey's men were not charging, Caesar's veterans halted their charge to catch their breath and re-form. After a short interval they resumed the charge, and both sides hurled javelins and drew swords.

At the moment of the infantry impact Pompey launched his cavalry on his left flank, supported by archers and slingers, against Caesar's horsemen. Although Caesar's cavalry fought well, they fell back. Then Caesar wheeled out with his six reserve cohorts. They charged with such force that Pompey's cavalry scattered. Pompey's archers and slingers, now exposed, were overwhelmed. Caesar then turned the fourth line against the left flank of Pompey's army and drove it in from the rear.

At the same time Caesar ordered forward his third line, which had been inactive to this point. This fresh force and the fourth line attacking from the rear set Pompey's army to flight. Caesar would not allow men to stop for plunder and instead pressed the pursuit. Pompey escaped with a handful of followers, reaching the coast and sailing for Egypt. Caesar's superior military leadership won against a capable commander who was forced into a fight. The end of the battle was not the end of the war, as Pompeians gathered in North Africa to resume the conflict.

Spencer C. Tucker

See also: Cavalry; Civil War II; Julius Caesar, Gaius; Pompeius Magnus, Gnaeus

References

Caesar. *War Commentaries of Caesar.* Translated by Rex Warner. New York: New American Library, 1960.

Goldsworthy, A. *The Army at War, 100 B.C.–A.D. 200.* Oxford, UK: Clarendon, 1996.

Griffin, Marian, ed. *A Companion to Julius Caesar.* Oxford, UK: Wiley-Blackwell, 2009.

Sabin, Philip, Hans Van Wees, and Michael Whitby, eds. *The Cambridge History of Greek and Roman Warfare,* Vol. 2. Cambridge: Cambridge University Press, 2007.

Philippi, Battle of

One of the chief justifications that Antony, Lepidus, and Octavian employed in the creation of the Second Triumvirate in 43 was the need to bring the assassins of Julius Caesar to justice. After settling affairs in Rome and leaving Lepidus behind, Antony and Octavian transported their army to Greece in mid-42 after eluding naval opposition. Brutus and Cassius, the leading assassins, had been gathering forces and resources in Anatolia for more than a year but did not cross the Hellespont until late summer. Both armies met near Philippi in Macedonia in October 42.

Brutus and Cassius, with 17 legions (reportedly 80,000 infantry) and 17,000 allied cavalry, arrived near Philippi first. They dug into their position facing west down the Via Egnatia so that a marsh anchored their left and a mountain anchored their right. Cassius held the left, with Brutus on the right.

Antony was first of the triumvirs to arrive because Octavian had been ill, but by late September both commanders were present with 19–20 legions at full strength (reportedly more than 100,000 infantry) and 38,000 cavalry. Octavian took the left, and Antony took the right, next to the swamp. The triumvirs offered battle several times, but Brutus and Cassius declined, certain that they could outlast their enemies. Antony tried to build a causeway in the swamp to outflank Cassius, but Cassius responded with a counterwork that cut off Antony's efforts.

These flanking works and counterworks led to battle on October 3. Antony ordered an assault on Cassius' fortifications. Antony's army moved forward, sweeping away Cassius' legions and capturing his camp. Cassius had sent some of his force south, and these units did not participate and could not break Antony's defenses. Defeated and unaware of what had transpired on Brutus' line, Cassius committed suicide. As Antony launched his assault, Brutus' men attacked Octavian's position despite not receiving the order to attack, surprising Brutus and Octavian. The soldiers overran

Philippi was the site of two key battles in 42 BCE when the forces of the Second Triumvirate under Antonius and Octavian met and defeated the forces of Brutus and Cassius, who had led the assassination plot against Caesar. (Lee L. Brice)

Octavian's position, smashing more than three legions and capturing his camp before Octavian's legions formed up to make a stand and force Brutus to withdraw. Octavian was not in camp, having fled to the swamp. The first day's battle was a draw, with Cassius and Octavian having each lost.

In the aftermath, Antony pressed Brutus' position from the west as Octavian finished the causeway in the swamp, forcing Brutus to extend his defense south. Brutus' position and supplies were still secure, as he had access to the sea. The triumvirs, however, were at a logistical disadvantage, since the province of Macedonia had been exploited by their enemy and could not provide food for the whole army for long. The assassin's fleet had cut their access to supplies in Italy.

Finally, Brutus' soldiers and allies grew tired of taking the defense to wear down the triumvirs and started demanding the signal for attack. Brutus allowed himself to be chivied into attacking on October 23. The assault may have begun well, but Antony was able to stop Brutus' advance and then began forcing his legions back. Before they could secure their own fortifications and re-form, Octavian's legions captured the gates and were able to hold them against Brutus' forces. The result was a rout, as Brutus' legions were cut down and his allies fled. Brutus escaped into the mountains with several legions but finally committed suicide, bringing the campaign to an end.

The total losses were probably staggering, given that it was largely a battle of trained veterans in which the action was crushing. In the aftermath, some of the defeated legions were permitted to enroll in the triumvirs' army; the rest of the defeated survivors were sent home, uncompensated. Soldiers in the triumvirs' army who had served out their time were demobilized and given land seized in Italy. Antony's reputation was lifted by the battle as a result of his superior leadership, while Octavian's reputation was diminished due to his poor performance in the first battle. When duties were split afterward, Antony went east to raise money with which to pay the troops, and Octavian had to settle the demobilized veterans and keep peace in Italy.

Lee L. Brice

See also: Aemilius Lepidus, Marcus; Antonius, Marcus; Cassius Longinus, Gaius; Civil War III; Greece; Julius Caesar Octavianus, Gaius; Junius Brutus, Marcus; Triumvirate, Second

References

Galinsky, Karl. *Augustus: Introduction to the Life of an Emperor.* Cambridge: Cambridge University Press, 2012.

MacKay, C. *The Breakdown of the Roman Republic: From Oligarchy to Empire.* Cambridge: Cambridge University Press, 2009.

Osgood, Josiah. *Caesar's Legacy: Civil War and the Emergence of the Roman Empire.* Cambridge: Cambridge University Press, 2006.

Southern, Patricia. *Mark Antony.* Charleston, SC: Tempus, 1998.

Piracy

Pirates were nonstate naval raiders. They were a potential problem for sea trade but were a much greater threat to coastal communities, which they raided. Pirates were more interested in acquisition of movable booty rather than territorial control. Ships permitted them freedom of movement to strike without warning and evade land-based patrols. Piracy was a problem throughout the ancient world but one that occasionally became serious enough to acquire military attention.

Pirates, like brigands, took advantage of weak military control wherever they could. As a result, they thrived on the fringes of warfare and on neglected coastlines wherever there was a power vacuum. Pirates would raid coastal communities or even lone travelers, pillaging and taking captives to ransom or sell into slavery elsewhere. Caesar, for example, was a victim of pirates while he was traveling to Anatolia.

Rome ignored piracy for centuries because it did not rise to a sufficient level of concern, but it became Rome's problem because of earlier policies in the eastern Mediterranean. During the third and second centuries, Rhodes was especially active in suppressing piracy in the eastern Mediterranean and the Aegean. However, in 167 BCE Rome took lucrative territory from Rhodes as well as its control of the mercantile center at Delos. The result was a loss of revenue, which led to Rhodes no longer being able to fight pirates as effectively, so pirates became an even greater problem.

Rome only acted when the situation deteriorated completely. Antony's father, Marcus Antonius Creticus, was sent to Cilicia in southern Anatolia in 102 to fight pirates. There were further campaigns, but in 67 Pompey was given overall command against the pirates for up to three years. He successfully defeated the pirates after three months, settling them elsewhere and cutting them off from traditional ports. Despite Pompey's success, actual pirates continued to be a problem of varying intensity until the end of the Roman Republic.

Pirate was not just an occupation; it was a label. Powerful leaders sometimes called their rivals pirates as a way of diminishing their status and legitimacy. The triumvirs labeled Domitius Ahenobarbus as a pirate in 43–42 when he led the fleet supporting Brutus and Cassius in 43–41. Domitius Ahenobarbus considered himself a liberator. Despite also fashioning his image as a liberator, Sextus Pompey received the same label from Octavian for the seizure of Sicily and the blockade of Italy, before and after 39. These labels were effective propaganda and political tools.

Lee L. Brice

See also: Antonius, Marcus; Fleet, Roman; Julius Caesar Octavianus, Gaius; Pompeius Magnus, Gnaeus; Pompeius Magnus, Sextus; Triumvirate, Second

References

de Souza, Philip. *Piracy in the Graeco-Roman World.* Cambridge: Cambridge University Press, 2002.

de Souza, Philip. "Rome's Contribution to Piracy." In *The Maritime World of Ancient Rome,* edited by Robert L. Hohlfelder, 71–96. Ann Arbor: University of Michigan Press, 2008.

Plutarch

Plutarch was born around 46 CE in the Greek city of Chaeronea. Our knowledge of his literary career remains incomplete. By 66, he had moved to Athens to study philosophy. In the subsequent years, Plutarch traveled throughout Greece and Rome, where he became acquainted with the emperors Trajan and Hadrian.

Plutarch composed at least 200 works. His primary 2 bodies of work are his *Moralia* and biographies. The *Moralia* consists of essays on various topics but is less useful for Roman history than it is for Greek history. More useful for Roman military history are the biographies in the *Parallel Lives* in which he paired a famous Greek and a Roman for the purpose of conveying lessons. Plutarch himself said that his works were biography rather than history, selected for the lessons they preserve. For this reason, the *Lives* must be used carefully as sources.

Unlike Polybius, Plutarch does not provide battle narratives, and although he does write about commanders, he often omits military details. However, some *Lives* cover periods in Roman history for which we have limited sources. There is much of value in the small details he shares via the biographies, because even though they were often written more than a century after the events that they describe, Plutarch had access to sources that no longer survive.

Plutarch died after 125. His legacy lasted much longer. One of the most influential Greek writers of the Roman Empire, Plutarch helped define the genres of biography and essay writing with his influential works.

Lee L. Brice

See also: Polybius

References

Lamberton, Robert. *Plutarch*. New Haven, CT: Yale University Press, 2001.

Plutarch. *Lives*. 11 vols. Translated by B. Perrin. Cambridge, MA: Harvard University Press, 1919.

Polybian Legion. *See* Legion, Manipular/Polybian

Polybius

Polybius was born circa 200 BCE at Megalopolis in Arcadia, Greece, into a wealthy landowning family. Although he became famous for his history of Rome, he was originally an important leader in the Achaean League. During 170–169, Polybius became cavalry commander of the Achaean League. After the Third Macedonian War, he and at least 1,000 other Achaeans were deported to Italy as hostages. For about 16 years, he lived in Rome as a detainee, but when trial never took place, he and the other Achaeans were given freedom.

While in Rome, Polybius became a mentor to Scipio Aemilianus and remained close to the family. Polybius accompanied Scipio on campaigns, including Spain in 151 and later Africa. In 146 during Scipio's destruction of Carthage in the Third Punic War, Polybius was present. He traveled to Corinth after it was razed in 146 and helped establish order in the new province, negotiating with an awareness of both sides' interests. He may have accompanied Scipio during the siege of Numantia in Spain around 134–133. Polybius died at about the age of 82.

Most of Polybius' works are lost, but his *Histories,* originally in 40 books, survives in 5 complete books and fragments or summaries of others. The *Histories* covered Mediterranean history from 220 to 167. His purpose was to show how Rome emerged with a large empire in so short a time. Influenced by the Greek historian Thucydides, Polybius attempted to get firsthand accounts, consulted documents, and frequently recorded oral discussions with witnesses. According to Polybius, the historian "should not try to astonish his readers by sensationalism and enumerate all the possible consequences of the events under consideration, but to simply record what really happened, however commonplace."

The surviving portions of Polybius' works are extremely informative on military matters as well as the history of the period. He provides many details such as treaties, troop strengths, casualty lists, indemnities, and costs. In addition to telling the story, Polybius explains how the military was organized and functioned and much more about how this army was successful.

Since Polybius was a participant in the period that he described, his work is not without various biases and criticisms of contemporaries. His work was popular and influenced numerous later Roman authors. In addition to its great value as a historical source, his constitutional analysis has been influential in regard to the early modern revolutionary period.

Lee L. Brice

See also: Cornelius Scipio Aemilianus Africanus, Publius; Greece; Macedonian Wars; Punic Wars, Consequences of the

References

Gibson, Bruce, and Thomas Harrison, eds. *Polybius and His World: Essays in Memory of F. W. Walbank.* Oxford: Oxford University Press, 2013.

Marincola, John, ed. *A Companion to Greek and Roman Historiography.* Oxford, UK: Wiley-Blackwell, 2007.

McGing, Brian. *Polybius: The Histories.* Oxford: Oxford University Press, 2010.

Polybius. *Histories.* Translated by R. Waterfield and B. McGing. Oxford: Oxford University Press, 2010.

Pompeius Magnus, Gnaeus

Born in 106 BCE, Gnaeus Pompeius Magnus, more commonly known as Pompey, had a remarkable political and military career. He fought under his father, Gnaeus Pompeius Strabo, in the Social War. After his father was killed in the civil war, in 83 Pompey raised three private legions and supported Sulla's return and march on Rome. At the time Pompey was 23 years old, but Sulla made him a commander in his army. Sulla then sent Pompey to Sicily and North Africa to mop up opposition. Returning to Rome in 81, Pompey celebrated a triumph, and Sulla gave him the nickname of Magnus in imitation of Alexander the Great, although Sulla may have been mocking Pompey's youth.

Following Sulla's death, Pompey continued to be sent on commands to eliminate rebels. He helped suppress the rebellion of Marcus Aemilius Lepidus the elder in 77 and then was sent to eliminate the last Marian supporter, Quintus Sertorius, in Spain during 77–72. Returning to Italy in 71 just as Crassus was victorious against Spartacus' army, Pompey caught some of the fugitives and then took credit for winning the war. Although this did not endear him to Crassus, they were both elected consuls for 70.

In 67 a special law gave Pompey an unprecedented three-year command against piracy, and he was victorious in six months' time. Another special law gave Pompey the command against Mithradates VI, replacing Lucullus who had been in command. Pompey defeated Mithradates quickly, forcing him to retreat to the Crimea. Since Pompey's command had not expired, he then settled affairs in the east as he saw fit, including

Pompey the Great was a successful Roman commander who supported Sulla during and after the First Civil War despite his youth. He went on to a distinguished career, fighting and winning wars in Africa, Spain, and Asia before leading the opposition to Caesar in the Second Civil War. (Alfredo Dagli Orti/The Art Archive/Corbis)

annexing Syria, arranging Judea, creating colonies, and getting familiar with the Ptolemaic dynasty in Egypt.

Returning to Rome in 62 wealthy and powerful, Pompey celebrated another triumph and requested land for his soldiers and approval of his eastern acts. When the optimate senatorial opposition, led by Lucullus, resisted this request for more than a year, Pompey formed a cabal (the First Triumvirate) with Caesar and Crassus in 60 to get what he wanted. Pompey's veterans and cash helped Caesar became consul, who then passed the laws they wanted. The triumvirate was renewed four years later, and after serving as consul in 55 Pompey became governor of Spain for five years but stayed in Rome, using legates to administer both Spanish provinces on his behalf.

The deaths of his wife Julia (Caesar's daughter) in 54 and Crassus in 53 broke Pompey's ties with Caesar, who had become wealthy and famous fighting in Gaul. In Rome, Pompey steered an independent course initially but began to support the optimates in the Senate as he became powerful in the chaos of 52–50. During 50, Caesar's supporters tried repeatedly to forge a compromise that would avoid war between the two men, but Pompey sided with the optimates. When time ran out at the end of 50, the Optimates asked Pompey to protect the state.

Once the civil war began, Pompey quickly lost the initiative and had to withdraw to Macedonia and then to Dyrrachium, while Caesar campaigned in Spain during 49–48. Caesar took up the pursuit of his opponent and, evading Pompey's command of the sea, landed forces in Illyria. Pompey and his allied forces outmaneuvered Caesar's smaller army near Dyrrhacium in the spring of 48 but failed to capitalize. Pompey then followed Caesar into Thessaly, where they met at Pharsalus. Despite having overwhelming superiority in manpower, Pompey was talked into a battle that he lost in August 48. Pompey fled to Egypt, only to be murdered on his arrival in September of the same year on the orders of Ptolemy XIII.

Pompey was a superb commander but earned a reputation for stealing other men's victories and ignoring the legal niceties of Roman political careers. In his later years as a defender of the status quo, he proved to be an ineffective campaigner and no match for Caesar.

Spencer C. Tucker

See also: Civil War I; Civil War II; Cornelius Sulla Felix, Lucius; Julius Caesar, Gaius; Licinius Crassus, Marcus; Licinius Lucullus, Lucius; Mithradates VI; Pharsalus, Battle of; Piracy; Pompeius Magnus, Sextus; Ptolemaic Dynasty; Senate; Sertorius, Quintus; Social War; Spartacus Slave War; Triumvirate, First

References

MacKay, Christopher. *The Breakdown of the Roman Republic: From Oligarchy to Empire.* Cambridge: Cambridge University Press, 2009.

Rosenstein, N., and R. Morstein-Marx, eds. *A Companion to the Roman Republic.* Oxford, UK: Blackwell, 2010.

Seager, Robin. *Pompey the Great.* Oxford, UK: Blackwell, 2002.

Pompeius Magnus, Sextus

Sextus Pompeius Magnus was born circa 67 BCE in Rome, the youngest son of Pompey. When Pompey lost at Pharsalus in 48, Sextus fled to the Roman province of Africa, where he played a role in organizing opposition. After Caesar's victory at Thapsus, Sextus joined his older brother Magnus in Spain, the last holdout of Pompeian forces. Their army faced Caesar at Munda in 45, while Sextus commanded the garrison of Córdoba. After Caesar won big again, his officers pursued the survivors, catching and executing Magnus, but Sextus escaped again.

In the following year, Sextus organized a naval and land force in Sicily. He won some minor victories against Caesar's governors in Hispania. After Caesar's assassination, the Senate pardoned Sextus and made him a naval commander, but the following year he was one of the enemies proscribed by the Second Triumvirate. Sextus welcomed fugitives to join him as he occupied Sicily.

Sextus built up a naval force sufficient to blockade grain shipments from reaching Italy and defeated several efforts by the triumvirs to stop him. In 39, facing food shortages and popular discontent in Rome, Antony and Octavian agreed to the Pact of Misenum, which ended the blockade and gave Sextus control of Sicily, Sardinia, and Achaia.

Once Octavian was secure in Rome, he accused Sextus of violating the agreement. In 38, Octavian unsuccessfully attacked Sicily several times, losing at sea each time. With the help of his friend Agrippa, who organized a fleet and training, in addition to receiving some ships from Antony and even Lepidus invading Sicily from Africa, Octavian arranged a new campaign. After maneuvering and skirmishes, Agrippa caught Sextus' fleet at Naulochus and destroyed it. Lepidus invaded successfully and moved against Messina, capturing it. Sextus was no longer a threat to Italy.

Sextus escaped to Anatolia, where he started raising forces, but was captured and executed by one of Antony's commanders in 35. The elimination of Sextus gave Octavian a free hand in the west.

Lee L. Brice

See also: Aemilius Lepidus, Marcus; Antonius, Marcus; Civil War II; Civil War III; Fleet, Roman; Julius Caesar, Gaius; Julius Caesar Octavianus, Gaius; Pompeius Magnus, Gnaeus; Triumvirate, Second

References

MacKay, Christopher. *The Breakdown of the Roman Republic: From Oligarchy to Empire.* Cambridge: Cambridge University Press, 2009.

Powell, Anton, and Kathryn Welch, eds. *Sextus Pompey.* Swansea, UK: Classical Press of Wales, 2002.

Welch, Kathryn. *Magnus Pius: Sextus Pompeius and the Transformation of the Roman Republic.* Swansea, UK: Classical Press of Wales, 2012.

Pompey. *See* Pompeius Magnus, Gnaeus

Proletarians

Romans divided the population into groups based on their wealth, the bottommost group being the proletarians (*proletarii*), those who were too poor to participate in military service. In military terms they were also called *capite censi,* meaning "those who have a head," referring to the only thing they could bring to battle and making them ineligible for service. In the military assembly (the Comitia Centuriata), they occupied one enormous century that probably voted last.

In the mid-second century BCE, Rome had so much difficulty raising legions that the property qualifications were lowered, and some commanders accepted proletarian volunteers. Marius, unable to raise or uncertain about raising legions in 107, accepted proletarian volunteers in large numbers. His action effectively ended the property qualification for military service, although Rome continued to use traditional draft. This opened up an untapped pool of manpower for the Roman Republic.

The problem was that these poor men had everything to gain through the rewards of military service and nothing to lose. As a result, they might consider themselves clients of their commander and perhaps more loyal to them than to the state's interests—client armies. The reality was that such loyalty was rare in the late Republic, appearing only with the commanders involved in the civil wars and even then not consistently.

Lee L. Brice

See also: Comitia Centuriata; Marius, Gaius

References

Erdkamp, P., ed. *A Companion to the Roman Army.* Oxford, UK: Wiley-Blackwell, 2011.

Keaveney, Arthur. *The Army in the Roman Revolution.* London: Routledge, 2007.

Ligt, Luuk de. *Peasants, Citizens and Soldiers: Studies in Demographic History of Roman Italy, 225 BC–AD 100.* Cambridge: Cambridge University Press, 2012.

Ptolemaic Dynasty

The Ptolemaic dynasty was one of the three Macedonian dynasties to have emerged in the Hellenistic world in the aftermath of Alexander's death in 323 BCE. Ptolemy I, a former commander in Alexander's army and then governor of Egypt, named himself king and pharaoh of Egypt in 305.

Ptolemy created an elaborate social and religious framework by mixing Egyptian and Greek culture, which legitimized his rule and that of his family while maintaining much of the traditional Egyptian bureaucracy.

Successive Ptolemies made alternate peace and war with other Hellenistic dynasties as each attempted to control more territory. Some queens were powerful leaders, as likely to lead armies as the kings. Despite the many wars, the Ptolemies usually controlled Egypt, Cyrene, Cyprus, and sometimes parts of the Levant.

Roman contacts with the dynasty started in the third century, mostly through diplomacy and trade. The dynasty maintained increasingly strong ties with Rome, in part to counter the power of the Seleucid dynasty in the early second century. Occasionally Rome became directly involved in Egyptian affairs, such as when Rome intervened diplomatically to eject Antiochus IV and when Pompey helped Ptolemy XII. The dynasty became clients of individual Romans in this way, though they were not yet client kings serving at Rome's pleasure.

By the time Caesar became involved in 48, the Ptolemies were the last of the major Hellenistic dynasties. Cleopatra VII shrewdly drew on Caesar and then Antony as military and political patrons, trading wealth and grain for her independent status. Antony married Cleopatra, had three children with her, and even restored some of the dynasty's former territory, but in doing so he and Cleopatra lost the goodwill of Rome. On her death in 30, the dynasty ended and Egypt became Octavian's property.

Lee L. Brice

See also: Antonius, Marcus; Cleopatra VII; Julius Caesar, Gaius; Julius Caesar Octavianus, Gaius; Seleucid Dynasty

References

Eckstein, Arthur. *Rome Enters the Greek East: From Anarchy to Hierarchy in the Hellenistic Mediterranean, 230–170 BC.* Oxford, UK: Wiley-Blackwell, 2008.

Manning, J. G. *The Last Pharaohs: Egypt under the Ptolemies, 305–30 BC.* Princeton, NJ: Princeton University Press, 2012.

Punic Wars

The Punic Wars (264–146 BCE), three conflicts between Rome and Carthage, made the reputations of many famous generals such as Scipio Africanus and Hannibal, but the historical significance of the wars rests on the outcome of the long struggle. By the conclusion of the Third Punic War, the Roman Republic had transformed from a city-state with Italian allies to holding a Mediterranean empire.

The First Punic War started with a small incident in Sicily. Mamertine mercenaries in Messana requested assistance against Syracuse. Rome declared war on Syracuse and sent aid in 264. The following year, Rome laid siege to Syracuse and forced it to make peace that included the loss of some allies. Carthage sent more troops to Sicily, and in response Rome moved against Acragas in 262, thus precipitating the First Punic War. Defeating the Carthaginian army, Rome captured and sacked Acragas. The war in Sicily was only one theater, as the conflict spread to the sea and later to Africa. Rome had seemed to be avoiding war with Carthage, but once the conflict with Syracuse was settled, both sides tumbled into conflict.

Realizing that the war would require them to fight at sea, the Romans created a fleet of ships and trained crews from scratch. Prior to the war, Rome had not been a naval power. One way that the Romans tried to make up for their lack of experience was by inventing the *corax*, a swinging gangway with a metal spike that they would drop on enemy ships before they could ram. Once the spike clamped the other ship, Roman soldiers could cross over and fight, as they did on land. Still, it took numerous losses before they could get the upper hand on the Carthaginian fleet. While the *corax* was an equalizer, it also made ships top-heavy, and so Rome lost fleets in bad weather until it stopped using the *corax* later in the war. The war dragged on as each side exchanged victories at sea and in Sicily.

Rome won a major naval victory and landed an army in North Africa at Tunis in 256, but that campaign ended in disaster the following year when the force fell to Carthaginian mercenaries and the survivors were lost in a storm off Sicily. The Romans captured Panormus in Sicily in 254 but then lost another large fleet the following year. The nine-year Roman siege of Lilybaeum began in 250 after a major Roman victory on land, but little else happened. Rome lost a large naval battle at Drepana in 249. Hamilcar Barca fought a successful guerrilla war in Sicily in 244–241, recapturing Eryx but achieving little else.

After major Roman naval victories in 242 at Drepana and in 241 off Sicily, Rome secured command of the sea, and Carthage made peace. Both sides were exhausted financially. Rome received Sicily as a province, along with an indemnity of 3,200 talents. The indemnity required so much of Carthage's resources that the unpaid mercenaries along with Carthaginian holdings in Libya revolted. A few years later, Rome took advantage of the chaos to seize Sardinia.

Chart 5 Key Events of the Punic Wars, 264–146 BCE

Event Name	Date	Nearby Locale	Key Commanders (if known)	Victor
Mamertines' Appeal	264	Sicily	—	—
Declaration of War	264	—	A. Claudius Caudex	—
Siege of Syracuse	264–263	Sicily	M. Valerius Maximus vs. Hieron II	Rome
Siege of Acragas	262–261	Sicily	L. Postumius Megelus, Q. Mamilius vs. Hannibal Gisco	Rome
Battle of Lipara	260	Naval, Sicily	Gn. Cornelius Scipio Asina vs. Boödes, Hannibal Gisco	Carthage
Battle of Mylae	260	Naval, Sicily	G. Duilius vs. Boödes, Hannibal Gisco	Rome
Battle of Economus	256	Naval, Africa	M. Atillus Regulus and L. Manlius Volso vs. Hamilcar	Rome
Battle of Adys	255	Africa	Regulus vs. Hamilcar, Hasdrubal	Rome
Battle of Tunis	255	Africa	Regulus vs. Xanthippus	Carthage
Capture of Acragas	254	Sicily		Carthage
Battle of Panormus	251–250	Sicily	L. Caecilieus Metellus vs. Hasdrubal	Rome
Siege of Lilybaeum	251–240	Sicily	various	Rome
Battle of Drepana	249	Naval, Sicily	P. Claudius Pulcher vs. Adherbal	Carthage
Stalemate	247–242	Sicily	— vs. Hamilcar Barca	—
Capture Drepana	242	Sicily	C. Lutatius Catulus vs. Hamilcar Barca	Rome
Capture Lilybeum	242	Sicily	Catulus vs. Hamilcar Barca	Rome
Battle of Aegates Islands	241	Naval, Aegates Islands	Catulus vs. Hanno	Rome
Peace	241	Sicily and Carthage		Rome
Truceless War	241–237	Africa	Mercenaries, Libyan Rebels vs. Hamilcar and Hanno	Carthage
Seizure of Sardinia	238	Sardinia		Rome

150

Event Name	Date	Nearby Locale	Key Commanders (if known)	Victor
Ebro River Treaty	226	Spain	Rome and Hasdrubal Barca	—
Siege of Saguntum	219	Spain	Hannibal Barca	Carthage
Gallic Uprising	218	Cisalpine Gaul	L. Manlius Vulso vs. Gauls (Celts)	Gauls
Battle of Lilybaeum	218	Naval, Sicily	M. Aemellius vs. —	Rome
Battle of Cissa	218	N. Spain	Gn. Cornelius Scipio Calvus vs. Hanno, Hasdrubal	Rome
Battle of Ticinus	218	N. Italy	P. Cornelius Scipio vs. Hannibal	Carthage
Battle of Trebia River	Dec. 218	N. Italy	Scipio, Ti. Sempronius Longus vs. Hannibal, Mago Barca	Carthage
Battle of Ebro River	217	Naval, Spain	Gn. Cornelius Scipio Calvus vs. Hasdrubal	Rome
Battle of Lake Trasimene	217	Etruria, Italy	G. Flaminius, Gn. Servilius Geminus vs. Hannibal	Carthage
Battle of Geronium	Oct. 217	Central Italy	M. Minucius Rufus, Q. Fabius Maximus vs. Hannibal	Carthage
Battle of Dertosa	216	Spain	Scipio Brothers vs. Hasdrubal	Rome
Battle of Cannae	216	Apulia, Italy	L. Aemilius Paullus, G. Tarentius Varro vs. Hannibal	Carthage
Capua Defects	216	Campania, Italy		Carthage
First Battle of Nola	216	Campania	M. Claudius Marcellus vs. Hannibal	Rome
Battle of Litana Forest	216	Cisalpine Gaul	L. Postumius Albinus vs. the Boii	Boii
Treaty with Philip V	215		Philip V of Macedon and Hannibal	—
Capture of Casilinum	215	Apulia, Italy	Hannibal Barca	Carthage
Second Battle of Nola	215	Campania	Marcellus vs. Hannibal	Draw
Syracuse Defects	214	Sicily and Hannibal		Carthage
Battle of Casilinum	214	Apulia	—	Rome
Battle of Beneventum	214	Samnium	Ti. Sempronius Gracchus vs. Hanno Barca	Rome

(Continued)

Event Name	Date	Nearby Locale	Key Commanders (if known)	Victor
Third Battle of Nola	214	Campania	Marcellus vs. Hannibal	Rome
First Macedonian War	214–205	Macedon	M. Valerius Laevinus vs. Philip V	Rome
Battle of Cornus	215	Sardinia	T. Manlius Torquatus vs. Hasdrubal the Bald	Rome
Siege of Syracuse	214–212	Sicily	Marcellus vs. Hieronymus, Hippocrates, Epicydes	Rome
Capture of Leontini	214	Sicily	Marcellus vs. Hippocrates, Epicydes	Rome
Battle of Acila	213	Sicily	Marcellus vs. Hippocrates	Rome
Ambush in Bruttium	Dec. 213	Bruttium	Gracchus vs. Hanno	Carthage
Battle of Tarentum	212	Lucania, Italy	Hannibal vs. Tarentines	Carthage
Siege of Capua	212–211	Campania	Q. Fulvius Flaccus and A. Claudius Pulcher vs. Capua, Hannibal	Rome
First Battle of Capua	212	Campania	Pulcher, Q. Flaccus vs. Hannibal	Draw
Battle of Beneventum	212	Samnium, Italy	Q. Flaccus vs. Hanno the Elder	Rome
Battle of Silarus	212	Campania	M. Centenius Penula vs. Hannibal	Carthage
Battle of Herdonia	212	Apulia	Gn. Fulvius Flaccus vs. Hannibal	Carthage
Second Battle of Capua	211	Campania	Q. Flaccus, Pulcher, Publius Sulpicius Galba and Gn. Fulvius Centumalus vs. Hannibal	Rome
Battles of Upper Baetis	211	Spain	Scipio Brothers vs. Hasdrubal Barca, Mago, and Hasdrubal Gisco	Carthage
Fall of Capua	211	Campania	Q. Flaccus, Pulcher, Galba and Centumalus vs. Hannibal	Rome
Second Battle of Herdonia	210	Apulia	Centumalus vs. Hannibal	Carthage
Battle of Numistro	210	Lucania	Marcellus vs. Hannibal	Draw

Event Name	Date	Nearby Locale	Key Commanders (if known)	Victor
Battle of Asculum	209	Apulia	Marcellus vs. Hannibal	Carthage
Fall of New Carthage	209	Spain	P. Cornelius Scipio Africanus* vs. —	Rome
Battle of Caulonia	209	Bruttium	— vs. Hannibal	Carthage
Fall of Tarentum	209	Lucania	Fabius Maximus vs. —	Rome
Ambush at Venusia	208	Samnium	T. Quinctius Crispinus, Marcellus vs. Hannibal	Carthage
Battle of Baecula	208	Spain	Africanus vs. Hasdrubal Barca	Rome
Battle of Grumentum	207	Lucania	G. Claudius Nero vs. Hannibal	Rome
Battle of Metaurus River	207	N. Italy	M. Livius Salinator, Nero vs. Hasdrubal Barca	Rome
Battle of Ilipa	206	Spain	Africanus vs. Hasdrubal Gisco, Mago Barca	Rome
Fall of Gades	206	Spain	—	Rome
Battles of Croton	204, 203	Bruttium	P. Sempronius Tuditanus, P. Licinius Crassus vs. Hannibal	Draw
Battle of Insubria	203	N. Italy	Cethegus vs. Mago	Rome
Siege of Utica	203	Africa	Africanus vs. Hasdrubal Gisco, Syphax	Rome
Battle of Great Plains	203	Africa	Africanus vs. Hasdrubal Gisco, Syphax	Rome
Battle of Zama	202	Africa	Africanus vs. Hannibal	Rome
Battle of Oroscopa	151	Africa	Numidia vs. Carthage	Numidia
Siege of Carthage	149–146	Carthage	P. Cornelius Scipio Aemilianus vs. Carthage	Rome
Razing of Carthage	146	Carthage	Aemilianus vs. —	Rome

* Name received later but used to distinguish him from his father.

Source: Dexter Hoyos, ed., *A Companion to the Punic Wars* (Oxford: Wiley-Blackwell, 2011).

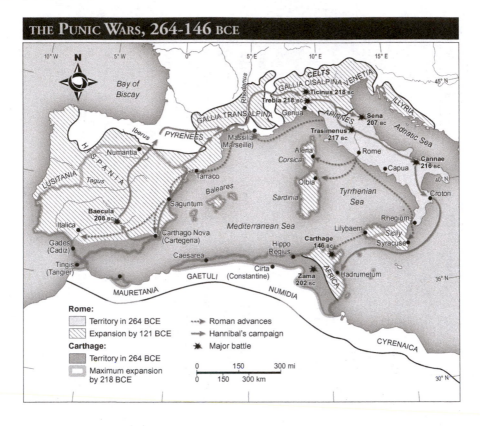

THE PUNIC WARS, 264-146 BCE

In response to the loss of Sicily and Sardinia, Carthage focused on expanding its activity in Spain. Carthaginian governors Hamilcar and then Hasdrubal pushed northward, extending Carthaginian control to the Ebro River. Hannibal became governor in 221 and continued to expand the territory, but in 219 he laid siege to the city of Saguntum, despite knowing that it was allied with Rome and that his siege would lead to war. Rome declared the Second Punic War. Saguntum fell after nine months, even as Publius Cornelius Scipio (father of Africanus) was en route.

Leaving his brother Hasdrubal to hold Spain, Hannibal marched toward Italy with some 50,000 men, 9,000 horses, and 40 elephants, evading Scipio's army in Gaul. Crossing the Alps by a difficult route and fighting tribes in the mountain passes, Hannibal lost many men and most of his elephants but also acquired numerous Gallic allied soldiers to make up for his losses.

Hannibal's strategy seems to have been to win away Rome's allies and thus cause it to lose and make peace on Carthage's terms. It was an immense risk. What Hannibal probably did not know, but that Polybius tells us, was that Rome had made a manpower survey just before the war broke out and found that it could draw upon a manpower pool of more than

250,000 men in Rome and Campania alone, plus more than 200,000 allies and more than 55,000 Roman and allied cavalry. Hannibal could win many victories and steal many allies but still bleed to death waiting for Rome to exhaust its manpower reserves. While modern readers can know how the war ended, the outcome of Hannibal's strategy was not a foregone conclusion in 218.

Rome recalled Scipio, and after a minor cavalry engagement he and Sempronius Longus met Hannibal in 218 at Trebia, where they lost decisively. Hannibal then pushed south and the following May defeated a large Roman force at Lake Trasimene. After re-forming his legions, in 217 Scipio with his army was sent to Spain with a second army, led by his brother Calvus, to try cutting off reinforcements from Hasdrubal. Hannibal continued to push south along the eastern coast of Italy as Scipio and Calvus fought in Spain.

After the defeats the new Roman commander, Fabius, employed an attrition strategy against Hannibal until 216, when Fabius was replaced due to public pressure. That same year Fabius' successors suffered at Cannae the greatest one-day defeat of Roman forces at Cannae. Numerous Greek cities in southern Italy changed sides after Cannae, including Capua and then Syracuse in 214, and Hannibal captured Tarentum in 212. He was also able in 215 to sign a treaty with Philip V of Macedon. No one then alive could know it, but the victory at Cannae was Hannibal's high-water mark.

Rome responded with special appeals to the gods and a return to Fabius' strategy. Despite the situation, most Roman allies did not change sides. Roman manpower reserves based on the alliance network enabled Rome to recover quickly and move against the cities that had defected. Hannibal was stuck in southern Italy for much of the next decade trying to protect his new allies as Rome ground away at them. He won battles, including the ambush of two consular armies, but received few reinforcements and little support from Carthage as Rome gradually recaptured the Greek cities and narrowed his scope for movement. Marcellus led the successful Roman conquest of Syracuse in 212, Capua fell in 211 despite Hannibal's feint on Rome, and Fabius recaptured Tarentum in 209. Each time, the captured cities were sacked as retribution and to make an example of them.

Active in Spain, the Scipio brothers won a series of engagements against Carthaginian forces, including defeating Hannibal's brother, Hasdrubal, in 216 and recapturing Saguntum in 212. In 211, however, while facing superior Carthaginian forces, both brothers died in separate battles. In 210 the young Scipio (soon to be Africanus) took command in Spain and had a number of significant victories, including the capture of New

Carthage. Hasdrubal was able to take an army out of Spain in 208 but was defeated and died at the Metaurus River the following year, before he could reach his brother with reinforcements. In 206 Scipio Africanus won the Battle of Ilipa, defeating a much larger Carthaginian force and securing the region for Rome.

Roman armies continued to keep Hannibal bottled up in the south while other armies captured his allies in Italy. The manpower reserves made a difference, as Roman armies sent north defeated the Gauls north of the Po River while additional armies were active in Spain and even Macedon and Roman fleets kept support from reaching Hannibal by sea. In 205, Scipio Africanus invaded Sicily and then North Africa, winning several victories. By 203, Carthage recalled Hannibal, and the following year Scipio defeated him at the Battle of Zama, effectively ending the war. In the peace settlement Carthage lost most of its fleet and all its elephants, returned all prisoners of war and deserters, and was banned from engaging in war without Rome's permission. Carthage also had to pay an indemnity of 10,000 talents over 50 years in addition to surrendering all its Spanish territory.

The Third Punic War began in 149 over a Roman ally, Masinissa, king of Numidia, who provoked Carthage with territorial demands. After negotiating unsuccessfully with Rome, Carthage raised an army and attacked Masinissa. Rome declared war in 149. The Carthaginians welcomed Rome and offered to turn over armaments. The Roman commander demanded that they abandon the city of Carthage, but this was too much to ask, and the Carthaginians fortified themselves for a siege. The so-called war was actually an extended siege of the city. Carthage held out from 149 to 146. In 146, however, Scipio Aemilianus sacked and razed Carthage, selling the inhabitants into slavery and spreading salt to symbolically ensure its infertility. Carthage became the Roman province of Africa.

James Emmons and Lee L. Brice

See also: Allies, Roman; Cannae, Battle of; Carthage; Cornelius Scipio Aemilianus Africanus, Publius; Cornelius Scipio Africanus, Publius; Fabius Maximus Verrucosus, Quintus; Fleet, Roman; Hannibal; Punic Wars, Causes of the; Punic Wars, Consequences of the; Siege; Syracuse; Zama, Battle of

References

Erdkamp, P., ed. *A Companion to the Roman Army.* Oxford, UK: Wiley-Blackwell, 2011.

Goldsworthy, A. *The Punic Wars.* London: Cassell, 2000.

Hoyos, Dexter. *The Carthaginians*. London: Routledge, 2010.

Hoyos, Dexter, ed. *A Companion to the Punic Wars*. Oxford, UK: Wiley-Blackwell, 2011.

Lazenby, J. F. *The First Punic War*. London: Routledge, 1996.

Lazenby, J. F. *Hannibal's War: A Military History of the Second Punic War*. Norman: University of Oklahoma Press, 1998.

Ligt, Luuk de. *Peasants, Citizens and Soldiers: Studies in Demographic History of Roman Italy. 225 BC–AD 100*. Cambridge: Cambridge University Press, 2012.

Polybius. *Histories*. Translated by R. Waterfield and B. McGing. Oxford: Oxford University Press, 2010.

Punic Wars, Causes of the

The First Punic War started with a small incident in Sicily. Relations between Rome and Carthage were friendly, and there was no suggestion of animosity before 264. The Mamertines, a Campanian mercenary force from Italy, took the Greek city of Messana in 289 BCE. Their depredations brought several armies against them, including Syracuse's tyrant Hiero II. Hard-pressed, the Mamertines sought aid first from Carthage and then from Rome. The first to respond were the Carthaginians, who installed a garrison of soldiers in the city.

Rome decided to send aid and declared war on Syracuse, not Carthage. Learning of this decision, the Mamertines ejected the Punic garrison. In response, Syracuse and Carthage laid siege against Messana. Rome sent the consul of 264 with an army to relieve Messana and press Syracuse, and the following year a new army defeated Syracuse, forcing it to make a treaty of alliance. However, Carthage did not intervene, and Rome still did not start war with Carthage. Only in 262, when Rome attacked Acragas, a Carthaginian ally, did the First Punic War truly start. A year later Rome began building its first navy. The war was not inevitable, as both sides were intent on avoiding direct conflict but still tumbled into war.

The Second Punic War may have grown out of the 241 treaty between Rome and Carthage, but it too was not inevitable, despite what later Roman sources suggest. In the wake of losing Sicily in 241, the Carthaginians had to fight their mercenaries who rebelled for back pay, but in 238 Rome took advantage of Carthage's troubles to seize Sardinia, breaking trust with Carthage. In turn, Carthage focused much of its energy on Spain, where it

ITALY BEFORE THE FIRST PUNIC WAR, 264 BCE

already had settlements. Spain was the only region in the western Mediterranean in which Carthage could seek enrichment. Three members of the Barcid family—Hamilcar, Hasdrubal, and Hannibal—successfully exploited Spain and expanded Carthaginian control. We can ignore Roman tales of the "hatred of the Barcids" as later fiction.

Rome and Carthage signed a treaty in 221 making the Ebro River the limit of Carthaginian expansion and Roman influence. However, the coastal city of Saguntum, south of the Ebro, had reportedly long been an ally of Rome. In 219, apparently with the permission of the government in Carthage, Hannibal attacked Saguntum, despite knowing that this would precipitate the Second Punic War. Hannibal departed Spain the following year. His strategy, to detach Rome's allies and force it to make peace on Carthaginian terms, correctly identified Rome's strength but was contingent upon too many variables.

The third and final conflict can be traced back to the treaty of 202, even if the trigger was in 149. That treaty had forbidden Carthage to maintain an army. The Roman ally, Masinissa, king of Numidia, moved to seize fertile Carthaginian territory in 153. Carthage, as required by the treaty, asked Rome to send an envoy to solve the issue. Cato the Elder, who had so often shouted "*Carthago delenda est!*" ("Carthage must be destroyed!"), was upset by the evidence of Carthaginian recovery and ruled in favor of Masinissa. Carthage responded by paying off its indemnity to Rome early and raising an army, moving against Masinissa in 150. The swift Roman response confirms sources that report Rome's decision to make war as soon as it could find a pretext. When Rome declared war in response, Carthage offered to hand over its armaments and hostages. The Roman commander in Utica demanded that they vacate the city of Carthage—permanently. They refused this insult, and so the siege of Carthage began. This final engagement was more of a siege than a war. There is no doubt that of the three wars, this war was the one that most obviously resulted from aggressive imperialism. At the same time, we must also recognize that Carthage had become an enemy on which Romans focused an immense amount of collective anxiety, much like the Celts. Fear is a strong motivator for conflict.

The three wars were all connected, more like a continuous conflict than three separate wars. There were complex causes in each case that cannot be reduced to brazen imperialism alone, even if this was present as a strong motivation in the third war. Imperialism clearly played a role in the final siege, but the prior two wars do not seem to have been the result of aggressive imperialism. Indeed, both sides tried to avoid the first war. No one alive during the first war could have guessed that by the time the conflict was over, Rome would control a Mediterranean empire.

Lee L. Brice

See also: Hannibal; Punic Wars; Punic Wars, Consequences of the; Siege; Syracuse

References

Erdkamp, P., ed. *A Companion to the Roman Army.* Oxford, UK: Wiley-Blackwell, 2011.

Goldsworthy, A. *The Punic Wars.* London: Cassell, 2000.

Hoyos, Dexter, ed. *A Companion to the Punic Wars.* Oxford, UK: Wiley-Blackwell, 2011.

Polybius. *Histories.* Translated by R. Waterfield and B. McGing. Oxford: Oxford University Press, 2010.

Punic Wars, Consequences of the

The Punic Wars ended in 146 BCE when Rome sacked Carthage. Most of the immediate consequences of the victory were predictable for both sides. The ultimate result of the wars was that Rome emerged as the dominant power in the Mediterranean world, already in control of a vast empire. The growing pains that resulted from such sudden expansion would contribute to the crisis in the late Roman Republic.

The immediate consequences of the First Punic War were several. During the war Rome acquired its first navy and learned how to manage it, and by the end of the war Rome controlled the seas in the western Mediterranean. The treaty granted Rome its first province, Sicily, except for Hiero's Syracuse. The indemnity that Carthage owed eliminated its ability to pay mercenaries, resulting in the Truceless War. Carthage fought the mercenaries and rebellions in Libya and Utica in 241–237. Rome seized Sardinia in 238 while Carthage was busy with its war, organizing it as a province with Corsica in 227. The creation of provinces forced Rome to adjust its magistracies for governors, so Rome expanded the number of praetors elected annually. In response to its losses, Carthage focused on Spain.

The most important consequence of the first war, however, was the continuing struggle with Carthage. The later wars were by no means inevitable, but both of them grew out of the initial clash of these two states. Rome became an imperial power outside Italy, and the Republic had to begin adjusting to both its new status and new strains.

The results of the Second Punic War were much more severe for both sides. Carthage had to surrender most of its war-making capacity, including its navy and elephants, surrendered all prisoners of war and deserters, lost Spain and much territory in North Africa, could not make war without Rome's permission, and had 50 years to pay a 10,000-talent indemnity. Hannibal was not killed after the war but became one of the political leaders at Carthage until fleeing under pressure from Rome. Carthage was hobbled but recovered via trade, paying the indemnity on time.

Rome experienced losses and gains from the war. In addition to immense population losses, Rome's relationship with its Italian allies was irreparably damaged. On the other hand, the end of the war provided Roman leaders with a chance to expand into Spain and get revenge on Macedon. These two regions would result in much warfare for Rome until 133, so that Rome expanded at a continuing price. There was immense enrichment too from the expansion and the indemnity. Expansion and enrichment led to additional strains on the Republic.

The most obvious result of the Third Punic War was the ruin of Carthage. Aemilianus sacked and razed the city, selling the survivors into slavery, and then spread salt on the site to ritually poison it. The territory that had been Carthage became a Roman province. Only then was Rome satisfied that Carthage had been smote forever.

It is also important to consider the accumulated consequences. In destroying the power of Carthage, Rome gained more than the trade routes of the once mighty city; it also won valuable lands close to home (Sicily, Sardinia, and Corsica) and across the sea (Spain and western North Africa), along with the fertile fields of Carthage, which became a major supplier of grain. Rome forged a navy, an experienced army, and the land to support them.

In the aftermath, two Hellenistic dynasties rapidly disappeared or withered, and the third diminished, leaving Rome dominant throughout the Mediterranean. As the premier power in the western Mediterranean, Rome was able to extend its influence east, which it did right after the Second Punic War, getting revenge on Macedon and then defeating the Seleucid Empire a few years later. The Ptolemies did not escape the Roman juggernaut, forming a relationship with Rome based on the need for support and protection.

The other immediate impacts during the war were much more widespread even if impossible to quantify. In addition to the battle deaths on both sides, an unknown number of men, women, and children died violently off the battlefield during the war. A number of city-states, including Carthage and Capua, had been entirely destroyed or depopulated. Agricultural production had suffered throughout much of the southern Italian mainland, causing additional economic, social, and medical problems. All of this meant an overall decline in the population in Italy that was spread unevenly but affected all economic levels, free and slave.

On the other hand, the flood of inexpensive slaves into Italy fueled agricultural specialization and hurt prospects for free laborers. Military-related growth enriched a few wealthy merchants and ship-builders as the number of expensive ships and the supplies needed by the military increased over time. The losses were great, but within 50 years after the war many regions had recovered (southern Italy, too would recover eventually, contrary to some traditional interpretations).

The nonagricultural economy suffered from some losses but recovered quickly. The population recovered rapidly too, but the limited available land would eventually mean farmers with smaller plots of land and therefore more poverty.

The Punic Wars set Rome on a course unimaginable to anyone living before or right after the wars and ushered in Rome's long-term dominance of the Mediterranean world and Europe.

Lee L. Brice

See also: Carthage; Cornelius Scipio Aemilianus Africanus, Publius; Greece; Hannibal; Macedonian Wars; Ptolemaic Dynasty; Punic Wars; Punic Wars, Causes of the; Rome; Seleucid Dynasty; Spanish Wars; Syracuse

References

Eckstein, Arthur. *Rome Enters the Greek East: From Anarchy to Hierarchy in the Hellenistic Mediterranean, 230–170 BC.* Oxford, UK: Wiley-Blackwell, 2008.

Erdkamp, P., ed. *A Companion to the Roman Army.* Oxford, UK: Wiley-Blackwell, 2011.

Hoyos, Dexter, ed. *A Companion to the Punic Wars.* Oxford, UK: Wiley-Blackwell, 2011.

Hoyos, Dexter, ed. *A Companion to Roman Imperialism.* Leiden: Brill, 2012.

Ligt, Luuk de. *Peasants, Citizens and Soldiers: Studies in Demographic History of Roman Italy, 225 BC–AD 100.* Cambridge: Cambridge University Press, 2012.

Pydna, Battle of

Rome, fearing Macedonian dominance of Greece again, declared war against Perseus, its king, in 171. Initially the Romans did poorly. The troops they sent to Greece landed on the east coast of Illyria and marched to Macedon, only to be defeated in three separate campaigns. Finally in 168, Rome sent out Paullus, a capable commander.

After taking command, Paullus retrained his forces and then set out in June 168. After fruitless initial engagements, he chased Perseus north. The Romans caught up with Perseus at the Leucus River, near Pydna. Paullus established camp in the foothills.

On the afternoon of June 22 during a truce to allow both sides to draw water from the Leucus, a misunderstanding led to a rush for weapons. Perseus, who had at his disposal some 4,000 cavalry and 40,000 infantry, organized more quickly with two phalanxes in the center, mercenaries on his left flank, and cavalry on his right. Paullus arranged two legions in his center, with cavalry on his left flank and some allied Italian light infantry, along with a few war elephants, on his right.

At first, Perseus enjoyed success as his phalangites crashed into the forming Roman legions. The mercenaries on his left also beat back a Roman counterattack by allied infantry. The phalanx could only operate effectively on flat ground, however, and as they advanced gaps opened up the phalanx line from the uneven terrain, as had occurred to his father's army at Cynoscephalae. Paullus seized the opportunity to send his troops and war elephants into the gaps. The result for Perseus was reported as 20,000 men killed and 11,000 taken prisoner, while Paullus lost 100 killed and 400 wounded. Perseus fled the field with his cavalry and was later captured.

The battle ended the Third Macedonian War and also extinguished Macedon as a threat to its neighbors. Perseus died in captivity in Italy.

Spencer C. Tucker

See also: Aemilius Paullus, Lucius; Cynoscephalae, Battle of; Greece; Macedonian Wars

References

Eckstein, Arthur. *Rome Enters the Greek East: From Anarchy to Hierarchy in the Hellenistic Mediterranean, 230–170 BC.* Oxford, UK: Wiley-Blackwell, 2008.

Hammond, N. G. L. "Battle of Pydna." *Journal of Hellenic Studies* 104 (1984): 31–47.

Pyrrhic Wars

Tarentum, the leading Greek city-state on the southern coast of Italy, saw the spread of Roman influence into the south during the late fourth century BCE as a threat to its own regional dominance. After unsuccessfully seeking to hire an army from several Greek city-states, Tarentum appealed to Pyrrhus, the king of Epirus, for assistance against Rome, and he accepted the opportunity.

Pyrrhus had a Macedonian-style army in Epirus and employed it successfully in various campaigns there and in northern Greece. He reportedly sought to use the Italian campaign as a platform from which to seize Syracuse. Crossing into Italy in the winter of 281–280, Pyrrhus brought a combined Epirot and mercenary force, including 22,500 infantry, 2,000 archers, 500 slingers, 3,000 cavalry, and 20 Indian elephants. Against this force, the Romans dispatched a force equivalent to four legions with cavalry support of uncertain numbers.

The two sides met in 280 near Heraclea. Pyrrhus arrayed his force in standard Macedonian fashion, with his tight phalanx in the center, hoplites on either side, and cavalry and light troops on either side of them anchoring the flanks. Pyrrhus also positioned his line at a riverbank to block the Romans crossing the ford there. The Roman commander, Laevinus, threw his cavalry upriver to come around behind Pyrrhus, a maneuver that worked perfectly, striking the Epirots in the rear. Pyrrhus' army started to break, and the Romans crossed the river to engage. The ensuing battle was hard-fought by both sides, with Pyrrhus breaking the Roman line when he committed his elephants. The Romans, unaccustomed to elephants, broke and fled toward the river. Sources report Roman losses as 7,000–15,000 men, a thorough defeat, but Pyrrhus' losses amounted to 4,000 men, a considerable number of his trained army.

Samnites and other hill tribes as well as Greek cities immediately flocked to Pyrrhus' side. These allies swelled his ranks, but phalanx tactics require much training and experience to work properly. Pyrrhus then moved toward Capua and Naples, with Laevinus in pursuit. Unable to lure these cities to join his cause, Pyrrhus marched north. The Senate ordered proletarians armed at public expense for the city's defense, and the other consular army, which had been north fighting Etruscans, won and moved south. Pyrrhus finally turned back less than 40 miles from Rome and marched back to Tarentum, having achieved nothing more.

Pyrrhus then negotiated with Rome for the freedom of the Greeks, Samnites, and Lucanians as well as the return of all their lands. The Senate rejected this demand as well as the gifts that Pyrrhus sent. The following year after recruiting more mercenaries in Greece, Pyrrhus took the field and pushed north. Rome sent both consuls south with an army of six to eight legions, including allies. Both sides met near Ausculum, where the first battle was indecisive, but the second battle was a draw, or Pyrrhic victory. Pyrrhus' losses, however, were again reportedly heavy, especially among his phalangites. Pyrrhus is quoted as quipping that if he had another victory like this, he would have no army left.

Attracted to an opportunity to take command of Syracuse, in 278 Pyrrhus departed for Sicily, where he stayed for two years. Rome took advantage of his departure to vigorously press its campaigns against Samnites, Lucanians, and Bruttians in southern Italy. Pyrrhus returned to

Italy in late 276 facing a different strategic situation. Rome had largely eliminated his support among the hill tribes and even captured the Greek city of Croton, another ally. Pyrrhus attacked Rhegium unsuccessfully with heavy losses soon after arriving.

In 275, both sides fielded armies. The Senate sent both consuls south into two parts of southern Italy. Pyrrhus had to divide his forces but focused his efforts on the force at Maleventum. Arriving to find the Romans in a wooded site again, he attempted a night march around them. The march went awry, and at dawn the Romans caught Pyrrhus' troops in disarray and sent them running. The next day, both sides met in a pitched battle. Pyrrhus sent in his elephants, but the Romans were ready and captured them. The battle was a complete loss for Pyrrhus, after which he left Italy for Greece. The Romans renamed the town Beneventum.

Pyrrhus did not keep the Greeks from conquest by Rome, but he did give his name to a type of battle in which the victor's losses are excessive.

Lee L. Brice

See also: Allies, Roman; Elephants, War; Greece; Rome; Samnite Wars; Syracuse

References

Cornell, T. J. *The Beginnings of Rome: Italy and Rome from the Bronze Age to the Punic Wars (1000–264 BC)*. London: Routledge, 1995.

Rosenstein, N. *Rome and the Mediterranean, 290–146 BC: The Imperial Republic*. Edinburgh, UK: Edinburgh University Press, 2012.

Rosenstein, N., and R. Morstein-Marx, eds. *A Companion to the Roman Republic*. Oxford, UK: Blackwell, 2010.

Q

Quaestor

Quaestors were the lowest level of the senatorial-level magistrates in Rome. Originally there were 2, but by 267 BCE there were 6, and by 82 there were 12, elected in the Tribal Assembly. Their primary duties were to act as treasurers. A quaestor typically served with each consular or praetorian army to keep track of all financial matters.

Candidates were usually 27 to 30 years old and had already served as military tribune or in a minor magistracy. Because they were the first level in the ladder of offices (*cursus honorum*), required for anyone wishing to run for praetor someday, every Roman commander had started his political career as a quaestor.

Quaestors did not have the power of imperium so they could not normally lead legions, but commanders would sometimes award their quaestor with temporary imperium as necessary. Lucullus, for example, successfully led Sulla's fleet against Mithradates, and later Cassius was quaestor with Crassus in 54 and proquaestor at the Battle of Carrhae in 53. After the defeat Cassius rallied the surviving troops and defended the province against being overrun by Parthia. By the end of the Roman Republic, quaestors were occasionally holding such irregular powers as circumstances required.

Lee L. Brice

See also: Cassius Longinus, Gaius; Imperium; Licinius Lucullus, Lucius; Tribunes, Military

References

Lintott, A. *The Constitution of the Roman Republic.* Oxford: Oxford University Press, 1999.

Nicolet, Claude. *The World of the Citizen in Republican Rome.* Translated by P. S. Falla. Berkeley: University of California Press, 1980.

Quinctius Flamininus, Titus

Titus Quinctius <u>Flamininus</u> was born circa 229 BCE. He participated in the Second Punic War, as a military tribune under Marcellus in 208, and in Tarentum in 205.

Flamininus was elected consul in 198 and was sent to command Roman forces in Greece. He persuaded a number of Greek cities and leagues to back Rome. The Second Macedonian War followed in 197. After forcing Philip V out of central Greece and following more maneuvering by both sides, Flamininus defeated Philip at the Battle of Cynoscephalae in 197. As a result, Philip was limited to Macedon, and the Aetolian League was forced to give up territorial claims.

Flamininus announced the following year at the Isthmian Games the "Freedom of the Greeks." The Greeks responded enthusiastically and even struck a gold coin with Flamininus' face on it, the first living Roman to appear on a coin.

In 194–193 Flamininus negotiated with the Seleucid king Antiochus III to keep him out of Greece, but these negotiations failed. In 191 Flamininus was at Thermopylae, but was not in command when Antiochus was defeated there. Flamininus later negotiated unsuccessfully with Prusia for Hannibal to be turned over to Rome.

Lee L. Brice

See also: Cynoscephalae, Battle of; Greece; Hannibal; Macedonian Wars; Punic Wars, Consequences of the; Seleucid Dynasty

References

Eckstein, Arthur. *Rome Enters the Greek East: From Anarchy to Hierarchy in the Hellenistic Mediterranean, 230–170 BC.* Oxford, UK: Wiley-Blackwell, 2008.

Hammond, N. G. L. "The Campaign and the Battle of Cynoscephalae in 197 B.C." *Journal of Hellenic Studies* 108 (1988): 60–82.

R

Rome

The city of Rome, traditionally founded in 753 BCE, was well situated for success and took advantage of opportunities. Located in central Italy along the Tiber River about 15 miles from the sea, Rome was far enough inland to avoid pirates but close enough to the coast to enjoy navigable river trade. Surrounded by the fertile land of the Latium plain, the tiny village that became Rome was originally settled on the southern/eastern bank of the Tiber, nestled on hills that provided some protection. Rome was also well located for trade since it occupied a good ford on the Tiber, and much land trade passed through the city.

Much of the early history written by Romans is semilegendary or mythical. Romans did not begin recording their history until centuries later. Amid the legendary pre-500 history, a few points stand out. Rome was not originally marked for greatness; it did not stand out among the numerous Latin cities in central Italy. Etruscan culture dominated the region north of the Tiber and heavily influenced Roman culture, but the Etruscans did not have a political empire or even a federation. During the seventh and sixth centuries if not before, Rome was perhaps under the control of kings. It was one of these legendary kings, Servius Tullius, who was credited with building the city's first walls, which were repeatedly rebuilt and enlarged as necessary into the second century. According to the Romans, they expelled the kings circa 509, traditionally, and once the dust settled they set up their *res publica* form of government, or the Roman Republic.

The Servian walls were said by the Romans to have been started in the sixth century by one of the kings, but were probably started in the fifth century and continuously updated through the second century. (Lee L. Brice)

Beginning soon thereafter, in the early fifth century Rome began to expand its influence by bringing other cities in Latium into its alliance. The relationship with the Latins was rocky, so not until 338 did Rome absorb this region. Wars with Etruscans started in the early fifth century and continued until the early third century, when Rome finally made all of it alliances. In the case of Veii, Rome absorbed the city, but usually Rome made an alliance treaty with the Etruscans and Latins. In addition to these indigenous peoples, there were tribes who had migrated into central Italy, including the Volsci, Aequi and Samnites. These tribes moved into the Appenines, and then the Volsci and Aequi raided Roman territory annually, sometimes joining Gallic raiding bands. Rome fought against these two tribes during the fifth and fourth centuries, finally forcing them to become allies.

Rome's expansion brought with it a number of military and commercial colonies and a series of treaties that created alliances. This left Rome with control of much of the territory between the Tiber River and the Po River. Allies were not under Roman control but were obligated to provide soldiers when called upon and could not fight other allies without Rome's permission. These alliances provided Rome with a deep manpower pool in wartime. One positive outcome of the spread of alliances was peace.

Rome also moved into central Italy, fighting a number of conflicts large and small with peoples there, especially the Samnites. Some cities joined Rome as allies seeking protection while others were forced to join, but every city that Rome conquered joined the alliance. Beginning in the early third century, Rome fought a series of wars against the Greek cities of the south. These cities hired a mercenary general, Pyrrhus, to fight on their behalf, but he eventually withdrew, and the Greeks had to also join the alliance. Rome lost many engagements in these wars but by 265 controlled the Italian peninsula south of the Po River.

By the time the Punic Wars and related conflicts ended in the late second century, Rome had acquired an overseas empire that it controlled directly through provinces governed by praetors, propraetors, and proconsuls. Nearly all of these territories had been acquired through warfare, although it is not possible to argue that Rome originally set out to conquer and control all of that territory. Certainly after 167 Roman imperialism was much more openly aggressive in terms of grabbing territory whenever possible, both to increase Rome and even more so as commanders sought increased status and wealth that could accrue to military glory. Commanders and their soldiers were in the field much longer and grew accustomed to the spoils of war.

By the first century, Rome had expanded far beyond the capabilities of a small city-state to control in the same way that it had begun to expand centuries earlier. This final Republican century saw the rise of especially powerful generals who used their armies to achieve new levels of status, power, and wealth and in the process eventually led to civil wars. Marius may not have actually invented 'client armies,' but he did create a much more professional army that later commanders used. Pompey added an immense eastern settlement, and Caesar added most of Gaul to the Roman empire.

After Caesar's assassination, no one could have predicted that the empire would survive intact. Octavian deserves much credit that it did so, regardless of one's opinion of his methods. Rome controlled a fully Mediterranean empire by the aftermath of the Battle of Actium and was on the verge of a new form of government—the Roman Empire.

Lee L. Brice

See also: Actium, Battle of; Allies, Roman; Civil War I; Civil War II; Etruscan Wars; Julius Caesar, Gaius; Julius Caesar Octavianus, Gaius; Latin Wars;

Marius, Gaius; Pompeius Magnus, Gnaeus; Punic Wars; Pyrrhic Wars; Samnite Wars

References

Boatright, Mary, Daniel Gargola, Noel Lenski, and Richard Talbert. *The Romans: From Village to Empire.* 2nd ed. Oxford: Oxford University Press, 2012.

Cornell, T. J. *The Beginnings of Rome: Italy and Rome from the Bronze Age to the Punic Wars (1000–264 BC).* London: Routledge, 1995.

Hoyos, Dexter, ed. *A Companion to Roman Imperialism.* Leiden: Brill, 2012.

Rosenstein, N., and R. Morstein-Marx, eds. *A Companion to the Roman Republic.* Oxford, UK: Blackwell, 2010.

S

Sacramentum. *See* Military Oath

Sallust

Gaius Sullustius Crispus, more commonly known as <u>Sallust</u>, was born circa 86 BCE in Amiternum from which he moved to Rome to pursue a political career. In the introduction to one of his works, the *Bellum Catilinae,* he mentions that as a youth he wanted to study and write history.

Sallust joined Caesar in 49 and commanded a legion. When Sallust was praetor, he tried unsuccessfully to quell a mutiny among Caesar's legions in 47. Sallust participated in the African campaign, but this assignment seems to have been the end of his military activity.

Sallust wrote a number of works that are valuable for military historians, including the *War of Catiline* and *The Jurgurthine War.* He also wrote the *Histories,* which covered events in Rome from 78 to 67 in five books, of which only fragments survive. Sallust's works are noteworthy because they are some of the first to describe a short period of history in greater detail. They have been criticized for inconsistencies in geography and chronology, and Sallust sometimes took liberties with historical accuracy (such as creating speeches for major figures), but those were common practices in his time.

After Sallust's death circa 35, his work was used and praised by the later historians Tacitus and Quintilian but was criticized by Livy. Its value as a source for military history is limited.

Christina Girod

See also: Civil War II; Jugurthine War; Julius Caesar, Gaius

References

Feldherr, A., ed. *Cambridge Companion to the Roman Historians*. Cambridge: Cambridge University Press, 2009.

Marincola, John, ed. *A Companion to Greek and Roman Historiography.* Oxford, UK: Wiley-Blackwell, 2007.

Samnite Wars

Samnites were an indigenous Oscan-speaking people in the central Apennines related to the Lucanians and Bruttians farther south. There were several Samnite tribes that settled independently but used a federation when necessary in war. They had expanded into parts of Campania during the fifth century BCE, occupying much of it except for the main cities of Capua and Naples.

In 343 when Samnites laid siege to Capua, the city appealed to Rome as subject allies for assistance. Rome, despite having made an alliance with the Samnites, declared the First Samnite War. The war ended in 341, Rome having lifted the siege and extended its influence to Capua and Naples.

The Second Samnite War began in 327 when the Samnites moved against Roman colonies in Campania and instigated a revolt. There was annual campaigning. The only large battle occurred in 321 at the Caudine Forks at the end of which an ambushed Roman army surrendered and had to pass under the yoke, meaning that those men were under obligation to the Samnites to not take up battle against them again. After this surrender there was a truce until 316, when hostilities started anew as Rome moved against the Samnites. Roman and Samnite forces exchanged raids and victories as the Romans suppressed any revolt in Campania, built the Appian Way to speed communication and assert control, and settled a ring of military colonies that gradually constricted Samnite movements. The Romans maintained an aggressive policy of subduing the Samnites in order to secure their own safety from the south. This war ended when the Romans invaded central Samnium in 304, capturing its stronghold and crushing the Samnites in a pitched battle.

The Third Samnite War began in 298 when Rome made an alliance with the Lucanians, who occupied the region south of Samnium. There was some successful campaigning in the south that year and the next. However, with Etruscans, Umbrians, and especially Gauls, the Samnites forged a broad alliance that was intended to stop Roman expansion. The result was the Battle of Sentinum in 295, the largest pitched battle yet fought in Italy. Rome won decisively despite heavy losses, and the alliance was broken.

Vigorous campaigns against the Samnites followed annually for the next several years so that by 291, Samnium was conquered and signed a treaty of alliance as subjects, losing some territory to Rome.

The wars ended, but the Samnites continued to resist Rome. They supported Pyrrhus in 280–275 and were crushed again as a result, losing more territory as the Romans settled colonies in Samnite territory. Some communities supported Hannibal in and after 216, costing them more land once Rome moved against them. Finally, during the Social Wars the Samnites were the strongest opposition, continuing to fight long after most other groups had surrendered. Sulla's revenge was to settle his veterans in Samnite areas and enlarge several colonies and towns. Afterward, Samnium no longer revolted.

Lee L. Brice

See also: Cornelius Sulla Felix, Lucius; Etruscan Wars; Hannibal; Latin Wars; Livy; Pyrrhic Wars; Rome; Social War

References

Bradley, Guy. *Early Rome to 290 B.C.: The Beginnings of the City and the Rise of the Republic*. Edinburgh, UK: Edinburgh University Press, 2013.

Cornell, T. J. *The Beginnings of Rome: Italy and Rome from the Bronze Age to the Punic Wars (1000–264 BC)*. London: Routledge, 1995.

Erdkamp, P., ed. *A Companion to the Roman Army*. Oxford, UK: Wiley-Blackwell, 2011.

Livy. *History of Rome*. 14 vols. Translated by B. O. Foster. Loeb Classical Library. Cambridge, MA: Harvard University Press, 1919.

Scipio Africanus the Elder. *See* Cornelius Scipio Africanus, Publius

Scipio Africanus the Younger. *See* Cornelius Scipio Aemilianus Africanus, Publius

Seleucid Dynasty

The Seleucid dynasty was one of the three Macedonian dynasties to have emerged in the Hellenistic world after Alexander's death in 323 BCE.

Antiochus III of the Seleucid Dynasty invaded Greece in 192. Rome responded quickly, defeating him in 191 at the Thermopylae pass and forcing him to withdraw his army from Greece. (Lee L. Brice)

Seleucus I, a former officer in Alexander's army and then governor of Babylon, named himself king of the region that stretched from Babylon to the Indus in 305 after Ptolemy had done so in Egypt.

Seleucus drew heavily on the local administrative and military institutions that Alexander had employed. Such a large empire required work to maintain, a task made more difficult as successive Seleucid kings made alternate peace and war with other Hellenistic dynasties as each attempted to control more territory.

Rome came to blows with the dynasty in the early second century. Antiochus III was an ally of Philip V of Macedon and may have aided him during his war with Rome. When Philip lost the Second Macedonian War, Antiochus invaded Thrace in 197. After peace negotiations failed and at the invitation of the Aetolian league, Antiochus invaded Greece in 192. Rome responded at the behest of its allies in Greece and Anatolia, defeating Antiochus at Thermopylae in 191. Rome took the war to Asia in 190 with help from Pergamum, defeating him at Magnesia in Anatolia the following year and forcing Antiochus to accept the Peace of Apamea in 188 in which he had to withdraw and relinquish control of Anatolia.

Antiochus IV defeated Egypt twice, but Rome forced him to evacuate his claims there and avoided renewed warfare. More revolts and the rising power of Parthia served to bring the Seleucid dynasty to an end late in the second century. The Romans finally annexed the remains of the empire in 64 as the province of Syria.

Lee L. Brice

See also: Cornelius Scipio Africanus, Publius; Greece; Macedonian Wars; Magnesia, Battle of

References

Eckstein, Arthur. *Rome Enters the Greek East: From Anarchy to Hierarchy in the Hellenistic Mediterranean, 230–170 BC.* Oxford, UK: Wiley-Blackwell, 2008.

Grainger, John D. *The Roman War of Antiochos the Great: Mnemosyne, Bibliotheca Classica Batava Supplementum.* Leiden: Brill.

Ma, John. *Antiochus III and the Cities of Western Asia Minor.* Oxford: Oxford University Press, 2000.

Sempronius Gracchus, Gaius

Born circa 153 BCE, Gaius Sempronius Gracchus was the son of Tiberius Sempronius Gracchus the Elder. Similar to many young men of wealthy plebeian families, Gaius began his political career with military service but distinguished himself through politics rather than military activity.

Most of Gaius' activity does not pertain to military history, but while he was tribune in 123–122 he proposed and had passed a number of laws that would impact the military later. Most of these laws are of uncertain date and were not tied to the military, but one law that turned out to have far-reaching implications pertained to arms and armor. His law required the Roman state to provide arms and armor for every man enlisted in the army. One impact of the law was eventual standardization of Roman military equipment. Another impact was that it became practicable for generals to accept poor volunteers, since the volunteers no longer had to provide equipment. Gaius tried to get his brother's land commission going again to relieve the shortage of recruits but without much of an impact.

Although Gaius died in 121, due to his reform efforts this one law had an immense impact on the military. Gaius' activities, like those of his brother, contributed to Sulla's frustration with the tribunate in 88.

Lee L. Brice

See also: Cornelius Sulla Felix, Lucius; Marius, Gaius; Sempronius Gracchus, Tiberius

References

Ligt, Luuk de. *Peasants, Citizens and Soldiers: Studies in Demographic History of Roman Italy, 225 BC–AD 100*. Cambridge: Cambridge University Press, 2012.

MacKay, Christopher. *The Breakdown of the Roman Republic: From Oligarchy to Empire*. Cambridge: Cambridge University Press, 2009.

Sempronius Gracchus, Tiberius

Born circa 163 BCE, <u>Tiberius</u> Sempronius <u>Gracchus</u> was closely connected with the Roman military tradition. His father, Tiberius Sempronius Gracchus the Elder, was a successful commander in various campaigns, especially in Spain, and his mother, Cornelia, was the daughter of Scipio Africanus. Similar to many young men of wealthy plebeian families, Tiberius began his political career with military service but distinguished himself through politics rather than military activity.

Tiberius fought in Carthage during the Third Punic War under Scipio Aemilianus. In 137 Tiberius served as quaestor during the Spanish Wars and was able to draw on his father's reputation to broker a treaty that saved many lives, despite being later rejected by the Senate. Tiberius then continued his political career until his death in 133 in a riot.

Tiberius' only other act that was important to Rome's military history was his creation of a commission to give land to the urban poor. According to our sources, there was a shortage of recruits who met the property qualification for military service. Tiberius expected that setting up a commission to distribute public land to the poor would lead to increasing the pool of manpower available to be drafted into the army, since the poor could not be drafted but landowning families would have sufficient wealth to be drafted. The land commission passed, but was stymied by senatorial opposition that led to Tiberius' own death in a riot.

Tiberius' direct impact may have been slight, but many later authors saw his and his brother's violent terms as tribunes as the beginning of the Roman Republic's slow decline. The issue of recruitment and manpower shortage is open to much debate in modern times, but there can be no doubt that the shortages were real enough to those living during this period.

Lee L. Brice

See also: Cornelius Scipio Aemilianus Africanus, Publius; Sempronius Gracchus, Gaius; Spanish Wars

References

Ligt, Luuk de. *Peasants, Citizens and Soldiers: Studies in Demographic History of Roman Italy 225 BC–AD 100*. Cambridge: Cambridge University Press, 2012.

MacKay, Christopher. *The Breakdown of the Roman Republic: From Oligarchy to Empire*. Cambridge: Cambridge University Press, 2009.

Senate

During much of the Roman Republic, the Senate was an advisory body to the consuls. Traditionally censors enrolled members, but in practice by the third century BCE, the Senate included all former magistrates, who served for life, about 300 men.

The Senate originally had no legally defined duties but acted from tradition. Its powers were thus ill-defined, but can be categorized as the power to distribute public funds, direct foreign policy, advise the consuls on laws and treaties, appoint magistrates not elected (dictators, proconsuls, and propraetors), and approve military triumphs and ovations. Usually,

The square building in the center of this image is the Curia, rebuilt by Diocletian on the site of the Julian Curia in the Roman Forum. The Senate met in the Curia, but it had burned down earlier so Caesar started to rebuild it in this new location, but it was finished by his son, Octavian. (Lee L. Brice)

men with military experience received the magistrate appointments. The power over financial expenditures meant that they could deny funds to an unpopular commander such as Marius. The power over foreign policy meant that they could refuse to put treaties to popular vote or not give a commander permission to leave his province under arms. They could deny a commander a triumph or reduce it to an ovation.

A development with unanticipated military repercussions was the emergence in the last century of the Republic of two factions: *populares* and *optimates*. *Populares* tended to support the interests of the people. *Optimates* were the ultraconservatives who focused on tradition and the interests of the elite. Neither faction constituted more than a small group, and voting by individuals fluctuated too much for them to be called political parties, but they could cause trouble by resisting compromise. Sulla was an optimate. *Optimates* blocked Pompey and Caesar, thus leading to the First Triumvirate, and optimates kept Caesar from making a compromise in 50, thus contributing to the start of Civil War II in 49.

Although the Senate had no military authority, through its powers as well as action or inaction it had great influence over Roman military activity and practices.

Lee L. Brice

See also: Civil War II; Civil War III; Julius Caesar, Gaius; Julius Caesar Octavianus, Gaius; Marius, Gaius; Pompeius Magnus, Gnaeus; Triumph; Triumvirate, First

References

Gruen, Erich. *The Last Generation of the Roman Republic.* Berkeley: University of California Press, 1995.

Lintott, A. *The Constitution of the Roman Republic.* Oxford: Oxford University Press, 1999.

Nicolet, Claude. *The World of the Citizen in Republican Rome.* Translated by P. S. Falla. Berkeley: University of California Press, 1980.

Sertorius, Quintus

Quintus <u>Sertorius</u> was born circa 126 BCE in Nursia. Nothing is known of his early career until he served in the wars against the Cimbri and Teutones in 102–101. He also performed well during the Social War, but Sulla intervened to block him from winning an election to tribune, so Sertorius supported Cinna after Sulla left Italy.

During the civil war that followed, Sertorius participated in Cinna's march on Rome in 87 and helped govern the city but later disagreed over preparations for Sulla's return and went to Spain as governor in 83. Sulla proscribed Sertorius, so he fled to North Africa for a year, returning to Spain in 80 as leader of an anti-Sullan revolt. Sertorius turned out to be a capable political and military leader, organizing a guerrilla war against the Roman commanders sent out to stop him, and by 77 he controlled most of Spain, governing it as if he were a Roman proconsul but still in revolt. Spain became the last theater of the civil war and thus attracted all remaining opponents of Sulla's original reforms.

Pompey was sent out to Spain in 77 as governor of Further Spain but also to stop Sertorius, who continued to receive support from more rebels. Although Sertorius was initially successful against Pompey, various errors and defeats forced him to take up guerrilla warfare again. Sertorius even made an alliance with Mithradates VI in 76. Sertorius' military losses in 75 led to diminishing support and increasing unpopularity in camp. Finally, he was murdered by one of his officers. Pompey returned to Rome and celebrated a triumph for the victory.

Lee L. Brice

See also: Civil War I; Cornelius Cinna, Lucius; Cornelius Sulla Felix, Lucius; Marius, Gaius; Mithradates VI; Pompeius Magnus, Gnaeus

References

Konrad, C. F. *Plutarch's Sertorius: a Historical Commentary.* Chapel Hill: University of North Carolina Press, 1994.

Matyszak, P. *Sertorius and the Struggle for Spain.* Barnsley, UK: Pen and Sword Military, 2013.

Sextus. *See* Pompeius Magnus, Sextus

Sicilian Slave Wars. *See* Slave Wars, Sicilian

Siege

Most of the Roman military activities that our sources record are battles, raids, and maneuvering. Sieges receive mention but little attention. Those that ancient authors describe in any detail are notable for an engineering feat. The reason that sieges do not receive more attention is because they tended to be gradual affairs where one side slowly undermined the other's defenses or starved them until an assault could win the day. A careful examination of Roman military history reveals, however, that sieges were often critical to Roman military success.

Roman siege methods were originally typical of Greek measures of the same period in that they consisted of surrounding a city with a fortified wall (circumvallation) and cutting off its food supply until it surrendered. If an external force trying to relieve the sieged city showed up, the Romans could build a second wall (contravallation) for protection. Engineering methods in these early sieges seem to have been limited to mining (tunnels), as we hear about in the war on Veii in the early fourth century BCE. Mining was not a simple process and required expertise and time to work well, but it was slow and not flashy until it worked, so it is not described in our sources.

Once the Greeks perfected siege engine technology from the east during the mid to late fourth century, the Romans began to adopt and adapt it in their campaigns. Torsion catapults became the Roman *ballista* and scorpion. These were important siege tools, more for their impact on enemy morale and keeping enemy troops from firing on Roman soldiers than for hammering at walls and towers. More sophisticated battering rams and siege towers appeared for assault and covering fire. Romans eventually employed ship-mounted siege platforms, as Alexander and the Hellenistic kings did. All of this equipment was not merely for show.

A blockade could last for many months or even years, with little for soldiers to do but stand guard duty and avoid enemy attacks. Soldiers had to be paid and fed and perhaps replaced, so a siege was expensive in many ways. Advances in siege technology sped up sieges and thus sped up campaigns and potentially shortened wars, saving money and manpower for the attacker. The investment was worth it. Defenders too invested when they could, as did Syracuse during the Roman siege of 214–212. Archimedes, the city's most famous resident, devised numerous defensive measures, and the city employed a number of measures adopted from the Carthaginians, including defensive cranes for lifting attacking ships from the water and dropping them from a height.

The Romans used siege often during the Punic Wars, perfecting their methods, and the Third Punic War was little more than a siege. Syracuse (214–212), Carthage (146), Numantia (133), and Piraeus (86) were all famous Roman sieges, but the most famous siege of the Roman Republic

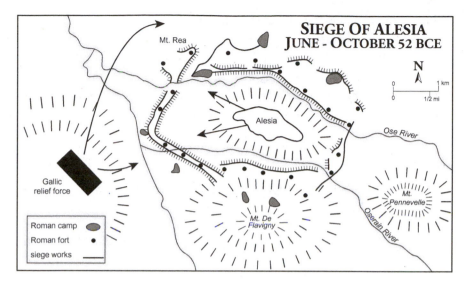

was Alesia (52). During the Gallic Wars, Caesar repeatedly used sieges effectively and described his measures and engineering in detail as a sign of his ingenuity and vision, but Alesia was presented as his crowning achievement. He used walls of circumvallation and contravallation stretching for miles over undulating terrain coupled with *ballista* and scorpion-armed towers, ditches, moats, hidden pits, and sharpened stakes. It was flashy and it worked, ending the war, but it still required perseverance on the part of his soldiers.

Siege was hard on soldiers. There was the tedium of a blockade siege and the need to avoid enemy attacks. Any aggression by the besiegers often took place at the walls or gates, meaning that the defenders knew where the action would be and the attackers would be in the open. When there was an assault the defenders were behind their walls, while the aggressors often had to charge in a predictable open space or wield the battering ram in a killing zone. Besiegers could count on high casualties in an aggressive siege. Josh Levithan has noted that given the lopsided nature of the conflict, it is unsurprising that the Romans observed the same practices for sieges, as had other states. A city that opened its gates willingly before a siege began could expect safety and relatively good treatment, but once the gate was closed and the ram touched the wall, the defenders knew that their city was subject to being sacked if the siege was successful. Pillaging and sacking were rewards for the soldiers' efforts, a chance for revenge, and punishment for those who had not surrendered as well as an example to the next city. It is little wonder, then, that ancient authors seldom described sieges in detail, despite their importance.

Lee L. Brice

See also: Artillery; Etruscan Wars; Gallic Wars; Julius Caesar, Gaius; Punic Wars; Syracuse

References

Levithan, J. *Roman Siege Warfare.* Ann Arbor: University of Michigan Press, 2014.

Levithan, J. "Roman Siege Warfare: Moral and Morale." In *New Approaches to Greco-Roman Warfare,* edited by Lee L. Brice, 127–148. Oxford, UK: Wiley-Blackwell, 2014.

Marsden, Eric W. *Greek and Roman Artillery: Historical Development.* Oxford, UK: Clarendon, 1969.

Signa Militaria. *See* Standards

Slaves and Camp Followers

The Roman military may have been well organized, but it was not a bureaucracy, so there were many services that needed to be provided by nonsoldiers, free and slave. Rome had a slave-based economy, so it should be no surprise that the Roman military used slaves and had a great impact on Roman slavery. Additionally, military captives could be sold into slavery for considerable profit. During the Republican period of greatest expansion (210–146 BCE), the price of slaves dropped immensely. In these ways, slavery was closely tied to the Roman military.

Every legion in the field had a remarkable amount of material to manage, including food, beasts of burden, building equipment, firewood, extra arms and armor, records, and much more. While soldiers may have carried much at times, especially on fast campaigns or raids, there were campaigns during which they did not carry everything, especially before Marius' reforms. In addition to carrying material and performing tasks, legions often required services provided by merchants, such as exchanging booty for coins, food, or companionship.

These dual kinds of tasks and services often fell to slaves and private merchants, who would have followed the legion to provide services, including slaves. In addition to these tasks, many officers also had slaves to do certain chores such as performing secretarial tasks, building fires, caring for horses, and the like. Although evidence for them is minimal, these two groups, free and slave, constituted camp followers. It is little wonder, then, that in most battle narratives authors mention the need to post units to guard the baggage, including slaves and camp followers. Marius tried to reduce the camp followers in his reforms.

A second way in which the military was connected with slaves was in the increasing provision of slaves. A fact of ancient warfare was that prisoners of war were liable to become slaves. Enslavement provided soldiers and commanders with mobile booty that they could quickly turn into wealth. At times, such as during the second century, so many slaves went on the market because of warfare that the price of slaves dropped to the point that every Roman family could own them and the wealthy could purchase many. Warfare was not the only means of acquiring more slaves, but at times it was a major source and had a huge impact on prices.

The final connection between the Roman military and slaves was in terms of emergency manpower. In times of emergencies such as the Punic Wars, slaves were enlisted, especially in the fleets. The Republic would sometimes require the wealthy to provide slaves to the military. The slaves would be freed, making them citizens and eligible for service, and then trained them for the navy. If they survived the military, these men remained free. In this way the military found a quick manpower source, and the wealthy shared the benefits of their wealth with the rest of society.

Lee L. Brice

See also: Fleet, Roman; Marius, Gaius; Punic Wars; Punic Wars, Consequences of the

References

Hoyos, Dexter, ed. *A Companion to the Punic Wars.* Oxford, UK: Wiley-Blackwell, 2011.

Joshel, Sandra. *Slavery in the Roman World.* Cambridge: Cambridge University Press, 2010.

Roth, J. P. *The Logistics of the Roman Army (264B.C.–A.D.235).* Leiden: Brill, 1999.

Slave War, Spartacus. *See* Spartacus Slave War

Slave Wars, Sicilian

Sicily had become the Roman Republic's first overseas province after victory in 241 BCE over Carthage in the First Punic War. Sicily was the principal grain producer for Rome and Italy. The wealth of imperial conquest enabled small numbers of the enormously rich Romans to acquire vast tracts of Sicilian land, where they employed slaves on a massive scale.

The first rebellion, which occurred during 135–132, was the result of maltreatment and abuse. The Roman historian Diodorus Siculus reports that the number of slave rebels swelled immensely, with modern estimates putting the number of rebellious slaves at no more than 70,000. Aristocratic disdain of servile populations led to a failure on the part of Rome to appreciate the situation's gravity, and the Roman military only won with considerable difficulty.

The second slave war, lasting from 104 to 100, resulted from an ill-advised Roman edict to liberate slaves in order to increase military manpower reserves. Under heavy pressure from aggrieved slave owners, Rome reneged on liberating the slaves and investigated slave rebellion, leading to actual revolt. The fighting was prolonged until Manius Aquillius finally prevailed. Although sources do not report the figures of this uprising, this second rebellion was nonetheless of immense scale. There were an estimated 30,000 slave casualties, and the rebellion's leaders were sent to the gladiatorial games in Rome.

Junius P. Rodriguez

See also: Punic Wars, Consequences of the; Spartacus Slave War

References

Joshel, Sandra R. *Slavery in the Roman World.* Cambridge: Cambridge University Press, 2010.

Shaw, Brent. *Spartacus and the Slave Wars: A Brief History.* Boston: Bedford/St. Martin's, 2001.

Social War

Also called the Marsic War and the Italic War, the Social War, named for the Latin term *socii* (allies), occurred during 91–87 BCE after attempts to grant Roman citizenship to allies failed. Italic peoples provided manpower for Roman armies in the unwritten expectation that they would get citizenship in return for loyalty. Although they had helped defeat many opponents, Rome had resisted extending citizenship to allies, despite several politicians' attempts. Numerous allies united to fight against Rome in 91, even seeking support from foreign rulers, including Mithradates VI, and minting their own coinage.

In fighting the allies, Rome faced a serious problem. Allies had fought alongside Rome for years and knew all their tactics and training. The war did not go well initially for Rome, and so it granted citizenship to all the Italic allies that had either not rebelled or had agreed to lay down their arms. The offer led many allies to withdraw, but in some areas fighting continued. This was a fortunate turn of events for the Italic allies, because they were now full citizens.

With numerous experienced commanders in the field, including Sulla and Marius, by 88 the war was mostly over, with the last holdouts losing in 87. It was a busy period, as Mithradates IV took advantage of the war to attack Romans in Anatolia. The extension of citizenship to Italy south of the Po River expanded the manpower pool for the legions and meant that auxiliary units would be specialists provided by peoples outside Italy, such as Gallic cavalry.

Lee L. Brice

See also: Allies, Roman; Cornelius Sulla Felix, Lucius; Marius, Gaius; Mithradates VI

References

Keaveney, Arthur. *Sulla, the Last Republican.* 2nd ed. London: Routledge, 2005.

MacKay, Christopher. *The Breakdown of the Roman Republic: From Oligarchy to Empire.* Cambridge: Cambridge University Press, 2009.

Spanish Wars

Rome acquired control of the Carthaginian parts of the Iberian Peninsula after the Second Punic War but did not organize it as provinces until 197 BCE. The Romans divided it into two provinces, Nearer Spain (Hispania Citerior) and Further Spain (Hispania Ulterior), but these provinces included only the coastal regions and a limited territory in the interior.

The Spanish Wars began in 197 as several peoples in both provinces rebelled against the Roman authorities. These rebellions were put down violently through military campaigns by a series of governors in the 190s. Leaders of the rebellions were sold into slavery. During 189, Aemilius Paullus pushed into Celtiberian territory in the center of the peninsula, winning a significant victory. This victory was followed up with more fighting, and finally in 179–178 Tiberius Sempronius Gracchus the Elder (father of the Gracchi brothers), governor of Nearer Spain, concluded a treaty with the indigenous Vascones people that enabled him to consolidate Roman control over the Celtiberian region, leading to treaties with the Celtiberians.

Roman governors of Spain were notorious for their corruption and their efforts to seek military glory even when there was peace. The result was repeated rebellions and the need for campaigning more often than not to restore peace disturbed by the prior governor. The Lusitanian tribes in the central and western part of the peninsula were especially resistant to Rome's attempts to expand. They raided all the way to the coast and signed no treaties until 155, when Gracchus the Elder negotiated a truce.

Soon afterward, however, the Lusitanians rose up under new leadership in 153. The Lusitanian war, a guerrilla war or insurgency, would last until 139, when their leader, Variathus, was murdered by his allies. Nearly simultaneous with the Lusitanian revolt, tribes in the central part of the peninsula revolted in what came to be called the Celtiberian War. This revolt devolved into another guerrilla war that would last until 133, when Scipio Aemilianus captured and sacked Numantia after a long siege. He sold the survivors into slavery and razed the city.

The so-called end of the Spanish Wars in 133 was not the end of resistance to Roman expansion, but it was the end of large-scale annual campaigns for a while. The first of the Spanish Wars may have provided booty for Rome, but by 155, service in Spain was not popular with soldiers, as there were limited opportunities for booty, and the fighting was not the pitched battles for which they had trained. Given their size and wealth of resources and agriculture, the two Spanish provinces remained extremely important to Rome. It is little wonder, then, that Sertorius and Pompey would both later exploit the peninsula for their own military goals.

Lee L. Brice

See also: Aemilius Paullus, Lucius; Pompeius Magnus, Gnaeus; Punic Wars, Causes of the; Punic Wars, Consequences of the; Sempronius Gracchus, Tiberius; Sertorius, Quintus; Siege

References

Hoyos, Dexter, ed. *A Companion to Roman Imperialism*. Leiden: Brill, 2012.

Lowe, B. *Roman Spain: Economy, Society and Culture*. London: Gerald Duckworth, 2009.

Silva, L. *Viriathus and the Lusitanian Resistance to Rome, 155–139 BCE*. Barnsley, UK: Pen and Sword Military, 2013.

Spartacus Slave War

Spartacus was a gladiator training in Capua when he became leader of a slave revolt. He was apparently of Thracian origin. According to one Roman source, he had been an allied (*auxilia*) soldier who had deserted and been captured, receiving the punishment of enslavement instead of death. While it is possible that the ancient source is correct, it is more likely that the story was a fiction invented by the Romans to explain Spartacus' military success. Attempts to extrapolate about Spartacus' life before the revolt from such limited and late sources are no better than speculation.

The slave war led by Spartacus began as a small local event in 73 when he and numerous other gladiators escaped from their training center in Capua. After raiding the countryside and attracting more followers among local slaves, they settled down on Vesuvius and elected multiple leaders, the most famous of whom were Spartacus and Crixus, a Gaul. The slaves then raided the local region, defeated a small Praetorian force sent against them, and after expanding their raiding defeated a larger force. Both of these victories brought more supporters from the local area and supplied weapons and armor from the defeated legionaries.

In 72 Spartacus and Crixus moved north in separate groups through the Apennines, pillaging as they went. Although Roman authors report a slave force of 70,000–120,000, that would be extreme exaggeration given the difficulties of ancient logistics and the Roman response, so 15,000–30,000 seems more appropriate. A new consular force of two legions was sent out, defeating Crixus and destroying most of his group before being defeated by Spartacus. The slaves elected additional leaders and then continued north, but once they reached Cisalpine Gaul they turned around and headed south again, presumably seeking rich territory for pillaging.

As the slaves marched south, the Senate gave command in the war and eight legions to Crassus. He trained his men aggressively and enforced strict obedience. Spartacus' army made it to the south, where they wintered.

When the slaves started to head north in early 71, Crassus blocked them. Despite losing a detachment, he was able to push Spartacus farther south into Bruttium right to Rhegium at the straits. Spartacus attempted to cross to Sicily but was unable to do so by any means. Roman sources suggest that he tried to employ pirates and that Crassus employed every means available to keep Spartacus from crossing.

Bottling up the slave force near Rhegium, Crassus tried to construct a wall to blockade the force and starve them out. Pompey, who had just returned from Spain, was ordered by the Senate to move south. Spartacus' army broke out of the siege, but Crassus caught up with them in Lucania, winning a decisive victory that destroyed most of the slaves, including Spartacus. Crassus had as many as 6,000 of the survivors crucified, a standard capital punishment for slaves and noncitizens, along the road to Capua.

Pompey destroyed a small group of slaves who had escaped Crassus and were heading north and then sent word to Rome, before Crassus, that he had defeated Spartacus' slave army. Crassus bore Pompey a grudge for having taken credit, but the two men were elected consuls for the following year. The Spartacus Slave War was the last large slave revolt in Roman history.

Lee L. Brice

See also: Licinius Crassus, Marcus; Pompeius Magnus, Gnaeus; Slave Wars, Sicilian

References

Joshel, Sandra R. *Slavery in the Roman World.* Cambridge: Cambridge University Press, 2010.

Shaw, Brent. *Spartacus and the Slave Wars: A Brief History.* Boston: Bedford/St. Martin's, 2001.

Winkler, M. M., ed. *Spartacus: Film and History.* Oxford, UK: Blackwell, 2007.

Standards

The standards (*signa militaria*) were the symbols of Roman units and a means of keeping men organized in battle. The standard consisted of a pole with a symbol on top and the unit honors stacked underneath. The standard-bearer (*signifer*) carried the standard in front of the unit.

In the Polybian legion, each maniple had two standards (one per century) on which the unit would orient itself. These unit standards seem to have typically had an open hand on top as if taking the military oath and then the unit honors stacked underneath. Each early legion carried five legionary standards that were carried in front of different parts of the legion *velites, hastati, principes, triarii,* and cavalry. These had one of five animal symbols on top: eagle, wolf, minotaur, boar, and horse. Sources do not report which parts of the legion had which symbol.

Marius made the eagle (*aquila*) in silver or gold the primary standard of every legion, with the other symbols subordinate but still in use. After his reforms, when the cohort was the primary unit, it was less important that different parts

Standards were the banners of the Roman legions with unit standards and one eagle standard per legion after Marius' reforms. Standards were carried by the *signifer* and would be decorated with all of the unit's honors and decorations. These are seen on Trajan's column in Trajan's Forum in Rome. (DEA/A. Dagli Orti/De Agostini/Getty Images)

had different symbols, so it was possible to make the eagle primary. As a result, the eagle standard came to be revered by each legion, not unlike a religious symbol. In the cohort legion, there were six of the century standards per cohort, with the primary standard being that of the leading maniple.

Loss of a standard in battle, especially the eagle, was significant and brought shame on the unit. The maniple standards were carried into battle so that soldiers knew where their unit was, based on the standards, but we do not know where in the battle line the standards were arranged. The legionary standards were present in battle but not in the first line, for safety. Commanders also relied on standards to watch the movement of units and would sometimes rely on its presence to rally their men, as Caesar did repeatedly during the Gallic Wars. In one instance, he even grabbed a standard and tossed it toward the enemy, telling his men to go get it if they wished to avoid the shame; they rallied, winning the battle.

The standards were an important part of each legion's identity as well as its battlefield success.

Lee L. Brice

See also: Gallic Wars; Julius Caesar, Gaius; Legion, Cohort; Legion, Manipular/Polybian; Marius, Gaius; Military Decorations

References

Keppie, L. J. F. *The Making of the Roman Army: From Republic to Empire.* Updated ed. Norman: University of Oklahoma Press, 1998.

Maxfield, V. *Military Decorations of the Roman Army.* Berkeley: University of California Press, 1981.

Pollard, N., and J. Berry. *The Complete Roman Legions.* London: Thames and Hudson, 2012.

Stipendium

The term stipendium came to have two meanings during the Roman Republic. One meaning was length of military service. During much of the Republic, the normal term of service seems to have been 6 continuous years, although men up to 46 years of age were expected to be available for up to 16 years in infantry or 10 years in cavalry as necessary.

The more common meaning was military pay. Rome introduced the stipendium in the fourth century BCE during the Etruscan Wars in order to help men cover their expenses, such as food, during extended campaign seasons. This stipendium was irregular, however, and it remains unclear whether they were paid in precious metal or in kind, as Rome did not yet have its own regular coinage. The need to pay soldiers during some of the extended wars of the fourth and third centuries forced Rome to adopt the minting of coins.

According to Polybius, in the early second century soldiers received 2 obols or 5 asses (coins) per day, which would have been 180 denarii in a year of 360 days. By 121 when coinage had been revalued, soldiers were earning 112.5 denarii. The pay rate for legionaries remained the same until sometime after 49, when Caesar doubled it to 225 denarii, to be paid in three parts during the year. This remained the rate of pay for soldiers until the end of the Republic.

The stipendium for centurions and other staff was greater, but its ratio to soldiers' pay is unknown. Military tribunes and other high-ranking officers received no pay from the state, although they had opportunities for enrichment.

The costs of uniforms, food, and replacement gear were standard deductions from all soldiers' annual pay throughout the Republic. They could earn more by selling war booty that they recovered or in bonuses paid after a triumph. During Civil War III, legionaries were initially promised immense bonuses in addition to their regular pay. Soldiers were unlikely to get wealthy, but for the poor who volunteered to serve after Marius' reforms, it was still an opportunity for improvement.

Lee L. Brice

See also: Julius Caesar, Gaius; Marius, Gaius; Triumph

References

Keppie, L. J. F. *The Making of the Roman Army: From Republic to Empire.* Updated ed. Norman: University of Oklahoma Press, 1998.

Nicolet, Claude. *The World of the Citizen in Republican Rome.* Translated by P. S. Falla. Berkeley: University of California Press, 1980.

Sulla, Lucius Cornelius. *See* Cornelius Sulla Felix, Lucius

Syracuse

Founded traditionally in 734 by Corinth, Syracuse became the preeminent Greek city in the west due to its large population and wealth. Syracuse had expended much of its energy over the years contesting with Carthage the domination of Sicily and usually controlling the eastern half of the island. Syracuse became militarily involved with Rome during the Punic Wars.

In 264, Mamertine mercenaries in Messana sought assistance from Rome and Carthage against Hieron II, tyrant of Syracuse. Hieron was trying to consolidate his control of eastern Sicily. Learning that Rome would respond, he allied with Carthage. The Roman response led to the First Punic War. Rome laid siege to Syracuse and forced Hieron to make peace and become an ally. When the war ended, Syracuse became the capital of the new province.

During the Second Punic War, Syracuse was one of numerous Greek cities that defected to Carthage after the Battle of Cannae. Rome responded vigorously, laying siege to the city. Archimedes, an inventor and engineer, helped Syracuse by inventing various devices to defeat Roman efforts. Despite those, Marcus Claudius Marcellus successfully captured and sacked the city in 211. The capture of Syracuse was a blow to Hannibal's logistical support. After the war, Syracuse remained the provincial capital and prospered.

Lee L. Brice

See also: Punic Wars; Punic Wars, Causes of the

References

Hoyos, Dexter, ed. *A Companion to the Punic Wars.* Oxford, UK: Wiley-Blackwell, 2011.

Smith, Christopher, and John Serrati, eds. *Sicily from Aeaneas to Augustus: New Approaches in Archaeology and History.* Edinburgh, UK: Edinburgh University Press, 2000.

T

Training

Roman sources are uninformative about details of legionary training during the Roman Republic, in large part because they and their audience took the topic for granted. A key problem with trying to reassemble training regimes for the Republic is that the most detailed source that survives dates from four centuries after the Republic. There are a number of features, however, that we can piece together.

Polybius, our best source for the second-century army, suggests that the best training focused on weapons training, care of weapons and armor, and maneuvers by both small and large units. He does not suggest how the Roman military accomplished this regime. On enlistment, a new recruit was called a tiro and was assigned to his unit. Socialization into the society of the legion and expectations began immediately, as did introduction to discipline through routine duties and training.

Soldiers were expected to be fit and to continue exercising during service. Gymnasium exercises and dance both served to develop fitness and flexibility. Soldiers learned to march with their gear. Scipio Africanus introduced (or reintroduced) a four-day training regime that included requiring men to run 4 miles while carrying all their gear on the first day in addition to the regular duties and then to rest completely on the third day. Carrying heavy packs was something that seems to have fallen out of use occasionally, because Marius reintroduced it a century later. He required his men to march 20 miles with full gear and their rations (60 pounds) within a set time or 24 miles with gear and rations at a quicker pace. Caesar similarly expected his men to march fast with full packs and trained them accordingly.

Africanus required his men to make a close inspection of their weapons and rubdown and clean them on the second day of his regime and to mock fight with wooden swords and spears on the fourth day. Marius introduced in his military reforms methods from gladiator training, such as use of a wooden sparring post with which men practiced shield use and stabbing out from behind the shield while instructors shouted. We know from Caesar that the instructors would accustom the men to judging killing distance by shouting out distances, especially the distance at which their enemy's weapons were effective. The training sword was wooden with a button on the end, and the sword and the shield may have been heavier than normal to build muscle strength and encourage freedom of movement in battle. Soldiers also learned how to throw the javelins and *pila* by throwing against a wooden pole under orders.

As we learn from Scipio and Marius, recruits and veterans would also practice live combat with weapons covered but in pairs, small units, and larger units. Drill was a regular duty for soldiers in camp. They also practiced maneuvering in groups and following orders. Some commanders also had their troops practice siege skills such as working a battering ram and entrenching and building fortifications. When Aemilianus took command in 134, he found the soldiers unprepared and so required them to build full fortifications, including ditches, and dismantle them daily. Civil engineering projects also served to inculcate discipline, obedience, and teamwork. Legions typically built roads and bridges but sometimes took on larger works. When Marius was preparing his legions for the campaigns against the Cimbri and Teutones, he had them build a canal.

Naval units also required extensive training. The kinds of tactics employed in trireme combat required skilled and disciplined crews to be effective. These strengths contributed to Roman success at sea. When the Romans built fleets, they had to train allies as well as Roman citizens and freed slaves, perhaps requiring non-Latin speakers to learn Latin commands. They had to train extensively to work together, but their naval successes were few until they became more experienced. When Octavian was fighting naval campaigns in 38–36, he was unable to make much headway until Agrippa arranged a closed lake for safe training of single and multiple vessels. In addition to training in weapon use and maintenance and staying fit, soldiers stationed aboard had to practice fighting on moving vessels.

All of the training and unit tasks contributed to internalizing discipline and obedience among the men. The tasks also brought them into the culture of the legions and the fleet and gave the men a shared identity that would help bond them in combat.

Lee L. Brice

See also: Aemilius Paullus, Lucius; Centurions; Cornelius Scipio Aemilianus Africanus, Publius; Cornelius Scipio Africanus, Publius; Discipline; Fleet; Julius Caesar, Gaius; Julius Caesar Octavianus, Gaius; Marius, Gaius; Polybius; Tribunes, Military; Vipsanius Agrippa, Marcus

References

Davies, R. W. "Joining the Roman Army." In *Service in the Roman Army,* edited by D. Breeze and V. Maxfield, 3–32. New York: Columbia University Press, 1989.

Goldsworthy, A. K. *The Roman Army at War, 100 B.C.–A.D. 200.* Oxford, UK: Clarendon, 1996.

Keppie, L. J. F. *The Making of the Roman Army: From Republic to Empire.* Updated ed. Norman: University of Oklahoma Press, 1998.

Tribunes, Military

Military tribunes (*tribuni militum*) were originally, in the sixth century BCE, the officers who led the units drawn from the tribes. Later, they were organized as the highest-ranking legionary officers, below the commander. Those assigned to each of the first four legions recruited each year were elected, and the consuls selected the tribunes for all subsequent legions. Polybius records that there were 24 military tribunes in the second century, 6 for each of the first four legions. Military tribunes were required to have 5 to 10 years of military experience and were drawn from the elite—equestrians or sons of senators. Because the military tribunate was a precursor to running for a higher magistracy, tribunes tended to be young, 25–35 years of age.

Polybius explains that the military tribunes were expected to work together in pairs. Two of them would rotate command of a legion for two months. Their responsibilities were administrative rather than tactical. The commander had ultimate authority, especially in combat, but the tribunes handled the day-to-day management of the legion, such as training, health, welfare, and discipline as well as constructing the fortifications as necessary. They reported to the commander daily.

Just because military tribunes did not have tactical responsibilities on the level of the commander does not mean they had no responsibilities in battle. The tribune was expected to assist the commander as necessary, perhaps by leading a wing of the battle line, and if the commander died or fled, then the tribune was expected to continue fighting in the commander's role if no legates were available. After the Battle of Cannae, Scipio (later Africanus), then a military tribune, rallied survivors at a nearby town and held off Hannibal's cavalry. At the Battle of Cynoscephalae, a tribune led part of a legion around behind Philip's line, smashing his phalanx and winning the battle.

In addition to its importance in maintaining the legions, the tribunate was also important for training officers. Ancient Rome lacked a military school or compulsory military training for youths, as in some Greek states, so the military tribunate provided young ambitious men with an opportunity to acquire the kind of military experience they would need if they were going to go into politics. There was no separation of civil and military institutions, so there were no professional military officers above the rank of centurion in the Roman Republic. Men who wanted to become commanders went into politics, starting with the office of quaestor. The military tribunate was a way to meet the requirements to run for a higher magistracy while also gaining valuable experience.

Also, since the first four tribunes were elected and the rest were appointed, the military tribunate gave these men a chance to hone their political skills. Men who had been incompetent previously were unlikely to be elected or selected, to their shame, so there was much pressure to perform well. A number of men who went on to political careers started out as military tribunes, such as Scipio Africanus and Pompey.

During Caesar's campaigns in Gaul he preferred employing legates to tribunes, so the post diminished in importance, but it still was an important post in the armies in Civil War III. Indeed, after tribunes sided with the soldiers in two mutinies, Octavian removed those men and increased the benefits of the military tribunes to create a social gulf between them and their legionaries. The duties of military tribunes may have changed over time, but they were an important part of the military and political fabric of Rome.

Lee L. Brice

See also: Cannae, Battle of; Cornelius Scipio Africanus, Publius; Cynoscephalae, Battle of; Discipline; Julius Caesar, Gaius; Legionary Commanders; Mutiny; Polybius; Pompeius Magnus, Gnaeus; Training

References

Brice, Lee L. "Disciplining Octavian: An Aspect of Roman Military Culture during the Triumviral Wars, 44–30 BCE." In *Warfare and Culture in World History,* edited by Wayne Lee, 35–60. New York: New York University Press, 2011.

Erdkamp, P., ed. *A Companion to the Roman Army.* Oxford, UK: Wiley-Blackwell, 2011.

Keppie, L. J. F. *The Making of the Roman Army, From Republic to Empire.* Updated ed. Norman: University of Oklahoma Press, 1998.

Nicolet, Claude. *The World of the Citizen in Republican Rome.* Translated by P. S. Falla. Berkeley: University of California Press, 1980.

Triumph

The triumph was the height of military celebration and the highest honor to which a Roman commander could usually aspire. It was a military parade awarded in recognition of achievements in warfare. Only the Senate could confer a triumph, and although many laws were thought to govern the process, it seems that political competition played as much of a role in the grant.

When the first actual triumph occurred is a matter of debate, but it seems not to have developed a format until the late fourth century BCE. A commander who thought that he had achieved success worthy of the triumph would send a report to the Senate in which he might hint at or even request a triumph. The Senate would then deliberate on the matter and let him know before he returned to Rome. The Senate would then request that the people vote in the Comitia Centuriata to grant the candidate permission to retain his imperium inside the walls of Rome. The people did not grant the triumph; they merely gave permission to hold onto military authority in the city if requested by the Senate. If the Senate thought that the achievement was good but not great, it might award an ovation, a lesser form of the triumph.

The triumph may originally have been an ad hoc parade, but by the second century it had evolved into a formalized ritual. The triumphal commander, or *triumphator,* would assemble a number of his troops, captives, booty, symbols, and banners in the Campus Martius. The parade (*pompa*) would then proceed through the city, entering at the triumphal gate and winding its way on a long path through much of the city to end at the Temple of Jupiter on the Capitoline hill. The *triumphator* would ride in a four-horse chariot accompanied by any of his youngest children or a slave holding a wreath to remind him of his mortality. He wore a special costume similar to the garb of Jupiter Optimus Maximus. Any older sons of the *triumphator*

After a battle the winning side would usually erect a trophy which often included a post with enemy armor attached to it. Standard Roman iconography often shows a female prisoner tied to the post. Such images were often displayed along with prisoners during Roman triumphs or military parades after a successful war. (Lee L. Brice)

would ride on horseback behind the chariot. The *triumphator's* lictors would march before him in special costume with wreaths on their fasces. Captives of all sorts, preferably in chains, would march, as would any freed prisoners, perhaps dressed as freedmen. The Senate and magistrates were supposed to march in the parade as a show of support. A large group of the *triumphator's* soldiers would march too, unarmed and singing songs or chants that made fun of the commander. The rude songs were a way of appeasing the gods and apparently amused the crowds. Caesar's men, for example, sang about their commander's reputation for sleeping around and suggested that all chaste women be locked away now that Caesar had returned. This aspect is one of several reminding us that the parade was religious as well as military in its significance.

In addition to all the participants, there would be placards identifying battle sites and provincial names. Carts full of booty and unique or fascinating spoils from the war as well as banners and musicians accompanied the parade. At the end of the procession, the *triumphator* would deposit booty at the temple, have some prisoners ritually killed, and formally surrender his imperium. The parade took as long as necessary and even multiple days in the case of Pompey, Caesar, and Octavian. There would often be additional events and public banquets associated with the celebration.

The triumph was not just a military celebration; it was also about status and politics. Once a commander triumphed, he was qualified to use the title of *triumphator* for the rest of his life, and it would be recalled at his death. Politicians did not campaign but instead ran on their record, so anything they could do to get the people's notice and give a positive impression was a worthy endeavor. Governors were sometimes accused of being overly aggressive in seeking triumphs by starting new conflicts and exaggerating the importance of victories. In addition to elections, the Senate appointed propraetors and proconsuls to lucrative assignments and was more likely to pick someone they favored and who had shown good military experience.

Since only the Senate could award a triumph, it was necessary to curry favor with that body, and the Senate could use its authority for political ends, as it did with Caesar. The triumph thus became an important part of the military, religious, social, and political web of Republican Rome. Traditional triumphs disappeared entirely within a decade of the end of the Republic.

Lee L. Brice

See also: Comitia Centuriata; Julius Caesar, Gaius; Imperium; Pompeius Magnus, Gnaeus; Senate

References

Beard, Mary. *The Roman Triumph.* Cambridge, MA: Harvard University Press, 2009.

Erdkamp, P., ed. *A Companion to the Roman Army.* Oxford, UK: Wiley-Blackwell, 2011.

Maxfield, V. *Military Decorations of the Roman Army.* Berkeley: University of California Press, 1981.

Tritle, Lawrence A., and J. Brian Campbell, eds. *The Oxford Handbook of Classical Military History.* Oxford: Oxford University Press, 2012.

Triumvirate, First

The First Triumvirate was the secret association, or cabal, formed in 60 BCE by Pompey, Crassus, and Caesar. Although such an association was not actually illegal and was strictly informal, these men used it to subvert traditional political activities and get what they each wanted.

In 60 BCE, Pompey had been waiting for two years for the Senate to grant his request that his men receive free land and that his extraordinary measures in the east be ratified. Crassus was irritated with the Senate because he had associates and debtors who were seeking rebates on tax contracts for which they had overbid and lost money. Caesar had returned from Spain seeking permission to hold a triumph and run for election as consul simultaneously, a combination that was illegal because a candidate had to be present, but a *triumphator* did not count as present until surrendering his imperium. His enemies, assuming that he would choose the triumph, arranged permission to do either the triumph or the election, but not both. The narrow optimate opposition in the Senate had blocked all three men.

These determined men banned together to pool their resources for success, and each had something to offer. Pompey and Crassus had their veterans and clients to call upon to vote as well as as much wealth they could employ bribing additional votes. Caesar decided to forego the triumph and brought only his candidacy and intellect. He was the binding force of their semisecret association and had Pompey marry his only daughter to seal the arrangement. Caesar was elected consul for 59. While in office, he arranged for Pompey's and Crassus' requests to pass and for his governorship to include both provinces of Gaul as well as Illyricum and to last for five years. Pompey's achievements in the east had completely raised the standards for military greatness, so Caesar needed time, and he was immune from prosecution as long as he held a magistracy.

As governor, Caesar created continuing opportunities for military glory in the Gallic Wars. Crassus and Pompey sought similar opportunities in 56, and the arrangement was renewed. Both men became consuls for 55, and they each became governors for five years, Pompey in Spain and Crassus in Syria. They also extended Caesar's term for five additional years to end on December 31, 50. Crassus went to Syria in 54 and started a war with Parthia. Pompey remained in Rome, governing through his legates.

Their cabal unraveled soon afterward. Crassus died at Carrhae and Caesar's daughter, Julia, who had married Pompey to secure their arrangement, had died in childbirth, leaving Pompey miserable and no longer tied to Caesar. The triumvirate was broken. Their informal association had worked in blocking the optimate opposition and giving each participant what he had wanted, but they had run roughshod over normal political process and hardened their opponents' resolve.

The important thing to recall is that all our sources knew where events would lead, so their accounts often have the feel of impending doom and tragedy. The people who lived through the period had no idea where things would lead. Civil war and the end of the Roman Republic were still not inevitable, though they became increasingly likely. The label "First Triumvirate" is a modern invention and is misleading because it gives the false impression that this cabal was a formal and permanent thing when in fact it was not.

Lee L. Brice

See also: Civil War II; Gallic Wars; Julius Caesar, Gaius; Licinius Crassus, Marcus; Pompeius Magnus, Gnaeus; Senate; Triumph

References

Gruen, Erich. *The Last Generation of the Roman Republic.* Berkeley: University of California Press, 1995.

MacKay, C. *The Breakdown of the Roman Republic: From Oligarchy to Empire.* Cambridge: Cambridge University Press, 2009.

Rosenstein, N., and R. Morstein-Marx, eds. *A Companion to the Roman Republic.* Oxford, UK: Blackwell, 2010.

Syme, R. *The Roman Revolution.* Oxford: Oxford University Press, 1938.

Triumvirate, Second

The Second Triumvirate was the formal constitutional arrangement forged in 43 BCE by Antony, Lepidus, and Octavian. It was the Second Triumvirate because modern historians had already assigned the misleading label "First Triumvirate" to the cabal of 60.

In the fall of 43, Antony had been declared an enemy and outlaw. He had been defeated at Mutina in April and then linked up with Lepidus, who was subsequently declared an outlaw. Octavian was at that time a suffect consul in northern Italy. He already had a law passed declaring the assassins of Caesar enemies and outlaws. Octavian was supposed to be hunting down Antony and Lepidus but was actually negotiating a pact with them. Their agreement, made at Bononia with their soldiers' support in October, became law in Rome in November.

Because by his abuse of power Caesar had made the office of dictator so unpalatable that it had been eliminated, these generals formally called their office "triumvirs for the restoration of the Republic." A triumvirate had originally been a commission of three minor magistrates that handled some element of public business, such as minting coins on behalf of the state. Each of these new triumvirs had the same powers as a dictator but for five years.

The triumvirs proscribed their enemies and sold off the property to raise money for their troops. The triumvirs also promised their soldiers bonuses equal to more than 15 years' pay in return for their support. Afterward, Antony and Octavian moved to Greece in 42 against Brutus and Cassius, winning decisively at Philippi. With the deaths of these two leading assassins, the anti-Caesar movement disappeared. Antony went east to chastise the assassin's allies and raise money for the troops, while Octavian had the task of resettling the veterans in Italy. Lepidus had stayed in Rome keeping the peace.

Octavian had difficulties settling the veterans because the land he gave them was seized from the current owners. He eventually restored order but not before a revolt in 41–40, usually called the Perusine War. Antony's wife Fulvia and his brother Lucius instigated the revolt, claiming to be concerned that Octavian was getting too much credit for settling affairs in Italy. They raised an army and after some maneuvering seized Perusia, where Octavian arrived and started a siege. His experienced troops won the siege in 40, and the leaders were permitted to leave Italy, although Fulvia died on her way to Antony.

Antony returned to Italy that same year, avoiding conflict with Octavian by the intervention of the soldiers on both sides. With the triumvirate renewed, Antony, who was now widowed, married Octavia, Octavian's sister. In their arrangement, Lepidus was still a triumvir but was assigned to Africa. The following year at Misenum, the triumvirs made an agreement with Sextus Pompey, who had been causing difficulties from Sicily. He received governorship of Sicily, Sardinia, Corsica, and Greece for five years. The agreement broke down the following year as renewed war between Sextus and Octavian erupted. The triumvirs renewed the triumvirate officially in 37, with their powers extended for five more years to 33 or early 32. Lepidus retained his post.

Octavian finally defeated Sextus at Naulochus in 36, capturing Sicily. Lepidus, who had invaded Sicily to help Octavian, found himself deposed from the triumvirate and sent to Rome after he tried to take credit for the victory. At about the same time, Antony was defeated in his attempt to invade Parthia. Octavian's military reputation in Rome was rising as Antony's was weakening. The triumvirate continued officially, but relations between Octavian and Antony were increasingly strained.

Octavian waged a war in Illyria in 35–33 as Antony successfully invaded Armenia in 34 with Cleopatra's support. Antony then made a number of political missteps, including public marriage to Cleopatra after which he divorced Octavia, breaking the only remaining connection between the two men. The triumvirate formally ended in 33 or 32, with everyone aware that warfare was highly likely. Octavian successfully raised sufficient support to declare war on Cleopatra the same year and won the Battle of Actium in 31.

Examination of this period reveals that it is difficult to separate Civil War III from the Second Triumvirate. The triumvirate merely provided constitutional cover for what three powerful men wished to impose on the Roman world. It is little wonder, then, that when Octavian was ready to restore order in 27, he called it restoring the Republic to the people. The triumvirate was a transitional period, although contemporaries had no way of realizing that.

Lee L. Brice

See also: Actium, Battle of; Aemilius Lepidus, Marcus; Antonius, Marcus; Cassius Longinus, Gaius; Civil War III; Cleopatra VII; Julius Caesar Octavianus, Gaius; Junius Brutus, Marcus; Philippi, Battle of; Pompeius Magnus, Sextus; Siege; Triumvirate, First

References

MacKay, C. *The Breakdown of the Roman Republic: From Oligarchy to Empire.* Cambridge: Cambridge University Press, 2009.

Osgood, Josiah. *Caesar's Legacy: Civil War and the Emergence of the Roman Empire.* Cambridge: Cambridge University Press, 2006.

Rosenstein, N., and R. Morstein-Marx, eds. *A Companion to the Roman Republic.* Oxford, UK: Blackwell, 2010.

Syme, R. *The Roman Revolution.* Oxford: Oxford University Press, 1938.

V

Vipsanius Agrippa, Marcus

Marcus Vipsanius Agrippa was born circa 63 BCE to an obscure family, and little is known about his childhood. Agrippa accompanied Octavian to Rome in 44 and helped him raise a private army later that year. Theirs was a close friendship that would last until Agrippa's death in 12.

Agrippa played a role in the Perusine War of 41. He was governor of Gaul in 38, crushing a revolt of the Aquitani in Gaul and crossing the Rhine to subdue the Germanic tribes. As consul in 37, Agrippa rebuilt Octavian's fleet and created an artificial harbor by linking Lake Avernus to the sea near Baiae so that his rowers had a safe place to train. He also invented a new form of grapnel that could be shot from a *ballista* and then used to pull the enemy close for deck-side combat.

With Agrippa's help, Octavian moved against Sextus in 36. Defeating Sextus' fleet near Mylae and then winning decisively the following month at Naulochus in a huge battle, Agrippa contributed immensely to Octavian's victory in Sicily. Agrippa was awarded a naval crown for his accomplishments in Sicily. He then served in Illyria during Octavian's campaign there in 35–34. As an aedile in 33, Agrippa undertook numerous popular public works that contributed to Octavian's success in winning over the Roman people.

By 31, Agrippa had established himself as a superior naval commander. In a series of naval actions, he seized important coastal bases in Greece and used them to disrupt Antony's sea routes of supply and communication. Agrippa's control of the sea made it possible for Octavian to safely transfer his army to a base north of Actium. Then he and Agrippa

Agrippa was a close friend of Octavian and an outstanding commander on land and sea. He fought at Philippi and engineered the naval defeats of Sextus Pompey in 36 BCE and of Antony and Cleopatra at Actium in 31. (Charles & Josette Lenars/Corbis)

blockaded Antony and Cleopatra's force on the Actium Peninsula. Their attempt to break out became the Battle of Actium on September 2. Agrippa's strategy successfully neutralized most of the enemy fleet and resulted in Octavian's complete victory, in which it did not matter that Antony escaped. Agrippa thus made it possible for Octavian to take sole control of the Mediterranean Sea and most of the Roman world.

Lee L. Brice

See also: Actium, Battle of; Antonius, Marcus; Civil War III; Cleopatra VII; Fleet, Roman; Julius Caesar Octavianus, Gaius; Military Decorations; Pompeius Magnus, Sextus

References

MacKay, Christopher. *The Breakdown of the Roman Republic: From Oligarchy to Empire.* Cambridge: Cambridge University Press, 2009.

Osgood, J. *Caesar's Legacy: Civil War and the Emergence of the Roman Empire.* Cambridge: Cambridge University Press, 2006.

Roddaz, Jean-Michel. *Marcus Agrippa.* Rome: École Française de Rome, 1984.

W

War Elephants. *See* Elephants, War

Z

Zama, Battle of

The Battle of Zama, fought in October 202 in North Africa, pitted the Roman commander Scipio Africanus against Hannibal. Scipio invaded North Africa in 204. After several successes, Carthage recalled Hannibal from Italy in 203.

Hannibal raised a new army to supplement his veterans and prepared to engage Scipio. Moving away from Carthage, probably in October, Hannibal seems to have camped at Zama Regia before the battle. His army included as many as 36,000 infantry, 4,000 cavalry, and 80 elephants. Scipio may have had 29,000 infantry and 6,000 cavalry. Hannibal seems to have had overall numerical advantage, but Scipio had more cavalry, which turned out to be decisive. The exact location of the battle remains a mystery, despite the battle's name.

Hannibal positioned war elephants in front. Behind these he placed his infantry in three lines. The first line consisted of seasoned mercenary troops, the second consisted of less experienced Carthaginian and Libyan troops, and the third line was Hannibal's seasoned veterans. Numidian cavalry protected Hannibal's left flank, and Carthaginian cavalry protected his right flank. Scipio placed his infantry facing the Carthaginian line of battle. His Italian cavalry was on the left flank, and his Numidian cavalry under Masinissa was on the right flank. Scipio's infantry was not in solid ranks but instead was subdivided into smaller maniples, with spaces between the lines to help absorb the shock of the Carthaginian war elephants. Scipio placed the maniples one behind the other. At the beginning of the battle, the gaps between maniples were filled by the light troops.

The battle began with Hannibal advancing his elephants toward the Roman lines. The elephants were not well trained, however, and many of them soon became disoriented by Roman trumpets and bugles and bolted, causing Hannibal's Numidian cavalry to stampede and allowing Masinissa's cavalry to rout the rest. Scipio's Roman cavalry defeated the Carthaginian cavalry on Hannibal's right, driving it from the field. Hannibal's initial infantry assault failed, but as it withdrew it ran into the veterans who were moving forward to engage. Scipio re-formed his infantry before Hannibal could strike, and his cavalry fell on Hannibal's veterans from the rear, cutting them to pieces and causing a rout.

The Romans won a decisive victory. Only Hannibal and some of the cavalry escaped to Hadrumetum. Zama was payback for Cannae. Well-trained Roman infantry, supported by a superior cavalry force, had annihilated a larger poorly trained infantry force that was weak in cavalry. As a result, Carthage sued for peace.

Spencer C. Tucker

See also: Allies, Roman; Cavalry; Cornelius Scipio Africanus, Publius; Hannibal; Punic Wars

References

Goldsworthy, A. *The Punic Wars.* London: Cassell, 2000.

Hoyos, Dexter, ed. *A Companion to the Punic Wars.* Oxford, UK: Wiley-Blackwell, 2011.

Lazenby, J. F. *Hannibal's War: A Military History of the Second Punic War.* Norman: University of Oklahoma Press, 1998.

Scullard, Howard. *Scipio Africanus: Soldier and Politician.* London: Thames and Hudson, 1970.

Documents

1. Polybius, Organization of a Manipular Legion

Polybius, a Greek living and writing between 167 and 146 BCE in Rome, provides the best description of how a manipular legion was organized. These were the types of legions used from circa 311 until 104. His description is thought to have come in part from an older manual for military tribunes, although he probably supplemented it by interviewing Roman officers and soldiers. Polybius was heavily influenced by the methodology of the earlier Greek historian Thucydides, so it would not be surprising if Polybius incorporated some eyewitness accounts along with a Roman manual. He was a Greek officer and had seen Roman legions in action before coming to Rome and during his association with the Scipio family.

The excerpt here is part of an extended discussion on what made the Roman military so successful. The part of his narrative preceding this passage includes his description of the process of enlistment (*dilectus*). There are inconsistencies in his report that probably resulted from the older nature of the manual he used. Perhaps also as a result of using older or multiple sources, his vocabulary is confused in places, such as when he calls maniples *ordines* or *vexilla,* but this is the only known vocabulary problem. Despite these problems, his account is consistent and full of valuable detail. What makes his description so important, in addition to his contemporary eyewitness accounts, is that it is the only continuous discussion on the organization of the pre-Marian legion. This passage is also useful because Polybius discusses how centurions were supposed to be selected and also discusses their duties.

6.21 The enrollment having been completed in this manner, those of the tribunes on whom this duty falls collect the newly-enrolled soldiers, and picking out of the whole body a single man whom they think the most suitable make him take the oath that he will obey his officers and execute their orders as far as is in his power. Then the others come forward and each in his turn takes his oath simply that he will do the same as the first man.

At the same time the consuls send their orders to the allied cities in Italy which they wish to contribute troops, stating the numbers required and the day and place at which the men selected must present themselves. The magistrates, choosing the men and administering the oath in the manner above described, send them off, appointing a commander and a paymaster.

The tribunes in Rome, after administering the oath, fix for each legion a day and place at which the men are to present themselves without arms and then dismiss them. When they come to the rendezvous, they choose the youngest and poorest to form the *velites;* the next to them are made *hastati;* those in the prime of life *principes;* and the oldest of all *triarii,* these being the names among the Romans of the four classes in each legion distinct in age and equipment. They divide them so that the senior men known as *triarii* number six hundred, the *principes* twelve hundred, the *hastati* twelve hundred, the rest, consisting of the youngest, being *velites.* If the legion consists of more than four thousand men, they divide accordingly, except as regards the *triarii,* the number of whom is always the same.

22 The youngest soldiers or *velites* are ordered to carry a sword, javelins, and a target (*parma*). The target is strongly made and sufficiently large to afford protection, being circular and measuring three feet in diameter. They also wear a plain helmet, and sometimes cover it with a wolf's skin or something similar both to protect and to act as a distinguishing mark by which their officers can recognize them and judge if they fight pluckily or not. The wooden shaft of the javelin measures about two cubits in length and is about a finger's breadth in thickness; its head is a span long hammered out to such a fine edge that it is necessarily bent by the first impact, and the enemy is unable to return it. If this were not so, the missile would be available for both sides.

23 The next in seniority called *hastati* are ordered to wear a complete panoply. The Roman panoply consists firstly of a shield (*scutum*), the convex surface of which measures two and a half feet in width and four feet

in length, the thickness at the rim being a palm's breadth. It is made of two planks glued together, the outer surface being then covered first with canvas and then with calf-skin. Its upper and lower rims are strengthened by an iron edging which protects it from descending blows and from injury when rested on the ground. It also has an iron boss (*umbo*) fixed to it which turns aside the most formidable blows of stones, pikes, and heavy missiles in general. Besides the shield they also carry a sword, hanging on the right thigh and called a Spanish sword. This is excellent for thrusting, and both of its edges cut effectually, as the blade is very strong and firm. In addition they have two *pila,* a brass helmet, and greaves. The *pila* are of two sorts— stout and fine. Of the stout ones some are round and a palm's length in diameter and others are a palm square. Fine *pila,* which they carry in addition to the stout ones, are like moderate-sized hunting-spears, the length of the haft in all cases being about three cubits. Each is fitted with a barbed iron head of the same length as the haft. This they attach so securely to the haft, carrying the attachment halfway up the latter and fixing it with numerous rivets, that in action the iron will break sooner than become detached, although its thickness at the bottom where it comes in contact with the wood is a finger's breadth and a half; such great care do they take about attaching it firmly. Finally they wear as an ornament a circle of feathers with three upright purple or black feathers about a cubit in height, the addition of which on the head surmounting their other arms is to make every man look twice his real height, and to give him a fine appearance, such as will strike terror into the enemy. The common soldiers wear in addition a breastplate of brass a span square, which they place in front of the heart and call the heart-protector (*pectorale*), this completing their accoutrements; but those who are rated above ten thousand drachmas wear instead of this a coat of chain-mail (*lorica*). The *principes* and *triarii* are armed in the same manner except that instead of the *pila* the *triarii* carry long spears (*hastae*).

24 From each of the classes except the youngest they elect ten centurions according to merit, and then they elect a second ten. All these are called centurions, and the first man elected has a seat in the military council. The centurions then appoint an equal number of rearguard officers (*optiones*). Next, in conjunction with the centurions, they divide each class into ten companies, except the *velites,* and assign to each company two centurions and two *optiones* from among the elected officers. The *velites* are divided equally among all the companies; these companies are called *ordines* or *manipuli* or *vexilla,* and their officers are called centurions or *ordinum ductores.* Finally these officers appoint from the ranks two of the finest and

bravest men to be standard-bearers (*vexillarii*) in each maniple. It is natural that they should appoint two commanders for each maniple; for it being uncertain what may be the conduct of an officer or what may happen to him, and affairs of war not admitting of pretexts and excuses, they wish the maniple never to be without a leader and chief. When both centurions are on the spot, the first elected commands the right half of the maniple and the second the left, but if both are not present the one who is commands the whole. They wish the centurions not so much to be venturesome and daredevil as to be natural leaders, of a steady and sedate spirit. They do not desire them so much to be men who will initiate attacks and open the battle, but men who will hold their ground when worsted and hard-pressed and be ready to die at their posts.

Source: Polybius, *The Histories, Vol. III,* 6.21–24. Translated by W. R. Paton. Loeb Classical Library (Cambridge, MA: Harvard University Press, 1923), 316–324.

2. Polybius, Setting up a Roman Fort

One aspect of Roman campaigning that distinguished the Roman military from Greek armies with which Polybius was familiar was the regular use of fortifications in any territory. Camp construction was a standard practice rather than law but one that the Romans seemed to have followed consistently. The fort was sufficiently standardized so that every soldier could find his way in the dark to his tent and to mustering points. Such camps were not intended for long-term defense. In such cases the Romans built them of stone but followed plans similar to Polybius' report.

Polybius describes an ideal plan for laying out a camp that reads as if it came right out of the same manual he employed for other aspects of the Roman legion. Roman archaeologists have found that much about his plan can be seen in excavated forts of the late Republic.

6.27 The manner in which they form their camp is as follows. When the site for the camp has been chosen, the position in it giving the best general view and most suitable for issuing orders is assigned to the general's tent (*praetorium*). Fixing an ensign on the spot where they are about to pitch it, they measure off round this ensign a square plot of ground each side of which is one hundred feet distant, so that the total area measure four *plethra*. Along one side of this square in the direction which seems to give the greatest facilities for watering and foraging, the Roman legions are disposed as follows. As I have said, there are six tribunes in each legion; and since each consul has always two Roman legions with him, it is evident that there are twelve tribunes in the army of each. They place then the tents of these all in one line parallel to the side of the square selected and fifty feet distant from it, to give room for the horses, mules, and baggage of the tribunes. These tents are pitched with their backs turned to the *praetorium* and facing the outer side of the camp, a direction of which I will always speak as "the front." The tents of the tribunes are at an equal distance from each other, and at such a distance that they extend along the whole breadth of the space occupied by the legions.

28 They now measure a hundred feet from the front of all these tents, and starting from the line drawn at this distance parallel to the tents of the tribunes they begin to encamp the legions, managing matters as follows. Bisecting the above line, they start from this spot and along a line drawn at right angles to the first, they encamp the cavalry of each legion facing each other and separated by a distance of fifty feet, the last-mentioned line being exactly half-way between them. The manner of encamping the cavalry and the infantry is very similar, the whole space occupied by the maniples and squadrons being a square. This square faces one of the streets or *viae* and is of a fixed length of one hundred feet, and they usually try to make the depth the same except in the case of the allies. When they employ the larger legions they add proportionately to the length and depth.

29 The cavalry camp is thus something like a street running down from the middle of the tribunes' tents and at right angles to the line along which these tents are placed and to the space in front of them, the whole system of *viae* being in fact like a number of streets, as either companies of infantry or troops of horse are encamped facing each other all along each. Behind the cavalry, then, they place the *triarii* of both legions in a similar arrangement, a company next to each troop, but with no space between, and facing in the contrary direction to the cavalry. They make the depth of each company half its length, because as a rule the *triarii* number only half the strength of the other classes. So that the maniples being often of unequal strength, the length of the encampments is always the same owing to the difference in depth. Next at a distance of 50 feet on each side they place the *principes* facing the *triarii,* and as they are turned towards the intervening

space, two more streets are formed, both starting from the same base as that of the cavalry, i.e. the hundred-foot space in front of the tribunes' tents, and both issuing on the side of the camp which is opposite to the tribunes' tents and which we decided to call the front of the whole. After the *principes,* and again back to back against them, with no interval they encamp the *hastati.* As each class by virtue of the original division consists of ten maniples, the streets are all equal in length, and they all break off on the front side of the camp in a straight line, the last maniples being here so placed as to face to the front.

30 At a distance again of 50 feet from the *hastati,* and facing them, they encamp the allied cavalry, starting from the same line and ending on the same line. As I stated above, the number of the allied infantry is the same as that of the Roman legions, but from these the *extraordinarii* must be deducted; while that of the cavalry is double after deducting the third who serve as *extraordinarii.* In forming the camp, therefore, they proportionately increase the depth of the space assigned to the allied cavalry, in the endeavor to make their camp equal in length to that of the Romans. These five streets having been completed, they place the maniples of the allied infantry, increasing the depth in proportion to their numbers; with their faces turned away from the cavalry and facing the agger and both the outer sides of the camp. In each maniple the first tent at either end is occupied by the centurions. In laying the whole camp out in this manner they always leave a space of 50 feet between the fifth troop and the sixth, and similarly with the companies of foot, so that another passage traversing the whole camp is formed, at right angles to the streets, and parallel to the line of the tribunes' tents. This they called *quintana,* as it runs along the fifth troops and companies.

31 The spaces behind the tents of the tribunes to the right and left of the *praetorium,* are used in the one case for the market and in the other for the office of the *quaestor* and the supplies of which he is in charge. Behind the last tent of the tribunes on either side, and more or less at right angles to these tents, are the quarters of the cavalry picked out from the *extraordinarii,* and a certain number of volunteers serving to oblige the consuls. These are all encamped parallel to the two sides of the agger, and facing in the one case the quaestors' depot and in the other the market. As a rule these troops are not only thus encamped near the consuls but on the march and on other occasions are in constant attendance on the consul and quaestor. Back to back with them, and looking towards the agger are the select infantry who

perform the same service as the cavalry just described. Beyond these an empty space is left a hundred feet broad, parallel to the tents of the tribunes, and stretching along the whole face of the agger on the other side of the market, *praetorium* and *quaestorium,* and on its further side the rest of the *equites extraordinarii* are encamped facing the market, *praetorium* and *quaestorium.* In the middle of this cavalry camp and exactly opposite the *praetorium* a passage, 50 feet wide, is left leading to the rear side of the camp and running at right angles to the broad passage behind the *praetorium.* Back to back with these cavalry and fronting the agger and the rearward face of the whole camp are placed the rest of the *pedites extraordinarii.* Finally the spaces remaining empty to the right and left next the agger on each side of the camp are assigned to foreign troops or to any allies who chance to come in.

The whole camp thus forms a square, and the way in which the streets are laid out and its general arrangement give it the appearance of a town. The *agger* is on all sides at a distance of 200 feet from the tents, and this empty space is of important service in several respects. To begin with it provides the proper facilities for marching the troops in and out, seeing that they all march out into this space by their own streets and thus do not come into one street in a mass and throw down or hustle each other. Again it is here that they collect the cattle brought into camp and all booty taken from the enemy, and keep them safe during the night. But the most important thing of all is that in night attacks neither fire can reach them nor missiles except a very few, which are almost harmless owing to the distance and the space in front of the tents.

32 Given the numbers of cavalry and infantry, whether 4000 or 5000, in each legion, and given likewise the depth, length, and number of the troops and companies, the dimensions of the passages and open spaces and all other details, anyone who gives his mind to it can calculate the area and total circumference of the camp. If there ever happen to be an extra number of allies, either of those originally forming part of the army or of others who have joined on a special occasion, accommodation is provided for the latter in the neighborhood of the *praetorium,* the market and *quaestorium* being reduced to the minimum size which meets pressing requirements, while for the former, if the excess is considerable, they add two streets, one at each side of the encampment of the Roman legions.

Whenever the two consuls with all their four legions are united in one camp, we have only to imagine two camps like the above placed in juxtaposition back to back, the junction being formed at the encampments of the *extraordinarii* infantry of each camp whom we described as being stationed facing the rearward agger of the camp. The shape of the camp is now oblong, its area double what it was and its circumference half as much again. Whenever both consuls encamp together they adopt this arrangement; but when the two encamp apart the only difference is that the market, *quaestorium,* and *praetorium* are placed between the two camps.

Source: Polybius, *The Histories,Vol. III,* 6.27–32. Translated by W. R. Paton. Loeb Classical Library (Cambridge, MA: Harvard University Press, 1923), 330–343.

3. Polybius on Punishments, Rewards, and Pay

In their descriptions of the Roman military, Polybius and Livy both bring up the benefits and punishments of being in the military. As with his description of the legion, Polybius seems to have found this material in a manual. The punishments that he describes are only some of the options open to commanders. The Romans understood that effective discipline was more than punishment, however, so Polybius devotes some attention to the honors that soldiers could earn.

A sign that his material came from a manual organized topically, he also discusses soldiers' pay abruptly after honors. Polybius clearly saw army pay as part of Rome's success.

The most serious physical punishment a commander could inflict on a unit was decimation. Livy's description of an actual decimation is one of several he presents in his history. Since Octavian was eventually interested in restoring what he saw as traditional discipline, Livy may have drawn more attention to these episodes than they actually merited in order to provide exempla for contemporaries.

6.37 A court-martial composed of all the tribunes at once meets to try him, and if he is found guilty he is punished by the *bastinado* (*fustuarium*). This is inflicted as follows: The tribune takes a cudgel and just touches the condemned man with it, after which all in the camp beat or stone him, in most cases dispatching him in the camp itself. But even those who manage to escape are not saved thereby: impossible! for they are not allowed to return to their homes, and none of the family would dare to receive such a man in his house. So that those who have of course fallen into this misfortune are utterly ruined. The same punishment is inflicted on the *optio* and on the *praefect* of the squadron, if they do not give the proper orders at the right time to the patrols and the *praefect* of the next squadron. Thus, owing to the extreme severity and inevitableness of the penalty, the night watches of the Roman army are most scrupulously kept.

While the soldiers are subject to the tribune, the latter are subject to the consuls. A tribune, and in the case of the allies a *praefect,* has the right of inflicting fines, of demanding sureties, and of punishing by flogging. The bastinado is also inflicted on those who steal anything from the camp; on those who give false evidence; on young men who have abused their persons; and finally on anyone who has been punished thrice for the same fault. Those are the offences which are punished as crimes, the following being treated as unmanly acts and disgraceful in a soldier—when a man boasts falsely to the tribune of his valor in the field in order to gain distinction; when any men who have been placed in a covering force leave the station assigned to them from fear; likewise when anyone throws away from fear any of his arms in the actual battle. Therefore the men in covering forces often face certain death, refusing to leave their ranks even when vastly outnumbered, owing to dread of the punishment they would meet with; and again in the battle men who have lost a shield or sword or any other arm often throw themselves into the midst of the enemy, hoping either to recover the lost object or to escape by death from inevitable disgrace and the taunts of their relations.

38 If the same thing ever happens to large bodies, and if entire maniples desert their posts when exceedingly hard pressed, the officers refrain from inflicting the bastinado or the death penalty on all, but find a solution of the difficulty which is both salutary and terror-striking. The tribune assembles the legion, and brings up those guilty of leaving the ranks, reproaches them sharply, and finally chooses by lots sometimes five, sometimes eight, sometimes twenty of the offenders, so adjusting the number thus chosen that they form as near as possible the tenth part of those guilty of coward-ice. Those on whom the lot falls are bastinadoed mercilessly in the manner above described; the rest receive rations of barley instead of wheat and are ordered to encamp outside the camp on an unprotected spot. As therefore the danger and dread of drawing the fatal lot affects all equally, as it is uncertain on whom it will fall; and as the public disgrace of receiving barley rations falls on all alike, this practice is that best calculated both inspire fear and to correct the mischief.

39 They also have an admirable method of encouraging the young soldiers to face danger. After a battle in which some of them have distinguished themselves, the general calls an assembly of the troops, and bringing forward those whom he considers to have displayed conspicuous valour, first of all speaks in laudatory terms of the courageous deeds of each and of anything else in their previous conduct which deserves commendation, and afterwards distributes the following rewards. To the man who has wounded an enemy, a spear; to him who has slain and stripped an enemy, a cup if he be in the infantry and horse trappings if in the cavalry, although the gift here was originally only a spear. These gifts are not made to men who have wounded or stripped an enemy in a regular battle or at the storming of a city, but to those who during skirmishes or in similar circumstances, where there is no necessity for engaging in single combat, have voluntarily and deliberately thrown themselves into the danger. To the first man to mount the wall at the assault on a city, he gives a crown of gold. So also those who have shielded and saved any of the citizens or allies receive honorary gifts from the consul, and the men they saved crown their preservers, if not under their own free will under compulsion from the tribunes who judge the case. The man thus preserved also reverences his preserver as a father all through his life, and must treat him in every way like a parent. By such incentives they excite to emulation and rivalry in the field not only the men who are present and listen to their words, but those who remain at home also. For the recipients of such gifts, quite apart from becoming famous in the army and famous too for the time at their homes, are especially distinguished in religious processions after their return, as no one is allowed to wear decorations except those on whom these honours for bravery have been conferred by the consul; and in their houses they hang up the spoils they won in the most conspicuous places, looking upon them as tokens and evidences of their valour. Considering all this attention given to the matter of punishments and rewards in the army and the importance attached to both, no wonder that the wars in which the Romans engage end so successfully and brilliantly.

As pay the foot-soldier receives two obols a day, a centurion twice as much, and a cavalry-soldier a drachma. The allowance of corn to a foot-soldier is about two-thirds of an Attic *medimnus* a month, a cavalry-soldier receives seven *medimni* of barley and two of wheat. Of the allies the infantry receive the same, the cavalry one and one-third *medimnus* of wheat and five of barley, these rations being a free gift to the allies; but in the case of the

Romans the quaestor deducts from their pay the price fixed for their corn and clothes and any additional arm they require.

Source: Polybius, *The Histories, Vol. III,* 6.37–39. Translated by W. R. Paton. Loeb Classical Library (Cambridge, MA: Harvard University Press, 1923), 353–361.

4. Polybius, Treatment of Spoils and Booty

Polybius did not merely have views on legionary organization, forts, and discipline but also felt that part of Rome's success was in the treatment of spoils and booty following a siege. This passage is another in which Polybius provides his audience with a direct commentary on how war ought to be conducted. The extent to which spoils were part of a siege is sometimes lost on readers. In this passage Polybius provides a more vivid sense of their importance. Since spoils were important to soldiers and income was important to the Republic, the way in which all spoils were managed was important to military success as a whole. Notice in this case that most of the population is not enslaved.

10.16 Next day the booty, both the baggage of the troops in the Carthaginian service and the household stuff of the townsmen and working classes, having been collected in the market, was divided by the tribunes among the legions on the usual system. The Romans after the capture of a city manage matters more or less as follows: according to the size of the town sometimes a certain number of men from each maniple, at other times certain whole maniples are told off to collect booty, but they never thus employ more than half their total force, the rest remaining in their ranks at times outside and at times inside the city, ready for the occasion. As their armies are usually composed of two Roman legions and two legions of allies, the whole four legions being rarely massed, all those who are told off to spoil bring the booty back each man to his own legion, and after it has been sold the tribunes distribute the profits equally among all, including not only those who were left behind in the protecting force, but the men who are guarding the tents, the sick, and those absent on any special service. I have already stated at some length in my chapters on the Roman state how it is that no one appropriates any part of the loot, but that all keep the oath they make when first assembled in camp on setting out for a campaign. So that when half of the army disperse to pillage and the other half keep their ranks and afford them protection, there is never any chance of the Romans suffering disaster owing to individual covetousness. For as all, both the spoilers and those who remain to safeguard them, have equal confidence that they will get their share of the booty, no one leaves the ranks, a thing which usually does injury to other armies.

17 For since most men endure hardship and risk their lives for the sake of gain, it is evident that whenever the chance presents itself it is not likely that those left in the protecting force or in the camp will refrain, since the general rule among us is that any man keeps whatever comes into his hands. And even if any careful king or general orders the booty to be brought in to form a common fund, yet everyone regards as his own whatever he can conceal. So that, as most of the men start pillaging, commanders cannot maintain any control and run the risk of disaster, and indeed many who have been successful in their object have, after capturing the enemy's camp or a town, not only been driven out but have met with complete disaster simply for the above reason. Commanders should therefore exercise the utmost care and foresight about this matter, so that as far as is possible the hope of equal participation in the booty when such a chance presents itself may be common to all.

The tribunes, then, were now dealing with the booty, but the Roman commander, when the whole of the prisoners, numbering little less than ten thousand, had been collected, ordered first the citizens with their wives and children, and next the working men, to be set apart.

Source: Polybius, The Histories, Vol. IV, 10.16–17.6. Translated by W. R. Paton. Loeb Classical Library (Cambridge, MA: Harvard University Press, 1925), 139–143.

5. Polybius, Prelude to Cannae, the Battle of the Trebia River

Roman authors picked up Greek historians' practices of recording battle narratives. The Punic Wars (218–202 BCE) were not the earliest conflict for which such narratives exist, but these may be the earliest with so many trustworthy details. Polybius' account of the battle may include eyewitness testimony as well as details from official reports. As part of the Scipionic family circle that developed in the mid-second century, Polybius had special access to family reports. He also, however, had a vested interest in minimizing any blame that might attach to Scipio while putting as much blame as possible on Sempronius.

The Battle of the Trebia River in December 218 was the second battle that Hannibal fought against Roman forces after invading Italy. He had defeated and wounded Publius Scipio (father of Africanus) at the Battle of the Ticinus earlier in the autumn. Tiberius Sempronius Longus, the other consul, arrived at the Trebia River with in-experienced troops, linked up with Scipio, and moved with four legions and allies against Hannibal. Polybius' narrative of the battle highlights a number of features that will reappear at Cannae in 216.

3.72 Tiberius, when he saw the Numidian horse approaching, sent out at first only his cavalry with orders to close with the enemy. He next dis-patched about six thousand javelineers on foot and then began to move his whole army out of the camp, thinking that the mere sight of them would decide the issue, so much confidence did his superiority in numbers and the success of his cavalry on the previous day give him. The time of year was about the winter solstice, and the day exceedingly cold and snowy, while the men and horses nearly all left the camp without having had their morning meal. At first their enthusiasm and eagerness sustained them, but when they had to cross the Trebia, swollen as it was owing to the rain that had fallen during the night higher up the valley than where the armies were, the infantry had great difficulty in crossing, as the water was breast-high. The consequence was that the whole force suffered much from cold and also from hunger, as the day was now advancing. The Carthaginians, on the contrary, who had eaten and drunk in their tents and looked after their horses, were all anointing and arming themselves around their fires. Hannibal, who was waiting for his opportunity, when he saw that the Romans had crossed the river, threw forward as a covering force his pikemen and slingers about eight thousand in number and led out his army. After advanc-ing for about eight stades he drew up his infantry, about twenty thousand in number, and consisting of Spaniards, Celts, and Africans, in a single line, while he divided his cavalry, numbering, together with the Celtic allies, more than ten thousand, and stationed them on each wing, dividing also his elephants and placing them in front of the wings so that his flanks were doubly protected. Tiberius now recalled his cavalry, perceiving that they could not cope with the enemy, as the Numidians easily scattered and retreated, but afterwards wheeled round and attacked with great daring—these being their peculiar tactics. He drew up his infantry in the usual

Roman order. They numbered about sixteen thousand Romans and twenty thousand allies, this being the strength of their complete army for decisive operations, when the Consuls chanced to be united. Afterwards placing his cavalry, numbering about four thousand, on each wing he advanced on the enemy in imposing style marching in order at a slow step.

73 When they were nearly at close quarters, the light-armed troops in the van of each army began the combat, and here the Romans laboured under many disadvantages, the efficiency of the Carthaginians being much superior, since the Roman javelineers had had a hard time since daybreak, and had spent most of their missiles in the skirmish with the Numidians, while those they had left had been rendered useless by the continued wet weather. The cavalry and the whole army were in much the same state, whereas just the opposite was the case with the Carthaginians, who, standing in their ranks fresh and in first-rate condition, were ready to give efficient support wherever it was required. So when the skirmishers had retired through the gaps in their line and the heavy-armed infantry met, the Carthaginian cavalry at once pressed on both flanks of the enemy, being greatly superior in numbers and the condition of themselves and their horses, having, as I explained above, started quite fresh. When the Roman cavalry fell back and left the flanks of the infantry exposed, the Carthaginian pike-men and the Numidians in a body, dashing past their own troops that were in front of them, fell on the Romans from both flanks, damaging them severely and preventing them from dealing with the enemy in their front. The heavy-armed troops on both sides, who occupied the advanced centre of the whole formation, maintained for long a hand-to-hand combat with no advantage on either side.

74 But now the Numidians issued from their ambuscade and suddenly attacked the enemy's centre from the rear, upon which the whole Roman army was thrown into the utmost confusion and distress. At length both of Tiberius' wings, hard pressed in front by the light-armed troops, turned and were driven by their pursuers back on the river behind them. After this, while the rear of the Roman centre was suffering heavy loss from the attack of the ambuscade, those in the van, thus forced to advance, defeated the Celts and part of the Africans, and after killing many of them broke through the Carthaginian line. But seeing that both their flanks had been forced off the field, they despaired of giving help there and of returning to their camp, afraid as they were of the very numerous cavalry and hindered by the river and the force and heaviness of the rain which was pouring down on their

heads. They kept, however, in close order and retired on Placentia, being not less than ten thousand in number. Of the remainder the greater part were killed near the river by the elephants and cavalry, but the few infantry who escaped and most of the cavalry retreated to join the body I just mentioned and with them got safely into Placentia.

Source: Polybius, *The Histories, Vol. II,* 3.72–74.8. Translated by W. R. Paton. Loeb Classical Library (Cambridge, MA: Harvard University Press, 1922), 179–184.

6. Polybius, The Disaster—Battle of Cannae

The Battle of Cannae in 216 was not just the largest single-day military disaster for Rome during the Republic; it was also Hannibal's high-water mark. The enormity of the victory was apparent to everyone. It galvanized Rome into responding vigorously and consistently. No one participating in the battle or events right afterward could know, however, that for the next decade Hannibal would remain caught in southern Italy, winning battles when he could force them but trying to salvage his strategy and survive.

As with the rest of Polybius' work, he had access to official documents and Scipio family reports and may have spoken with eyewitnesses. He also wrote his narrative with the full knowledge of how events would play out for Hannibal. It is not surprising, then, that Polybius makes it appear neat and tidy, as if Hannibal was clairvoyant. Scipio (soon to be Africanus) distinguished himself as a military tribune in the aftermath but does not figure in Polybius' report.

3.110 Next day the Consuls broke up their camp and advanced towards the place where they heard that of the enemy was. Coming in view of them on the second day, they encamped at a distance of about fifty stadia from them. Aemilius, seeing that the district round was flat and treeless, was opposed to attacking the enemy there as they were superior in cavalry, his advice being to lure them on by advancing into a country where the battle would be decided rather by the infantry. As Terentius, owing to his inexperience, was of the contrary opinion, difficulties and disputes arose between the generals, one of the most pernicious things possible. Terentius was in command next day—the two Consuls according to the usual practice commanding on alternate days—and he broke up his camp and advanced with the object of approaching the enemy in spite of Aemilius' strong protests and efforts to prevent him. Hannibal met him with his light-armed troops and cavalry and surprising him while still on the march disordered the Romans much. They met, however, the first charge by advancing some of their heavy infantry, and afterwards sending forwards also their javelineers and cavalry got the better in the whole engagement, as the Carthaginians had no considerable covering force, while they themselves had some companies of their legions fighting mixed with the light-armed troops. The fall of night now made them draw off from each other, the attack of the Carthaginians not having had the success they hoped. Next day, Aemilius, who neither judged it advisable to fight nor could now withdraw the army in safety, encamped with two-thirds of it on the bank of the river Aufidus. This is the only river which traverses the Apennines, the long chain of mountains separating all the Italian streams, those on one side descending to the Tyrrhenian sea and those on the other to the Adriatic. The Aufidus, however, runs right through these mountains, having its source on the side of Italy turned to the Tyrrhenian Sea and falling into the Adriatic. For the remaining portion of his army he fortified a position on the farther side of the river, to the east of the ford, at a distance of about ten stadia from his own camp and rather more from that of the enemy, intending thus to cover the foraging parties from his main camp across the river and harass those of the Carthaginians.

112 Next day he ordered all his troops to look to their persons and their accoutrements, and on the day following he drew up his army along the river with the evident intention of giving battle as soon as possible. Aemilius was not pleased with the ground, and seeing that the Carthaginians would soon have to shift their camp in order to obtain supplies, kept quiet, after securing his two camps by covering forces. Hannibal, after waiting for some time without anyone coming out to meet him, withdrew again the rest of his army into their entrenchments, but sent out the Numidians to intercept the water-bearers from the lesser Roman camp. When the Numidians came up to the actual palisade of the camp and prevented the men from watering, not only was this a further stimulus to Terentius, but the soldiers displayed great eagerness for battle and ill brooked further delay. For nothing is more trying to men in general than prolonged suspense, but when the issue has once been decided we make a shift to endure patiently all that men regard as the depth of misery.

When the news reached Rome that the armies were encamped opposite each other and that engagements between the outposts occurred every day, there was the utmost excitement and fear in the city, as most people dreaded the result owing to their frequent previous reverses, and foresaw and anticipated in imagination the consequences of total defeat. All the oracles that had ever been delivered to them were in men's mouths, every temple and every house was full of signs and prodigies, so that vows, sacrifices, supplicatory processions and litanies pervaded the town. For in seasons of danger the Romans are much given to propitiating both gods and men, and there is nothing at such times in rites of the kind that they regard as unbecoming or beneath their dignity.

113 Next day it was Terentius' turn to take the command, and just after sunrise he began to move his forces out of both camps. Crossing the river with those from the larger camp he at once put them in order of battle, drawing up those from the other camp next to them in the same line, the whole army facing south. He stationed the Roman cavalry close to the river on the right wing and the foot next to them in the same line, placing the maniples closer together than was formerly the usage and making the depth of each many times exceed its front. The allied horse he drew up on his left wing, and in front of the whole force at some distance he placed his light-armed troops. The whole army, including the allies, numbered about eighty thousand foot and rather more than six thousand horse. Hannibal at the same time sent his slingers and pikemen over the river and stationed them in front, and leading the rest of his forces out of camp he crossed the stream in two places and drew them up opposite the enemy. On his left close to the river he placed his Spanish and Celtic horse facing the Roman cavalry, next to these half his heavy-armed Africans, then the Spanish and Celtic infantry, and after them the other half of the Africans, and finally, on his right wing, his Numidian horse. After thus drawing up his whole army in a straight line, he took the central companies of the Spaniards and Celts and advanced with them, keeping the rest of them in contact with these companies, but gradually falling off, so as to produce a crescent-shaped formation, the line of the flanking companies growing thinner as it was prolonged, his object being to employ the Africans as a reserve force and to begin the action with the Spaniards and Celts.

114 The Africans were armed in the Roman fashion, Hannibal having equipped them with the choicest of the arms captured in the previous battles. The shields of the Spaniards and Celts were very similar, but the swords were entirely different, those of the Spaniards thrusting with as deadly effect as they cut, but the Gaulish sword being only able to slash

and requiring a long sweep to do so. As they were drawn up in alternate companies, the Gauls naked and the Spaniards in short tunics bordered with purple, their national dress, they presented a strange and impressive appearance. The Carthaginian cavalry numbered about ten thousand, and their infantry, including the Celts, did not much exceed forty thousand. The Roman right wing was under the command of Aemilius, the left under that of Terentius, and the centre under the Consuls of the previous year, Marcus Atilius and Gnaeus Servilius. Hasdrubal commanded the Carthaginian left, Hanno the right, and Hannibal himself with his brother Mago the centre. Since the Roman army, as I said, faced south and the Carthaginians north, they were neither of them inconvenienced by the rising sun.

115 The advanced guards were the first to come into action, and at first when only the light infantry were engaged neither side had the advantage; but when the Spanish and Celtic horse on the left wing came into collision with the Roman cavalry, the struggle that ensued was truly barbaric; for there were none of the normal wheeling evolutions, but having once met they dismounted and fought man to man. The Carthaginians finally got the upper hand, killed most of the enemy in the melee, all the Romans fighting with desperate bravery, and began to drive the rest along the river, cutting them down mercilessly, and it was now that the heavy infantry on each side took the place of the light-armed troops and met. For a time the Spaniards and Celts kept their ranks and struggled bravely with the Romans, but soon, borne down by the weight of the legions, they gave way and fell back, breaking up the crescent. The Roman maniples, pursuing them furiously, easily penetrated the enemy's front, since the Celts were deployed in a thin line while they themselves had crowded up from the wings to the centre where the fighting was going on. For the centres and wings did not come into action simultaneously, but the centres first, as the Celts were drawn up in a crescent and a long way in advance of their wings, the convex face of the crescent being turned towards the enemy. The Romans, however, following up the Celts and pressing on to the centre and that part of the enemy's line which was giving way, progressed so far that they now had the heavy-armed Africans on both of their flanks. Hereupon the Africans on the right wing facing to the left and then beginning from the right charged upon the enemy's flank, while those on the left faced to the right and dressing by the left, did the same, the situation itself indicating to them how to act. The consequence was that, as Hannibal had designed, the Romans, straying too far in pursuit of the Celts, were caught between the two divisions of the enemy, and they now no longer kept their compact

formation but turned singly or in companies to deal with the enemy who was falling on their flanks.

116 Aemilius, though he had been on the right wing from the outset and had taken part in the cavalry action, was still safe and sound; but wishing to act up to what he had said in his address to the troops, and to be present himself at the fighting, and seeing that the decision of the battle lay mainly with the legions, he rode along to the centre of the whole line, where he not only threw himself personally into the combat and exchanged blows with the enemy but kept cheering on and exhorting his men. Hannibal, who had been in this part of the field since the commencement of the battle, did likewise.

The Numidians meanwhile on the right wing, attacking the cavalry opposite them on the Roman left, neither gained any great advantage nor suffered any serious loss owing to their peculiar mode of fighting, but they kept the enemy's cavalry out of action by drawing them off and attacking them from all sides at once. Hasdrubal, having by this time cut up very nearly all the enemy's cavalry by the river, came up from the left to help the Numidians, and now the Roman allied horse, seeing that they were going to be charged by him, broke and fled. Hasdrubal at this juncture appears to have acted with great skill and prudence; for in view of the fact that the Numidians were very numerous and most efficient and formidable when in pursuit of a flying foe he left them to deal with the Roman cavalry and led his squadrons on to where the infantry were engaged with the object of supporting the Africans. Attacking the Roman legions in the rear and delivering repeated charges at various points all at once, he raised the spirits of the Africans and cowed and dismayed the Romans. It was here that Lucius Aemilius fell in the thick of the fight after receiving several dreadful wounds, and of him we may say that if there ever was a man who did his duty by his country both all through his life and in these last times, it was he. The Romans as long as they could turn and present a front on every side to the enemy, held out, but as the outer ranks continued to fall, and the rest were gradually huddled in and surrounded, they finally all were killed where they stood, among them Marcus and Gnaeus, the Consuls of the preceding year, who had borne themselves in the battle like brave men worthy of Rome. While this murderous combat was going on, the Numidians following up the flying cavalry killed most of them and unseated others. A few escaped to Venusia, among them being the Consul Gaius Terentius, who disgraced himself by his flight and in his tenure of office had been most unprofitable to his country.

117 Such was the outcome of the battle at Cannae between the Romans and Carthaginians, a battle in which both the victors and the vanquished displayed conspicuous bravery, as was evinced by the facts. For of the six thousand cavalry, seventy escaped to Venusia with Terentius, and about three hundred of the allied horse reached different cities in scattered groups. Of the infantry about ten thousand were captured fighting but not in the actual battle, while only perhaps three thousand escaped from the field to neighbouring towns. All the rest, numbering about seventy thousand, died bravely. Both on this occasion and on former ones their numerous cavalry had contributed most to the victory of the Carthaginians, and it demonstrated to posterity that in times of war it is better to give battle with half as many infantry as the enemy and an overwhelming force of cavalry than to be in all respects his equal. Of Hannibal's army there fell about four thousand Celts, fifteen hundred Spaniards and Africans, and two hundred cavalry.

Source: Polybius, *The Histories, Vol. II*, 3.110, 112–117.6. Translated by W. R. Paton. Loeb Classical Library (Cambridge, MA: Harvard University Press, 1922), 272–274, 278–291.

7. Polybius, Roman Siege I, Capture of Carthago Nova

Although it receives less press than the battlefield narratives, siege was a much more important element of successful Roman campaigns and wars. Sieges could be expensive in resources of all types, but Rome had sufficient manpower reserves and infrastructure to prosecute them more successfully than many of its opponents. Because of the expense of extended sieges and the impatience they engender, commanders often sought a way to assault the fortifications and win suddenly. One of the most difficult kinds of siege assault was an escalade in which the attackers would throw ladders against a fort and try to climb over the walls.

We are fortunate in having an instance of this tactic in the Punic Wars. Scipio (soon to be Africanus) attacked and captured the stronghold of Carthago Nova this way in 209. Polybius may have understandably heightened the genius and foresight of Scipio in his account, but the assault was still a great success. Notice the many different elements of the success that included infantry and fleet cooperating. Also, Polybius confirms that he visited the site in person to confirm details of his narrative.

10.11 Such being the situation of the place, the Roman camp was protected on its inner side without any fortification by the lagoon and by the outer sea. The intervening space, which connects the city with the mainland and which lay in the middle of his camp, was also left unentrenched by Scipio, either to intimidate the enemy or to adapt it to his own particular purpose, so that there should be no impediment to sorties from his camp and subsequent retirement into it. The circumference of the city was formerly not more than twenty stades—I am quite aware that many state it to be forty, but this is not true, as I speak not from report but from my own careful observation—and at the present day it has still further shrunk.

Scipio, then, when the fleet arrived in due time, decided to call a meeting of his troops and address them, using no other arguments than those which had carried conviction to himself and which I have above stated in detail. After proving to them that the project was feasible, and pointing out briefly what loss its success would entail on the enemy and what an advantage it would be to themselves, he went on to promise gold crowns to those who should be the first to mount the wall and the usual rewards to such as displayed conspicuous courage. Finally he told them that it was Neptune who had first suggested this plan to him, appearing to him in his sleep, and promising that when the time for the action came he would render such conspicuous aid that his intervention would be manifest to the whole army. The combination in this speech of accurate calculation, of the promise of gold crowns, and therewithal of confidence in the help of Providence created great enthusiasm and ardour among the lads.

12 Next day, encircling the city from the sea by ships furnished with all kinds of missiles under the command of Laelius, and sending forward on the land side two thousand of his strongest men together with the ladder-bearers, he began the assault at about the third hour. Mago, who was in command of the place, divided his regiment of a thousand men into two, leaving half of them on the citadel and stationing the others on the eastern hill. After the rest, he armed two thousand of the strongest with such arms as were to be found in the town, and posted them near the gate leading to the isthmus and the enemy's camp: the others he ordered to do their best to defend the whole of the wall. As soon as Scipio had given the signal for the assault by bugle, Mago sent the armed citizens out through the gate, feeling sure of striking terror into the enemy and entirely defeating their design. They delivered a vigorous assault on the Romans who had issued from the camp and were now drawn up on the isthmus, and a sharp

engagement ensued, accompanied by vehement shouts of encouragement from both sides, those in the camp and those in the town respectively cheering on their own men. But as the assistance sent to either side was not equal, the Carthaginians arriving through a single gate and from a distance of nearly two stades and the Romans from close by and from several points, the battle for this reason was an unequal one. For Scipio had purposely posted his men close to the camp itself in order to entice the enemy as far out as possible, well knowing that if he destroyed those who were so to speak the steel edge of the population of the town he would cause universal dejection, and none of those inside would venture out of the gate. However, for some time the battle was hotly contested, as both sides had picked out their best men. But finally, as reinforcements continued to come up from the camp, the Carthaginians were forced back, by sheer weight, and took to flight, many of them falling in the actual battle or in the retreat but the greater number being trodden down by each other in entering the gate. When this took place the city people were thrown into such panic that even the defenders of the walls fled. The Romans very nearly succeeded in entering together with the fugitives, and at any rate set up their scaling ladders in full security.

13 Scipio took part in the battle, but consulted his safety as far as possible; for he had with him three men carrying large shields, who holding these close covered the surface exposed to the wall and thus afforded him protection. So that passing along the side of his line on higher ground he contributed greatly to the success of the day; for he could both see what was going on and being seen by all his men he inspired the combatants with great spirit. The consequence was that nothing was omitted which was necessary in the engagement, but the moment that circumstances suggested any step to him he set to work at once to do what was necessary.

When the front rank advanced confidently to mount the ladders, it was not so much the numbers of the defenders which made the assault hazardous as the great height of the wall. Those on the wall consequently plucked up courage when they saw the difficulties of the assailant. For some of the ladders broke, as owing to their height so many mounted them at the same time, while on others those who led the way grew dizzy owing to their elevated position, and a very slight resistance on the part of the besieged sufficed to make them throw themselves off the ladders. Also whenever the defenders adopted the expedient of throwing beams or suchlike things from the battlements the whole of those on the ladders would be swept off and fall to the ground. Yet in spite of all these difficulties nothing could restrain the dash and fury of the Romans, but while the first scalers were still falling the vacant places were instantly taken by the next in order. The hour, however, was now advanced, and as the soldiers were worn out by fatigue, Scipio recalled the assailants by bugle.

14 The garrison were now overjoyed at having, as they thought, repelled the danger, but Scipio, who was now waiting for the fall of the tide, got ready five hundred men with ladders on the shore of the lagoon and recruited his force at the isthmus and by the gate. Then after addressing his soldiers he gave them still more ladders than before so that the whole extent of the wall was covered with escaladers. When the signal for attack was sounded and the assailants setting up the ladders against the wall mounted it everywhere in the most daring manner, the defenders were thrown into great confusion and became very despondent. They had thought they were delivered from peril, and now they saw they were menaced again by a new assault. As at the same time they had run out of ammunition and their losses were so severe as to dispirit them, they supported the assault with difficulty, but nevertheless offered a stubborn resistance. Just when the escalading attack was at its height the tide began to ebb and the water gradually receded from the edge of the lagoon, a strong and deep current setting in through the channel to the neighbouring sea, so that to those who were not prepared for the sight the thing appeared incredible. But Scipio had his guides ready and bade all the men he had told off for this service enter the water and have no fear. He indeed possessed a particular talent for inspiring confidence and sympathy in his troops when he called upon them. Now when they obeyed and raced through the shallow water, it struck the whole army that it was the work of some god. So that now remembering Scipio's reference to Neptune and the promise he made in his speech their courage was redoubled, and under cover of their shields they forced their way in dense order to the gate and began to try to cut down the doors with axes and hatchets. Meanwhile those who reached the wall through the lagoon finding the battlements deserted not only set up their ladders unmolested, but ascended them and occupied the wall without striking a blow, the defenders having been diverted to other quarters, especially to the isthmus and gate there, and having never conceived it possible that the enemy would reach the wall from the lagoon, while above all there was such disorderly shouting and such crowding and confusion that they could neither hear nor see to any effect.

15 The Romans, having once taken the wall, at first marched along it sweeping the enemy off it, the nature of their arms being very well adapted for such a service. Upon reaching the gate some of them descended and began to cut through the bolts, upon which those outside began to force their way in, while the escaladers at the isthmus had now overpowered the defence and established themselves on the battlements. Finally, when the walls had been taken in this manner, those who entered through the gate occupied the hill on the east after dislodging its defenders. When Scipio thought that a sufficient number of troops had entered he sent most of them, as is the Roman custom, against the inhabitants of the city with orders to kill all they encountered, sparing none, and not to start pillaging until the signal was given. They did this, I think, to inspire terror, so that when towns were taken by the Romans one would often see not only the corpses of human beings, but dogs cut in half, and the dismembered limbs of other animals, and on this occasion such scenes were very many owing to the numbers of those in the place. Scipio himself, with about a thousand men, proceeded to the citadel. On his approach Mago at first attempted to resist, but afterwards, when he saw that the city had undoubtedly been captured, he sent a message begging for his life and surrendered the citadel. After this, upon the signal being given, the massacre ceased and they began pillaging. At nightfall such of the Romans as had received orders to that effect, remained in the camp, while Scipio with his thousand men bivouacked in the citadel, and recalling the rest from the houses ordered them, through the tribunes, to collect the booty in the market, each maniple separately, and sleep there, keeping guard over it. Summoning also the light-armed troops from the camp he stationed them on the easternmost hill. Such was the manner in which the Romans gained possession of Spanish Carthage.

Source: Polybius, *The Histories,* Vol. *IV,* 10.11–15. Translated by W. R. Paton. Loeb Classical Library (Cambridge, MA: Harvard University Press, 1925), 126–139.

8. Polybius, Victory at the Battle of Zama

The Second Punic War concluded after the Battle of Zama in October 202 BCE. This battle saw what many observers consider the two best generals of the war, Hannibal and Africanus, face each other in Africa. Scipio prepared for the battle meticulously and made sure he had planned for reasonable contingencies. His army was experienced and trusted him entirely. Hannibal also seemed to have planned as best he could to defend his home turf, but he and his men were undoubtedly at a disadvantage, pressed against a wall of expectations. In the actual battle, Africanus demonstrated that he had learned the lesson about planning and having reliable cavalry.

All the usual strengths and weaknesses of Polybius' methodology and biases are present in this battlefield narrative. He used verifiable sources and may have spoken to participants on both sides. He visited the site and the surroundings. Polybius composes a careful narrative driven by hindsight and his need to make Africanus appear brilliant. Africanus won of course, so it was not difficult to make him look good, but Polybius may have played down the contributions of other officers in the process. Read the narrative carefully.

15.9 After this conversation, which held out no hopes of reconciliation, the two generals parted from each other. On the following morning at daybreak they led out their armies and opened the battle, the Carthaginians fighting for their own safety and the dominion of Africa, and the Romans for the empire of the world. Is there anyone who can remain unmoved in reading the narrative of such an encounter? For it would be impossible to find more valiant soldiers, or generals who had been more successful and were more thoroughly exercised in the art of war, nor indeed had Fortune ever offered to contending armies a more splendid prize of victory, since the conquerors would not be masters of Africa and Europe alone, but of all those parts of the world which now hold a place in history; as indeed they very shortly were. Scipio drew up his army in the following fashion. In front he placed the *hastati* with certain intervals between the maniples and behind them the *principes,* not placing their maniples, as is the usual Roman custom, opposite to the intervals separating those of the first line, but directly behind these latter at a certain distance owing to the large number of the enemy's elephants. Last of all he placed the *triarii.* On his left wing he posted Gaius Laelius with the Italian horse, and on the right wing Massanissa with the whole of his Numidians. The intervals of the first maniples he filled up with the cohorts of *velites,* ordering them to open the action, and if they were forced back by the charge of the elephants to retire, those who had time to do so by the straight passages as far as the rear of the whole army, and those who were overtaken to the right or left along the intervals between the lines.

10 Having made these preparations he rode along the lines and addressed his troops in a few words suitable to the occasion. "Bear in mind," he said,

"your past battles and fight like brave men worthy of yourselves and your country. Keep it before your eyes that if you overcome your enemies not only will you be unquestioned masters of Africa, but you will gain for yourselves and your country the undisputed command and sovereignty of the rest of the world. But if the result of the battle be otherwise, those of you who have fallen bravely in the fight will lie for ever shrouded in the glory of dying thus for their country, while those who save themselves by flight will spend the remainder of their lives in misery and disgrace. For no place in Africa will be able to afford you safety, and if you fall into the hands of the Carthaginians it is plain enough to anyone who gives due thought to it what fate awaits you. May none of you, I pray, live to experience that fate. Now that Fortune offers us a choice of the most glorious of prizes, how utterly craven, in short how foolish shall we be, if we reject the greatest of goods and choose the greatest of evils from mere love of life. Go, therefore, to meet the foe with two objects before you, emperor victory or death. For men animated by such a spirit must always overcome their adversaries, since they go into battle ready to throw their lives away."

11 Such was the substance of Scipio's harangue. Hannibal placed in front of his whole force his elephants, of which he had over eighty, and behind them the mercenaries numbering about twelve thousand. They were composed of Ligurians, Celts, Balearic Islanders, and Moors. Behind these he placed the native Libyans and Carthaginians, and last of all the troops he had brought over from Italy at a distance of more than a stade from the front lines. He secured his wings by cavalry, placing the Numidian allies on the left and the Carthaginian horse on the right. He ordered each commanding officer of the mercenaries to address his own men, bidding them be sure of victory as they could rely on his own presence and that of the forces that he had brought back with him. As for the Carthaginians, he ordered their commanders to set before their eyes all the sufferings that would befall their wives and children if the result of the battle were adverse. They did as they were ordered, and Hannibal himself went the round of his own troops, begging and imploring them to remember their comradeship of seventeen years and the number of the battles they had previously fought against the Romans. "In all these battles," he said, "you proved so invincible that you have not left the Romans the smallest hope of ever being able to defeat you. Above all the rest, and apart from your success in innumerable smaller engagements, keep before your eyes the battle of the Trebia fought against the father of the present Roman general, bear in mind the battle of the Trasimene against Flaminius, and that of Cannae against Aemilius, battles with which

the action in which we are about to engage is not worthy of comparison either in respect to the numbers of the forces engaged or the courage of the soldiers." He bade them, as he spoke thus, to cast their eyes on the ranks of the enemy. Not only were they fewer, but they were scarcely a fraction of the forces that had formerly faced them, and for courage they were not to be compared with those. For then their adversaries were men whose strength was unbroken and who had never suffered defeat, but those of to day were some of them the children of the former and some the wretched remnant of the legions he had so often vanquished and put to flight in Italy. Therefore he urged them not to destroy the glorious record of themselves and their general, but, fighting bravely, to confirm their reputation for invincibility. Such was the substance of the harangues of the two generals.

12 When all was ready for battle on both sides, the Numidian horse having been skirmishing with each other for some time, Hannibal ordered the drivers of the elephants to charge the enemy. When the trumpets and bugles sounded shrilly from all sides, some of the animals took fright and at once turned tail and rushed back upon the Numidians who had come up to help the Carthaginians, and Massanissa attacking simultaneously, the Carthaginian left wing was soon left exposed. The rest of the elephants falling on the Roman *velites* in the space between the two main armies, both inflicted and suffered much loss, until finally in their terror some of them escaped through the gaps in the Roman line with Scipio's foresight had provided, so that the Romans suffered no injury, while others fled towards the right and, received by the cavalry with showers of javelins, at length escaped out of the field. It was at this moment that Laelius, availing himself of the disturbance created by the elephants, charged the Carthaginian cavalry and forced them to headlong flight. He pressed the pursuit closely, as likewise did Massanissa. In the meanwhile both phalanxes slowly and in imposing array advanced on each other, except the troops which Hannibal had brought back from Italy, who remained in their original position. When the phalanxes were close to each other, Romans fell upon their foes, raising their war-cry and clashing their shields with their spears as is their practice, while there was a strange confusion of shouts raised by the Carthaginian mercenaries, for, as Homer says, their voice was not one, but

Mixed was the murmur, and confused the sound,
Their names all various,
as appears from the list of them I gave above.

13 As the whole battle was a hand-to-hand affair [the men using neither spears nor swords], the mercenaries at first prevailed by their courage and skill, wounding many of the Romans, but the latter still continued to advance, relying on their admirable order and on the superiority of their arms. The rear ranks of the Romans followed close on their comrades, cheering them on, but the Carthaginians behaved like cowards, never coming near their mercenaries nor attempting to back them up, so that finally the barbarians gave way, and thinking that they had evidently been left in the lurch by their own side, fell upon those they encountered in their retreat and began to kill them. This actually compelled many of the Carthaginians to die like men; for as they were being butchered by their own mercenaries they were obliged against their will to fight both against these and against the Romans, and as when at bay they showed frantic and extraordinary courage, they killed a considerable number both of their mercenaries and of the enemy. In this way they even threw the cohorts of the *hastati* into confusion, but the officers of the *principes,* seeing what was happening, brought up their ranks to assist, and now the greater number of the Carthaginians and their mercenaries were cut to pieces where they stood, either by themselves or by the *hastati*. Hannibal did not allow the survivors in their flight to mix with his own men but, ordering the foremost ranks to level their spears against them, prevented them from being received into his force. They were therefore obliged to retreat towards the wings and the open ground beyond.

14 The space which separated the two armies still on the field was now covered with blood, slaughter, and dead bodies, and the Roman general was placed in great difficulty by this obstacle to his completing the rout of the enemy. For he saw that it would be very difficult to pass over the ground without breaking his ranks owing to the quantity of slippery corpses which were still soaked in blood and had fallen in heaps and the number of arms thrown away at haphazard. However, after conveying the wounded to the rear and recalling by bugle those of the *hastati* who were still pursuing the enemy, he stationed the latter in the fore part of the field of battle, opposite the enemy's centre, and making the *principes* and *triarii* close up on both wings ordered them to advance over the dead. When these troops had surmounted the obstacles and found themselves in a line with the *hastati* the two phalanxes closed with the greatest eagerness and ardour. As they were nearly equal in numbers as well as in spirit and bravery, and were equally well armed, the contest was for long doubtful, the men falling where they stood out of determination, and Massanissa and Laelius, returning

from the pursuit of the cavalry, arrived providentially at the proper moment. When they fell on Hannibal's army from the rear, most of the men were cut down in their ranks, while of those who took to flight only quite a few escaped, as the cavalry were close on them and the country was level. More than fifteen hundred Romans fell, the Carthaginian loss amounting to twenty thousand killed and nearly the same number of prisoners.

Source: Polybius, *The Histories, Vol. IV,* 15.9–14. Translated by W. R. Paton. Loeb Classical Library (Cambridge, MA: Harvard University Press, 1925), 485–498.

9. Polybius, Revenge at the Battle of Cynoscephalae

After the Second Punic War, Rome took advantage of an opportunity in 200 to assist its allies in the Greek world and get some revenge in the bargain. During the war Philip had signed a treaty with Hannibal, so Rome had good reasons for wanting to chastise him militarily. Philip V continued to exercise hegemony over much of Greece. Rome's allies, Pergamum and the Aetolian League, requested that he be expelled, so Rome declared war. Flamininus arrived in 198 and was able the following year to maneuver Philip into proximity for a battle. In the days before the battle, both sides were blind as to the location of the other. Their light troops stumbled into each other in the fog, and the battle began. This is the first battle narrative we have in which the Romans used elephants and was one of the few battles in which the beasts were successful.

Flamininus was not one of Polybius' favorite Roman generals because of his interference in later Greek affairs. Despite that animosity, Polybius liked Philip V even less, so he does narrate events in such a way that Flamininus earned the victory. Yet the careful reader will notice that at the end of the narrative it is not Flamininus but a nameless military tribune who delivered the winning blow by a careful maneuver. Polybius' detailed description suggests that he visited the site, and as was his usual practice, he probably interviewed participants on both sides. This discussion is also important because the description of the Battle of Cynoscephalae is the first detailed account we have of a Macedonian phalanx in action against a legion.

18.20 Next day both armies, dissatisfied with the ground near Pherae, as it was all under cultivation and covered with walls and small gardens, retired from it. Philip for his part began to march towards Scotussa, hoping to procure supplies from that town and afterwards when fully furnished to find ground suitable for his own army. But Flamininus, suspecting his purpose, put his army in motion at the same time as Philip with the object of destroying the corn in the territory of Scotussa before his adversary could get there. As there were high hills between the two armies in their march neither did the Romans perceive where the Macedonians were marching to nor the Macedonians the Romans. After marching all that day, Flamininus having reached the place called Eretria in Phthiotis and Philip the river Onchestus, they both encamped at those spots, each ignorant of the position of the other's camp. Next day they again advanced and encamped, Philip at the place called Melambium in the territory of Scotussa and Flamininus at the sanctuary of Thetis in that of Pharsalus, being still in ignorance of each others' whereabouts. In the night there was a violent thunderstorm accompanied by rain, and next morning at early dawn all the mist from the clouds descended on the earth, so that owing to the darkness that prevailed one could not see even people who were close at hand. Philip, however, who was in a hurry to effect his purpose, broke up his camp and advanced with his whole army, but finding it difficult to march owing to the mist, after having made but little progress, he entrenched his army and sent off his covering force with orders to occupy the summits of the hills which lay between him and the enemy.

21 Flamininus lay still encamped near the sanctuary of Thetis and, being in doubt as to where the enemy were, he pushed forward ten squadrons of horse and about a thousand light-armed infantry, sending them out with orders to go over the ground reconnoitring cautiously. In proceeding towards the pass over the hills they encountered the Macedonian covering force quite unexpectedly owing to the obscurity of the army. Both forces were thrown somewhat into disorder for a short time but soon began to take the offensive, sending to their respective commanders messengers to inform them of what had happened. When in the combat that ensued the Romans began to be overpowered and to suffer loss at the hands of the Macedonian covering force they sent to their camp begging for help, and Flamininus, calling upon Archedamus and Eupolemus the Aetolians and two of his military tribunes, sent them off with five hundred horse and two thousand foot. For the Romans, encouraged by the arrival of the reinforcements, fought with redoubled vigour, and the Macedonians, though defending themselves gallantly, were in their turn pressed hard, and upon being completely overmastered, fled to the summits and sent to the king for help.

22 Philip, who had never expected, for the reasons I have stated, that a general engagement would take place on that day, had even sent out a fair number of men from his camp to forage, and now when he heard of the turn affairs were taking from the messengers, and as the mist was beginning to clear, he called upon Heraclides of Gyrton, the commander of the Thessalian horse, and Leo, who was in command of the Macedonian horse, and dispatched them, together with all the mercenaries except those from Thrace, under the command of Athenagoras. Upon their joining the covering force the Macedonians, having received such a large reinforcement, pressed hard on the enemy and in their turn began to drive the Romans from their heights. But the chief obstacle to their putting the enemy entirely to rout was the high spirit of the Aetolian cavalry who fought with desperate gallantry. For as much as the Aetolian infantry is inferior in the equipment and discipline required for a general engagement, by so much is their cavalry superior to that of other Greeks in detached and single combats. Thus on the present occasion they so far checked the spirit of the enemy's advance that the Romans were not as before driven down to the level ground, but when they were at a short distance from it turned and steadied themselves. Flamininus, upon seeing that not only had his light infantry and cavalry given way, but that his whole army was flustered owing to this, led out all his forces and drew them up in order of battle close to the hills. At the same time one messenger after another from the covering force came running to Philip shouting, "Sire, the enemy are flying: do not lose the opportunity: the barbarians cannot stand before us: the day is yours now: this is your time"; so that Philip, though he was not satisfied with the ground, still allowed himself to be provoked to do battle. The above-mentioned hills are, I should say, called "The Dog's Heads" (Cynoscephalae): they are very rough and broken and attain a considerable height. Philip, therefore, foreseeing what difficulties the ground would present, was at first by no means disposed to fight, but now urged on by these excessively sanguine reports he ordered his army to be led out of the entrenched camp.

23 Flamininus, having drawn up his whole army in line, both took steps to cover the retreat of his advanced force and walking along the ranks addressed his men. His address was brief, but vivid and easily understood by his hearers. For pointing to the enemy, who were now in full view, he said to his men, "Are these not the Macedonians whom, when they held the pass leading to Eordaea, you under Sulpicius attacked in the open and forced to retreat to the higher ground after slaying many of them? Are these not the same Macedonians who when they held that desperately

difficult position in Epirus you compelled by your valour to throw away their shields and take to flight, never stopping until they got home to Macedonia? What reason, then, have you to be timid now when you are about to do battle with the same men on equal terms? What need for you to dread a recurrence of former danger, when you should rather on the contrary derive confidence from memory of the past! And so, my men, encouraging each other dash onto the fray and put forth all your strength. For if it be the will of Heaven, I feel sure that this battle will end like the former ones." After speaking thus he ordered those on the right to remain where they were with the elephants in front of them, and taking with him the left half of the army, advanced to meet the enemy in imposing style. The advanced force of the Romans thus supported by the infantry of the legions now turned and fell upon their foes.

24 Philip at this time, now that he saw the greater part of his army drawn up outside the entrenchment, advanced with the peltasts and the right wing of phalanx, ascending energetically the slope that led to the hills and giving orders to Nicanor, who was nicknamed the elephant, to see that the rest of his army followed him at once. When the leading ranks reached the top of the pass, he wheeled to the left, and occupied the summits above it; for, as the Macedonian advanced force had pressed the Romans for a considerable distance down the opposite side of the hills, he found these summits abandoned. While he was still deploying his force on the right his mercenaries appeared hotly pursued by the Romans. For when the heavy-armed Roman infantry had joined the light infantry, as I said, and gave them their support in the battle, they availed themselves of the additional weight thus thrown into the scale, and pressing heavily on the enemy killed many of them. When the king, just after his arrival, saw that the light infantry were engaged not far from the hostile camp he was overjoyed, but now on seeing his own men giving way in their turn and in urgent need of support, he was compelled to go to their assistance and thus decide the whole fate of the army on the spur of the moment, although the greater portion of the phalanx was still on the march and approaching the hills. Receiving those who were engaged with the enemy, he placed them all, both foot and horse, on his right wing and ordered the peltasts and that part of the phalanx he had with him to double their depth and close up towards the right. Upon this being done, the enemy being now close upon them, orders were sent out to the men of the phalanx to lower their spears and charge, while the light infantry were ordered to place themselves on the flank. At the same moment Flamininus, having received his advanced force into the gaps between the maniples, fell upon the enemy.

25 As the encounter of the two armies was accompanied by deafening shouts and cries, both of them uttering their war-cry and those outside the battle also cheering the combatants, the spectacle was such as to inspire terror and acute anxiety. Philip's right wing acquitted themselves splendidly in the battle, as they were charging from higher ground and were superior in the weight of their formation, the nature of their arms also giving them a decided advantage on the present occasion. But as for the rest of his army, those next to the force actually engaged were still at a distance from the enemy and those on the left had only just surmounted the ridge and come into view of the summits. Flamininus, seeing that his men could not sustain the charge of the phalanx, but that since his left was being forced back, some of them having already perished and others retreating slowly, his only hope of safety lay in his right, hastened to place himself in command there, and observing that those of the enemy who were next the actual combatants were idle, and that some of the rest were still descending to meet him from the summits and others had halted on the heights, placed his elephants in front and led on his legions to the attack. The Macedonians now, having no one to give them orders and being unable to adopt the formation proper to the phalanx, in part owing to the difficulty of the ground and in part because they were trying to reach the combatants and were still in marching order and not in line, did not even wait until they were at close quarters with the Romans, but gave way thrown into confusion and broken up by the elephants alone.

26 Most of the Romans followed up these fugitives and continued to put them to the sword: but one of the tribunes with them, taking not more than twenty maniples and judging on the spur of the moment what ought to be done, contributed much to the total victory. For noticing that the Macedonians under Philip had advanced a long way in front of the rest, and were by their weight forcing back the Roman left, he quitted those on the right, who were now clearly victorious, and wheeling his force in the direction of the scene of combat and thus getting behind the Macedonians, he fell upon them in the rear. As it is impossible for the phalanx to turn right about face or to fight man to man, he now pressed his attack home, killing those he found in his way, who were incapable of protecting themselves, until the whole Macedonian force were compelled to throw away their shields and take to flight, attacked now also by the troops who had yielded before their frontal charge and who now turned and faced them. Philip at first, as I said, judging from the success of those under his own leadership, was convinced that his victory was complete, but now on suddenly seeing that the Macedonians were throwing away their shields and that the enemy had attacked them in the rear, retired with a

small number of horse and foot to a short distance from the scene of action and remained to observe the whole scene. When he noticed that the Romans in pursuit of his left wing had already reached the summits, he decided to fly, collecting hastily as many Thracians and Macedonians as he could. Flamininus, pursuing the fugitives and finding when he reached the crest of the ridge that the ranks of the Macedonian left were just attaining the summits, at first halted. The enemy were now holding up their spears, as is the Macedonian custom when they either surrender or go over to the enemy, and on learning the significance of this he kept back his men, thinking to spare the beaten force. But while he was still making up his mind some of the Romans who had advanced further fell on them from above and began to cut them down. Most of them perished, a very few escaping after throwing away their shields.

Source: Polybius, *The Histories, Vol. V,* 18.20–26. Translated by W. R. Paton. Loeb Classical Library (Cambridge, MA: Harvard University Press, 1926), 128–144.

10. Polybius, Macedonian Phalanx versus the Roman Legion

The Macedonian phalanx dominated warfare in the eastern Mediterranean world after 353. The phalanx was so effective that once introduced, it rendered all prior forms of regional warfare obsolete. However, that dominance grew in the east before the emergence of the fully developed legion and was unmolested by another power, such as Carthage or Rome. The description of the Battle of Cynoscephalae is the first detailed account we have of a Macedonian phalanx in action against a legion. Pyrrhus had of course employed a phalanx against the Romans and won, but the narratives of those battles are inadequate. Polybius follows up his narrative of Cynoscephalae with a lengthy analysis of why the phalanx lost to the legion.

Polybius had an additional goal in his Cynoscephalae battle narrative. He seems to have tried demonstrating to his Greek contemporaries that the phalanx was not invincible. Doing so would show Greeks that they did not have to be afraid of Macedonian kings and their phalanx. Polybius does not lie about events, but he crafted his narrative in such a way as to help him make that case. Polybius' analysis is informative, but careful readers will notice that Philip lost the battle more because his units entered the battle piecemeal than because half his phalanx failed to perform.

18.29 That when the phalanx has its characteristic virtue and strength nothing can sustain its frontal attack or withstand the charge can easily be understood for many reasons. For since, when it has closed up for action, each man, with his arms, occupies a space of three feet in breadth, and the length of the pikes is according to the original design sixteen cubits, but as adapted to actual need fourteen cubits, from which we must subtract the distance between the bearer's two hands and the length of the weighted portion of the pike behind which serves to keep it couched—four cubits in all—it is evident that it must extend ten cubits beyond the body of each hoplite when he charges the enemy grasping it with both hands. The consequence is that while the pikes of the second, third, and fourth ranks extend farther than those of the fifth rank, those of that rank extend two cubits beyond the bodies of the men in the first rank, when the phalanx has its characteristic close order as regards both depth and breadth, as Homer expresses it in these verses:

Spear crowded spear,
Shield, helmet, man press'd helmet, man, and shield;
The hairy crests of their resplendent casques
Kiss'd close at every nod, so wedged they stood.

This description is both true and fine, and it is evident that each man of the first rank must have the points of five pikes extending beyond him, each at a distance of two cubits from the next.

30 From this we can easily conceive what is the nature and force of a charge by the whole phalanx when it is sixteen deep. In this case those further back and the fifth rank cannot use their pikes so as to take any active part in the battle. They therefore do not severally level their pikes, but hold them slanting up in the air over the shoulders of those in front of them, so as to protect the whole formation from above, keeping off by this serried mass of pikes all missiles which, passing over the heads of the first ranks, might fall on those immediately in front of and behind them. But these men by the sheer pressure of their bodily weight in the charge add to its force, and it is quite impossible for the first ranks to face about.

Such being in general and in detail the disposition of the phalanx, I have now, for purposes of comparison, to speak of the peculiarities of the

Roman equipment and system of formation and the points of difference in both. Now in the case of the Romans also each soldier with his arms occupies a space of three feet in breadth, but as in their mode of fighting each man must move separately, as he has to cover his person with his long shield, turning to meet each expected blow, and as he uses his sword both for cutting and thrusting it is obvious that a looser order is required, and each man must be at a distance of at least three feet from the man next him in the same rank and those in front of and behind him, if they are to be of proper use. The consequence will be that one Roman must stand opposite two men in the first rank of the phalanx, so that he has to face and encounter ten pikes, and it is both impossible for a single man to cut through them all in time once they are at close quarters and by no means easy to force their points away, as the rear ranks can be of no help to the front rank either in thus forcing the pikes away or in the use of the sword. So it is easy to see that, as I said at the beginning, nothing can withstand the charge of the phalanx as long as it preserves its characteristic formation and force.

31 What then is the reason of the Roman success, and what is it that defeats the purpose of those who use the phalanx? It is because in war the time and place of action is uncertain and the phalanx has only one time and one place in which it can perform its peculiar service. Now, if the enemy were obliged to adapt themselves to the times and places required by the phalanx when a decisive battle was impending, those who use the phalanx would in all probability, for the reasons I stated above, always get the better of their enemies; but if it is not only possible but easy to avoid its onset why should one any longer dread an attack of a body so constituted? Again, it is acknowledged that the phalanx requires level and clear ground with no obstacles such as ditches, clefts, clumps of trees, ridges and water courses, all of which are sufficient to impede and break up such a formation. Every one would also acknowledge that it is almost impossible except in very rare cases to find spaces of say twenty stades or even more in length with no such obstacles. 8 But even if we assume it to be possible, supposing those who are fighting against us refuse to meet us on such ground, but force round sacking the cities and devastating the territory of our allies, what is the use of such a formation? For by remaining on the ground that suits it, not only is it incapable of helping its friends but cannot even ensure its own safety. For the arrival of supplies will easily be prevented by the enemy, when they have undisturbed command of the open country. But if the phalanx leaves the ground proper to it and attempts any action, it will be easily overcome by the enemy. And again, if it is decided to engage the enemy on

level ground, but instead of availing ourselves of our total force when the phalanx has its one opportunity for charging, we keep out of action even a small portion of it at the moment of the shock, it is easy to tell what will happen from what the Romans always do at present, 32 the likelihood of the result I now indicate requiring no argument but only the evidence of actual facts. For the Romans do not make their line equal in force to the enemy and expose all the legions to a frontal attack by the phalanx, but part of their forces remain in reserve and the rest engage the enemy. Afterwards whether the phalanx drives back by its charge the force opposed to it or is repulsed by this force, its own peculiar formation is broken up. For either in following up a retreating foe or in flying before an attacking foe, they leave behind the other parts of their own army, upon which the enemy's reserve have room enough in the space formerly held by the phalanx to attack no longer in front but appearing by a lateral movement on the flank and rear of the phalanx. When it is thus easy to guard against the opportunities and advantages of the phalanx, but impossible to prevent the enemy from taking advantage of the proper moment to act against it, the one kind of formation naturally proves in reality superior to the other. Again, those who employ the phalanx have to march through and encamp in every variety of country; they are compelled to occupy favourable positions in advance, to besiege certain positions and to be besieged in others, and to meet attacks from quarters the least expected. For all such contingencies are parts of war, and victory sometimes wholly and sometimes very largely depends on them. Now in all these matters the Macedonian formation is at times of little use and at times of no use at all, because the phalanx soldier can be of service neither in detachments nor singly, while the Roman formation is efficient. For every Roman soldier, once he is armed and sets about his business, can adapt himself equally well to every place and time and can meet attack from every quarter. He is likewise equally prepared and equally in condition whether he has to fight together with the whole army or with a part of it or in maniples or singly. So since in all particulars the Romans are much more serviceable, Roman plans are much more apt to result in success than those of others. I thought it necessary to speak on this subject at some length because many Greeks on the actual occasions when the Macedonians suffered defeat considered the event as almost incredible, and many will still continue to wonder why and how the phalanx comes to be conquered by troops armed in the Roman fashion.

Source: Polybius, *The Histories, Vol. V,* 18.29–32. Translated by W. R. Paton. Loeb Classical Library (Cambridge, MA: Harvard University Press, 1926), 150–159.

11. Livy, A Centurion's Long Career

Livy, writing at the end of the first century BCE, drew on earlier authors' histories as well as annalistic accounts kept by priests and officials. The source for the testimony here is unknown, but it could have come from official records. In the process of discussing the enlistment of men for the Third Macedonian War in 171, Livy provides the following testimony of a centurion, Spurius Ligustinus. What stands out from his account is that he participated in several major battles and campaigns and served under numerous distinguished generals. He treated each campaign as distinct service, returning home each time—demonstrating that Rome's military was not permanent or fully professionalized. In addition to the promotions even to the top centurion post, he enjoyed the honor of being an *evocatus,* a selection for marching in a triumph.

The passage is important because it provides an example of a centurion's career in detail that does not usually survive. Admittedly, Ligustinus' career was probably unusual, which is why Livy reports it; its exceptional quality stood out in his source. That said, there is no reason why it was not genuine. Among the specifics included are the names of the officers who promoted Ligustinus, the places where he served, and the numerous honors he received, all of which are useful for reconstructing details of military service, especially the careers of centurions, about which we know less than we would like for much of the Roman Republic.

34. After the consul had said what he wanted to say, one of those who were appealing to the tribunes—Sp. Ligustinus—begged the consul and the tribunes to allow him to say a few words to the Assembly. They all gave him permission, and he is recorded to have spoken to the following effect: "Quirites, I am Spurius Ligustinus, a Sabine by birth, a member of the Crustuminian tribe. My father left me a *jugerum* of land and a small cottage in which I was born and bred, and I am living there today. As soon as I came of age my father gave me to wife his brother's daughter. She brought nothing with her but her personal freedom and her modesty, and together with these a fruitfulness which would have been enough even in a wealthy house. We have six sons and two daughters. Four of our sons wear the *toga virilis,* two the *praetexta,* and both the daughters are married. I became a soldier in the consulship of P. Sulpicius and C. Aurelius. For two years I was a common soldier in the army, fighting against Philip in Macedonia; in the third year T. Quinctius Flamininus gave me in consideration of my courage the command of the tenth company of the *hastati.* After Philip and the Macedonians were vanquished and we were brought back to Italy and disbanded, I at once volunteered to go

with the consul M. Porcius to Spain. Men who during a long service have had experience of him and of other generals know that of all living commanders not one has shown himself a keener observer or more accurate judge of military valour. It was this commander who thought me worthy of being appointed first centurion in the *hastati*. Again I served, for the third time, as a volunteer in the army which was sent against Antiochus and the Aetolians. I was made first centurion of the *principes* by Manius Acilius. After Antiochus was expelled and the Aetolians subjugated we were brought back to Italy. After that I twice took service for a year at home. Then I served in Spain, once under Q. Fulvius Flaccus and again under Ti. Sempronius Gracchus. I was brought home by Flaccus amongst those whom, as a reward for their courage, he was bringing home to grace his triumph. I joined Tiberius Gracchus at his request. Four times, within a few years, have I been first centurion in the *triarii;* four-and-thirty times have I been rewarded for my courage by my commanders; I have received six civic crowns. I have served for twenty-two years in the army and I am more than fifty years old. But even if I had not served my full time and my age did not give me exemption, still, P. Licinius, as I was able to give you four soldiers for one, namely, myself, it would have been a right and proper thing that I should be discharged. But I want you to take what I have said simply as a statement of my case. So far as anyone who is raising troops judges me to be an efficient soldier, I am not going to plead excuses. What rank the military tribunes think that I deserve is for them to decide; I will take care that no man shall surpass me in courage; that I always have done so, my commanders and fellow-campaigners bear witness. And as for you, my comrades, though you are only exercising your right of appeal, it is but just and proper that as in your early days you never did anything against the authority of the magistrates and the senate, so now, too, you should place yourselves at the disposal of the senate and the consuls and count any position in which you are to defend your country as an honourable one."

Source: Titus Livius [Livy], *The History of Rome, Vol. 6,* 42.34. Translated by Rev. Canon Roberts (New York: E. P. Dutton, 1912).

12. Caesar, Cohort Legion in Combat

The Gallic Wars began in 58 soon after Caesar arrived in his provinces. He was initially successful in stopping Germanic incursions against Roman allies. Some Gauls welcomed Caesar as a protector, but many tribes saw his actions as unwelcome interference. In 57 Caesar moved north against the Belgae, a coalition of tribes in northern Gaul, because they had attacked a Roman ally. Belgic Nervi ambushed Caesar's army during a march along the Sambre River, attacking as it was building a fort. The attack was a complete surprise and required Caesar to respond quickly. He won the battle, but his account gives the credit to his legate Labienus, whose swift return turned the tide.

This passage, written by Caesar in 52 or 51 after the war concluded, is useful for highlighting a number of issues. The role of officers in battle receives great emphasis, especially centurions. The number of centurions killed and wounded emphasizes the forward position that they were expected to take in combat. Caesar himself is in the thick of things and relies heavily on the standards to know what unit he was rallying. The fort was still part of Roman practice. Construction seems to have been further along than initially indicated. The presence of camp followers is something of a surprise too for readers, who expect Caesar to have kept a lean marching order. Notice also Caesar's easy literary style and his use of third person for himself, both signs of his intended audience back in Rome.

21—Caesar, having given the necessary orders, hastened to and fro into whatever quarter fortune carried him, to animate the troops, and came to the tenth legion. Having encouraged the soldiers with no further speech than that "they should keep up the remembrance of their wonted valor, and not be confused in mind, but valiantly sustain the assault of the enemy"; as the latter were not further from them than the distance to which a dart could be cast, he gave the signal for commencing battle. And having gone to another quarter for the purpose of encouraging [the soldiers], he finds them fighting. Such was the shortness of the time, and so determined was the mind of the enemy on fighting, that time was wanting not only for affixing the military insignia, but even for putting on the helmets and drawing off the covers from the shields. To whatever part any one by chance came from the works (in which he had been employed), and whatever standards he saw first, at these he stood, lest in seeking his own company he should lose the time for fighting.

22—The army having been marshaled, rather as the nature of the ground and the declivity of the hill and the exigency of the time, than as the method and order of military matters required; while the legions in the different places were withstanding the enemy, some in one quarter, some in another, and the view was obstructed by the very thick hedges intervening, as we have before remarked, neither could proper reserves be posted, nor could the necessary measures be taken in each part, nor could all the commands be issued by one person. Therefore, in such an unfavorable state of affairs, various events of fortune followed.

23—The soldiers of the ninth and tenth legions, as they had been stationed on the left part of the army, casting their weapons, speedily drove the Atrebates (for that division had been opposed to them), who were breathless with running and fatigue, and worn out with wounds, from the higher ground into the river; and following them as they were endeavoring to pass it, slew with their swords a great part of them while impeded (therein). They themselves did not hesitate to pass the river; and having advanced to a disadvantageous place, when the battle was renewed, they [nevertheless] again put to flight the enemy, who had returned and were opposing them. In like manner, in another quarter two different legions, the eleventh and the eighth, having routed the Veromandui, with whom they had engaged, were fighting from the higher ground upon the very banks of the river. But, almost the whole camp on the front and on the left side being then exposed, since the twelfth legion was posted in the right wing, and the seventh at no great distance from it, all the Nervii, in a very close body, with Boduognatus, who held the chief command, as their leader, hastened toward that place; and part of them began to surround the legions on their unprotected flank, part to make for the highest point of the encampment.

24—At the same time our horsemen, and light-armed infantry, who had been with those, who, as I have related, were routed by the first assault of the enemy, as they were betaking themselves into the camp, met the enemy face to face, and again sought flight into another quarter; and the camp-followers who from the Decuman Gate, and from the highest ridge of the hill had seen our men pass the river as victors, when, after going out for the purposes of plundering, they looked back and saw the enemy parading in our camp, committed themselves precipitately to flight; at the same time there arose the cry and shout of those who came with the baggage-train: and they (affrighted), were carried some one way, some another. By all these circumstances the cavalry of the Treviri were much alarmed (whose reputation for courage is extraordinary among the Gauls, and who had come to Caesar, being sent by their state as auxiliaries), and, when they saw our camp filled with a large number of the enemy, the legions hard pressed and almost held surrounded, the camp-retainers, horsemen, slingers, and Numidians fleeing on all sides divided and scattered, they, despairing of our affairs, hastened home, and related to their state that the Romans were routed and conquered, [and] that the enemy were in possession of their camp and baggage-train.

25—Caesar proceeded, after encouraging the tenth legion, to the right wing; where he perceived that his men were hard pressed, and that in consequence of the standards of the twelfth legion being collected together in one place, the crowded soldiers were a hinderance to themselves in the fight; that all the centurions of the fourth cohort were slain, and the standard-bearer killed, the standard itself lost, almost all the centurions of the other cohorts either wounded or slain, and among them the chief centurion of the legion P. Sextius Baculus, a very valiant man, who was so exhausted by many and severe wounds, that he was already unable to support himself; he likewise perceived that the rest were slackening their efforts, and that some, deserted by those in the rear, were retiring from the battle and avoiding the weapons; that the enemy [on the other hand] though advancing from the lower ground, were not relaxing in front, and were [at the same time] pressing hard on both flanks; he also perceived that the affair was at a crisis, and that there was not any reserve which could be brought up, having therefore snatched a shield from one of the soldiers in the rear (for he himself had come without a shield), he advanced to the front of the line, and addressing the centurions by name, and encouraging the rest of the soldiers, he ordered them to carry forward the standards, and extend the companies, that they might the more easily use their swords. On his arrival, as hope was brought to the soldiers and their courage restored, while every one for his own part, in the sight of his general, desired to exert his utmost energy, the impetuosity of the enemy was a little checked.

26—Caesar, when he perceived that the seventh legion, which stood close by him, was also hard pressed by the enemy, directed the tribunes of the soldiers to effect a junction of the legions gradually, and make their charge upon the enemy with a double front; which having been done, since they brought assistance the one to the other, nor feared lest their rear should be surrounded by the enemy, they began to stand their ground more boldly, and to fight more courageously. In the mean time, the soldiers of the two legions which had been in the rear of the army, as a guard for the baggage-train, upon the battle being reported to them, quickened their pace, and were seen by the enemy on the top of the hill; and Titus Labienus, having gained possession of the camp of the enemy, and observed from the higher ground what was going on in our camp, sent the tenth legion as a relief to our men, who, when they had learned from the flight of the horse and the sutlers in what position the affair was, and in how great danger the camp and the legion and the commander were involved, left undone nothing [which tended] to dispatch.

27—By their arrival, so great a change of matters was made, that our men, even those who had fallen down exhausted with wounds, leaned on their shields, and renewed the fight: then the camp-retainers, though unarmed, seeing the enemy completely dismayed, attacked [them though] armed; the horsemen too, that they might by their valor blot the disgrace of their flight, thrust themselves before the legionary soldiers in all parts of the battle. But the enemy, even in the last hope of safety, displayed such great courage, that when the foremost of them had fallen, the next stood upon them prostrate, and fought from their bodies; when these were overthrown, and their corpses heaped up together, those who survived cast their weapons against our men [thence], as from a mound, and returned our darts which had fallen short between [the armies]; so that it ought not to be concluded, that men of such great courage had injudiciously dared to pass a very broad river, ascend very high banks, and come up to a very disadvantageous place; since their greatness of spirit had rendered these actions easy, although in themselves very difficult.

Source: Julius Caesar, *The Commentaries of Caesar: Caesar's Gallic War,* 1st ed., 2.21–27. Translated by W. A. McDevitte and W. S. Bohn (New York: Harper and Brothers, 1869).

13. Plutarch, Rome versus Parthia at the Battle of Carrhae

Crassus arrived as governor of Syria in 54. Eager to earn military renown equal to Pompey and Caesar, Crassus took advantage of internal Parthian divisions to invade Parthia. His first campaign in 54 had been successful in capturing territory, but he needed more support, so he had returned to Syria and planned a second invasion in 53. The Parthian general Surena, who had good information from spies about Crassus' plans, anticipated this campaign that ended at the Battle of Carrhae. In addition to the Parthians, Crassus' plan was also hindered by his unfamiliarity with desert tactics, his inexperienced legions, and his own command failure to stay along his intended supply route and keep his army together. Surena drew Crassus into the desert and then attacked. Not all the blame for the defeat should be set on Crassus and his son, as Plutarch does; Antony would meet with a similar near disaster in 37.

This passage by Plutarch, a Roman Greek writing in the early second century CE, is useful for its insight into Parthian arms and tactics as well as for Roman errors of command. The lack of Parthian infantry was normal, as their cavalry was more important and practical. The Parthians used two tactics in combination during this battle. The *cataphract* cavalry could not charge the legion in square because it was densely packed, so the cavalry would feign charge to force the Romans to stand closer together. The horse archers would feign retreat to draw the Romans out and then wheel around to fire while drawing their enemy into a *cataphract* charge, both of which they do in this description.

23 Most of the officers, accordingly, thought they ought to bivouac and spend the night there, and after learning as much as they could of the number and disposition of the enemy, to advance against them at day-break. But Crassus was carried away by the eagerness of his son and the cavalry with him, who urged him to advance and give battle, and he therefore ordered that the men who needed it should eat and drink as they stood in the ranks. And before they were all well done with this, he led them on, not slowly, nor halting from time to time, as is usual on the way to battle, but with a quick and sustained pace until the enemy came in sight, who, to the surprise of the Romans, appeared to be neither numerous nor formidable. For Surena had veiled his main force behind his advance guard, and concealed the gleam of their armour by ordering them to cover themselves with robes and skins. But when they were near the Romans and the signal was raised by their commander, first of all they filled the plain with the sound of a deep and terrifying roar. For the Parthians do not incite themselves to battle with horns or trumpets, but they have hollow drums of distended hide, covered with bronze bells, and on these they beat all at once in many quarters, and the instruments give forth a low and dismal tone, a blend of wild beast's roar and harsh thunder peal. They had rightly judged that, of all the senses, hearing is the one most apt to confound the soul, soonest rouses its emotions, and most effectively unseats the judgment.

24 While the Romans were in consternation at this din, suddenly their enemies dropped the coverings of their armour, and were seen to be themselves blazing in helmets and breastplates, their Margianian steel glittering keen and bright, and their horses clad in plates of bronze and steel. Surena himself, however, was the tallest and fairest of them all, although his effeminate beauty did not well correspond to his reputation for valour, but he was dressed more in the Median fashion, with painted face and parted

hair, while the rest of the Parthians still wore their hair long and bunched over their foreheads, in Scythian fashion, to make themselves look formidable. And at first they purposed to charge upon the Romans with their long spears, and throw their front ranks into confusion; but when they saw the depth of their formation, where shield was locked with shield, and the firmness and composure of the men, they drew back, and while seeming to break their ranks and disperse, they surrounded the hollow square in which their enemy stood before he was aware of the manoeuvre. And when Crassus ordered his light-armed troops to make a charge, they did not advance far, but encountering a multitude of arrows, abandoned their undertaking and ran back for shelter among the men-at-arms, among whom they caused the beginning of disorder and fear, for these now saw the velocity and force of the arrows, which fractured armour, and tore their way through every covering alike, whether hard or soft.

But the Parthians now stood at long intervals from one another and began to shoot their arrows from all sides at once, not with any accurate aim (for the dense formation of the Romans would not suffer an archer to miss even if he wished it), but making vigorous and powerful shots from bows which were large and mighty and curved so as to discharge their missiles with great force. At once, then, the plight of the Romans was a grievous one; for if they kept their ranks, they were wounded in great numbers, and if they tried to come to close quarters with the enemy, they were just as far from effecting anything and suffered just as much. For the Parthians shot as they fled, and next to the Scythians, they do this most effectively; and it is a very clever thing to seek safety while still fighting, and to take away the shame of flight.

25 Now as long as they had hopes that the enemy would exhaust their missiles and desist from battle or fight at close quarters, the Romans held out; but when they perceived that many camels laden with arrows were at hand, from which the Parthians who first encircled them took a fresh supply, then Crassus, seeing no end to this, began to lose heart, and sent messengers to his son with orders to force an engagement with the enemy before he was surrounded; for it was his wing especially which the enemy were attacking and surrounding with their cavalry, in the hope of getting in his rear. Accordingly, the young man took thirteen hundred horsemen, of whom a thousand had come from Caesar, five hundred archers, and eight cohorts of the men-at-arms who were nearest him, and led them all to the charge. But the Parthians who were trying to envelop him, either because, as some say, they encountered marshes, or because they were manoeuvring to

attack Publius as far as possible from his father, wheeled about and made off. Then Publius, shouting that the men did not stand their ground, rode after them, and with him Censorinus and Megabacchus, the latter distinguished for his courage and strength, Censorinus a man of senatorial dignity and a powerful speaker, and both of them comrades of Publius and nearly of the same age. The cavalry followed after Publius, and even the infantry kept pace with them in the zeal and joy which their hopes inspired; for they thought they were victorious and in pursuit of the enemy, until, after they had gone forward a long distance, they perceived the ruse. For the seeming fugitives wheeled about and were joined at the same time by others more numerous still. Then the Romans halted, supposing that the enemy would come to close quarters with them, since they were so few in number. But the Parthians stationed their mail-clad horsemen in front of the Romans, and then with the rest of their cavalry in loose array rode round them, tearing up the surface of the ground, and raising from the depths great heaps of sand which fell in limitless showers of dust, so that the Romans could neither see clearly nor speak plainly, but, being crowded into a narrow compass and falling upon one another, were shot, and died no easy nor even speedy death. For, in the agonies of convulsive pain, and writhing about the arrows, they would break them off in their wounds, and then in trying to pull out by force the barbed heads which had pierced their veins and sinews, they tore and disfigured themselves the more.

Thus many died, and the survivors also were incapacitated for fighting. And when Publius urged them to charge the enemy's mail-clad horsemen, they showed him that their hands were riveted to their shields and their feet nailed through and through to the ground, so that they were helpless either for flight or for self-defence. Publius himself, accordingly, cheered on his cavalry, made a vigorous charge with them, and closed with the enemy. But his struggle was an unequal one both offensively and defensively, for his thrusting was done with small and feeble spears against breastplates of raw hide and steel, whereas the thrusts of the enemy were made with pikes against the lightly equipped and unprotected bodies of the Gauls, since it was upon these that Publius chiefly relied, and with these he did indeed work wonders. For they laid hold of the long spears of the Parthians, and grappling with the men, pushed them from their horses, hard as it was to move them owing to the weight of their armour; and many of the Gauls forsook their own horses, and crawling under those of the enemy, stabbed them in the belly. These would rear up in their anguish, and die trampling on riders and foemen indiscriminately mingled. But the Gauls were distressed above all things by the heat and their thirst, to both of which they were unused; and most of their horses had perished by being driven against the long spears. They were therefore compelled to retire upon the men-at-arms, taking with them Publius, who was severely wounded. And seeing a sandy hillock near by, they all retired to it, and fastened their horses in the centre; then locking their shields together on the outside, they thought they could more easily defend themselves against the Barbarians. But it turned out just the other way. For on level ground, the front ranks do, to some extent, afford relief to those who are behind them. But here, where the inequality of the ground raised one man above another, and lifted every man who was behind another into greater prominence, there was no such thing as escape, but they were all alike hit with arrows, bewailing their inglorious and ineffectual death.

Now there were with Publius two Greeks, of those who dwelt near by in Carrhae, Hieronymus and Nicomachus. These joined in trying to persuade him to slip away with them and make their escape to Ichnae, a city which had espoused the Roman cause and was not far off. But Publius, declaring that no death could have such terrors for him as to make him desert those who were perishing on his account, ordered them to save their own lives, bade them farewell, and dismissed them. Then he himself, being unable to use his hand, which had been pierced through with an arrow, presented his side to his shield-bearer and ordered him to strike home with his sword. In like manner also Censorinus is said to have died; but Megabacchus took his own life, and so did the other most notable men. The survivors fought on until the Parthians mounted the hill and transfixed them with their long spears, and they say that not more than five hundred were taken alive. Then the Parthians cut off the head of Publius, and rode off at once to attack Crassus.

26 His situation was as follows. After ordering his son to charge the Parthians and receiving tidings that the enemy were routed to a great distance and hotly pursued, and after noticing also that his own immediate opponents were no longer pressing him so hard (since most of them had streamed away to where Publius was), he recovered a little courage, and drawing his troops together, posted them for safety on sloping ground, in immediate expectation that his son would return from the pursuit. Of the messengers sent by Publius to his father, when he began to be in danger, the first fell in with the Barbarians and were slain; the next made their way

through with difficulty and reported that Publius was lost unless he received speedy and abundant aid from his father. And now Crassus was a prey to many conflicting emotions, and no longer looked at anything with calm judgement. His fear for the whole army drove him to refuse, and at the same time his yearning love for his son impelled him to grant assistance; but at last he began to move his forces forward.

At this point, however, the enemy came up with clamour and battle cries which made them more fearful than ever, and again many of their drums began bellowing about the Romans, who awaited the beginning of a second battle. Besides, those of the enemy who carried the head of Publius fixed high upon a spear, rode close up and displayed it, scornfully asking after his parents and family, for surely, they said, it was not meet that Crassus, most base and cowardly of men, should be the father of a son so noble and of such splendid valour. This spectacle shattered and unstrung the spirits of the Romans more than all the rest of their terrible experiences, and they were all filled, not with a passion for revenge, as was to have been expected, but with shuddering and trembling.

27 Even as he spoke such words of encouragement, Crassus saw that not many of his men listened with any eagerness, but when he also bade them raise the battle cry, he discovered how despondent his army was, so weak, feeble, and uneven was the shout they made, while that which came from the Barbarians was clear and bold. Then, as the enemy got to work, their light cavalry rode round on the flanks of the Romans and shot them with arrows, while the mail-clad horsemen in front, plying their long spears, kept driving them together into a narrow space, except those who, to escape death from the arrows, made bold to rush desperately upon their foes. These did little damage, but met with a speedy death from great and fatal wounds, since the spear which the Parthians thrust into the horses was heavy with steel, and often had impetus enough to pierce through two men at once. After fighting in this manner till night came on, the Parthians withdrew, saying that they would grant Crassus one night in which to bewail his son, unless, with a better regard for his own interests, he should consent to go to Arsaces instead of being carried there.

Source: Plutarch, *The Parallel Lives, Vol. III*, "Life of Crassus," 23.5–26.4, 27.1–2. Translated by Bernadotte Perrin. Loeb Classical Library (Cambridge, MA: Harvard University Press, 1916), 386–400, 402.

14. Caesar, Roman Siege II, Capture of Massilia

Sieges remained an important part of campaigning during the civil wars at the end of the Roman Republic. Caesar's army was experienced and capable in siege warfare, having employed it often during the Gallic Wars. When civil war broke out in 49, Caesar captured Rome and Italy as Pompey withdrew to Greece. Before going after Pompey, Caesar had to contend with the Pompeian strongholds in and near Spain, so he marched west. Finding Massilia on the Gallic coast held against him, Caesar had his legate Trebonius start a siege in 49 while Decimus Brutus, in charge of Caesar's fleet, controlled the harbor.

This siege narrative, written in 45 when the civil war ended, highlights several features common to Caesar's sieges. Speed was paramount, as Caesar could not afford to have his legions tied down against Massilia, so his men kept up an active siege. Unlike the earlier siege of New Carthage, Caesar's men built elaborate siege works to aid in taking the city and used artillery on towers to clear the ramparts of the enemy. The scale of the works and engines are common details in Caesar's *Commentaries*. Also unlike New Carthage, the defenders try the usual responses to siege, some of which work well, but they are still defeated.

2.10 When, by means of this tower, they thought they had sufficiently provided for the security of the works around it, they resolved to build a gallery sixty feet long, of wood, two feet in thickness, to extend from the brick tower to the tower of the enemy, and the very walls of the town. The form of the gallery was this: First, two beams of equal length were laid upon the ground, at the distance of four feet from one another; and in these were fixed little pillars five feet high, joined at the top by beams designed to support the roof of the gallery. Over these were laid rafters, two feet square, fastened strongly with nails and plates of iron. The upper part of the roof was composed of square laths, four inches thick, which were placed at a small distance one from another, to bear the tiles that were to be laid upon them. Thus was the whole finished with a sloping roof, which being partly composed of tiles and mortar, was proof against fire, and had besides a covering of hides, to hinder the mortar from being washed away by spouts of water. Over all we threw strong mattresses, to screen the hides from fire and stones. This work was finished close by the brick tower, under cover of four mantles, and immediately carried forward upon rollers, in the manner ships are launched, till it unexpectedly reached the very tower of the enemy.

11 The Marseillians astonished at so threatening and unlooked-for a machine, pushed forward with levers the largest stones they could find, and tumbled them from the top of the wall upon the gallery. But the strength of the wood resisted the violence of their blows, so that they fell to the ground without doing any hurt. Observing this, they changed their design, and poured down upon us burning barrels of pitch and tallow. But these likewise rolled along the roof without damage, and falling upon the ground, were afterwards thrust away with forks and long poles. Meanwhile our soldiers, under protection of the gallery, were endeavouring with their levers to undermine the enemy's tower. The gallery itself was defended by the tower of brick whence our engines played without intermission insomuch that the enemy, driven from their tower and walls, were at last obliged to abandon their defence. By degrees the tower being undermined, part of it fell down, and the rest was so shaken that it could not stand long.

Upon this the enemy, alarmed at so unexpected a misfortune, discouraged by the downfall of the tower, awed by such a testimony of the wrath of the gods, and dreading the plunder and devastation of their city, came forth in the habit of suppliants, and with outstretched hands, besought the compassion of the army and generals.

14 But the Marseillians, a nation without faith, aimed at nothing further in all this, than to find a time and opportunity to deceive us, and put in practice the treacherous purpose they had formed. For after some days, our men suspecting no danger, but relying upon the good faith of the enemy, while some were retired to their tents, others laid down, to rest in the trenches, overpowered by the long fatigue they had undergone, and all the arms laid up and removed out of sight, suddenly they sallied from the town, and the wind being high, and favourable to their design, set fire to the works. The flame in a moment spread itself on all sides, insomuch that the battery, the mantles, the tortoise, the tower, the machines, and the gallery were entirely destroyed, before it was possible to discover whence the disaster arose. The suddenness of the accident made our men immediately run to their arms, where every one took what came first to hand. Some sallied out upon the enemy, but were checked by the arrows and darts poured upon them from the town; insomuch that the Marseillians, sheltered by their walls, burnt without any difficulty the tower of brick and the gallery. Thus the labour of many months was destroyed in an instant, by the treachery of an enemy, and the violence of the wind. Next day they made the same attempt, favoured by the same wind, and with yet

greater assurance, against the tower and terrace of the other attack. They approached them boldly, and threw plenty of fire upon them; but our men, grown wise by their late misfortune, had made all necessary preparations for their defence, so that after losing many men, they were obliged to retreat into the city, without effecting their purpose.

15 Trebonius immediately resolved to repair his loss, in which he found himself warmly seconded by the zeal of the soldiers. They saw the works, which had cost so much labour and toil, destroyed by the perfidy of a people, who made no scruple of violating the most sacred engagements: they saw that their credulity had been abused, and that they were become the jest of their enemies, which grieved and provoked them at the same time. But it was still difficult to determine whence they might be supplied with wood, to repair all these works. There was none in the neighbourhood of Marseilles, the trees having been all cut down for a great way round. They resolved therefore to raise a terrace of a new kind, and such as history no where mentions before that time. They raised two walls of brick, each six feet thick, and distant from one another, nearly the breadth of the former mount. Over these they laid a floor, and to render it firm, besides its being supported on either side, placed pillars underneath between the walls, to bear it up where it was weakest, or had a greater stress of weight to support. There were moreover cross beams, which rested upon niches in the wall; and to render the several floors proof against fire, hurdles were laid over them, which were afterwards covered with clay. The soldiers, thus sheltered over head by the roof, on the right and left by walls, and before by a breast-work, brought the necessary materials without danger, and by the eagerness with which they laboured, soon completed the whole, leaving overtures in convenient places to sally out upon occasion.

22 The Marseillians, overwhelmed with profusion of calamities, reduced to the utmost distress by famine, worsted in two different engagements by sea, weakened by continual sallies, assaulted by a heavy pestilence, occasioned by the length of the siege, and their constant change of diet (for they were obliged to feed upon old meal and musty barley, which had been long treasured up in their magazines against an accident of this kind), their tower being overthrown, a great part of their walls undermined, and no prospect of relief from armies or the provinces, which were now all reduced under Caesar's power, they resolved to surrender in good earnest. But some days before, Domitius, who was apprized of their intentions, having prepared three ships (two of which he assigned to his followers, and

embarked in person on board the third), took occasion, during a storm, to make his escape. Some of Brutus' galleys, which he had ordered to keep constantly cruising before the port, chancing to get sight of him, prepared to give chase. That in which Domitius was, escaped under favour of the tempest; but the two others, alarmed at seeing our galleys so near them, re-entered the port. Caesar spared the town, more in regard to its antiquity and reputation, than any real merit it could plead. He obliged the citizens however to deliver up their arms, machines, and ships of war, whether in the port or arsenal; to surrender all the money in their treasury; and to receive a garrison of two legions. Then sending the rest of the army into Italy, he himself set out for Rome.

Source: Julius Caesar, *The Commentaries of Caesar: Caesar's Civil War,* 2.10–11, 14–15, 22. Translated by William Duncan (St. Louis: Edwards and Bushnell, 1856).

15. Caesar, Roman versus Roman, Battle of Pharsalus

The Battle of Pharsalus occurred in August 48 between Caesar and Pompey. The passage here includes numerous valuable details. Both commanders were experienced and extremely capable. The precharge speech includes Caesar's justification for the war—that it is not his fault. His *Commentaries* often return to this point. The reader gets a good sense of how noisy and dusty the battle must have been. This battle narrative provides a good example of why the cohort legion was an improvement over the maniple. Cohorts allowed Caesar the flexibility to try a novel arrangement without complicating his control. Both sides included veteran legions whose experience shows in the initial charge, when Pompey's men remained steady while Caesar's stop midcharge to dress their lines and catch their breath. As usual, in his *Commentaries* Caesar is everywhere at once, a reminder that he composed this account in 45 to convey in part his version of events.

3.85 Pompeius, who had his camp on the hill, kept drawing up his line on the lowest spurs of the mountain, apparently always waiting to see whether Caesar would approach close up to the unfavourable ground. Caesar, thinking that Pompeius could by no means be enticed out to a battle, judged that his most convenient plan of campaign was to move his camp from that place, and to be always on the march, with the view of getting his supplies more conveniently by moving camp and visiting various places and at the same time of meeting with some opportunity of fighting on the route, and of wearing out the army of Pompeius, which was unaccustomed to hard work, by daily marches. After making these arrangements, when the signal for starting had now been given and the tents had been unstretched, it was noticed that a little while before, contrary to its daily custom, Pompeius' line had advanced somewhat further from the rampart, so that it seemed possible for a battle to be fought in no disadvantageous position. Then Caesar, addressing his men, when his force was just at the gates, said: "We must put off our march for the present and think of giving battle, as we have always demanded. Let us be prepared in heart for a conflict; we shall not easily hereafter find an opportunity." At once he leads out his troops in light order. . . .

88 Caesar, having approached the camp of Pompeius, observed that his line was drawn up as follows: On the left wing were the two legions which had been handed over by Caesar at the beginning of the civil strife by de-cree of the senate, one of which was called the First, the other the Third. At that place was Pompeius himself. Scipio occupied the middle of the line with the Syrian legions. The Cilician legion, united with the Spanish co-horts, which, as we explained, had been brought over by Afranius, was stationed on the right wing. These legions Pompeius regarded as the strongest under his command. The rest he had interposed between the cen-tre and the wings and had made up the number of one hundred and ten cohorts. These forces amounted to forty-five thousand men, and about two thousand reserves who had come to him from the beneficiaries of his for-mer armies; and these he had distributed throughout the whole force. Seven remaining cohorts he had placed on garrison duty in the camp and the neighbouring forts. A stream with difficult banks protected his right wing; for which reason he had stationed his whole cavalry and all his arch-ers and slingers opposite the enemy on the left wing.

89 Caesar, observing his previous custom, had posted his Tenth Legion on the right wing, and his Ninth on the left, though it had been seriously attenuated by the Dyrrachian battles. To this legion he added the Eighth, so that he almost made the two into one, having given orders that the one should support the other. He had eighty cohorts posted in his lines, mak-ing a total of twenty-two thousand men; seven cohorts he had left as a protection for the camp. He had placed Antonius in command on the left wing, P. Sulla on the right, and Gn. Domitius in the centre. He himself

confronted Pompeius. At the same time, having noticed the arrangements mentioned above, fearing lest his right wing should be surrounded by the multitude of cavalry, he hastily withdrew individual cohorts from the third line and out of these constructed a fourth line, stationing it opposite the cavalry, explaining what his object was and reminding them that the day's victory depended on the valour of these cohorts. At the same time he commanded the third line and the whole army not to join battle without orders from himself, saying that when he wished this to be done he would give the signal with a flag.

90 When, according to the custom of war, he was exhorting his army to battle, and setting forth his unbroken record of kindness to his men, he particularly reminded them that he could call his troops to witness with what zeal he had sought peace, what negotiations he had conducted through Vatinius in conferences and through Aulus Clodius with Scipio, how at Oricum he had urged Libo about the sending of envoys. He had never, he said, wished to squander the blood of his soldiers or to deprive the republic of either of its armies. After delivering this speech, the soldiers clamouring for action and burning with zeal for the fight, he gave the signal with a trumpet.

91 There was in Caesar's army a reservist, G. Crastinus, who in the previous year had served under him as first centurion in the Tenth Legion, a man of remarkable valour. On the signal being given: "Follow me," said he, "you who have been my comrades, and give your commander your wonted loyal service. This one battle alone remains; when it is over he will recover his dignity and we our liberty." At the same time, looking at Caesar, he says: "To-day, General, I will give you occasion to thank me alive or dead." Having said this, he ran forward first from the right wing, and about one hundred and twenty picked men of the same cohort, serving as volunteers, followed him.

92 Between the two lines there was only as much space left as was necessary for the charge of each army. But Pompeius had previously ordered his men to await Caesar's attack without moving from their position, and to allow his line to fall into disorder. He is said to have done this on the advice of G. Triarius, in order that the first charge and impetus of the troops might be broken and their line spread out, and that so the Pompeians marshalled in their proper ranks might attack a scattered foe. He hoped, too, that the javelins would fall with less effect if the men were kept in their

place than if they themselves discharged their javelins and advanced; also that by having a double distance to run Caesar's soldiers would be breathless and overdone with fatigue. Now this seems to us to have been an irrational act on the part of Pompeius, because there is a certain keenness of spirit and impetuosity implanted by nature in all men which is kindled by the ardour of battle. This feeling it is the duty of commanders not to repress but to foster, nor was it without good reason that the custom was instituted of old that signals should sound in every direction and the whole body of men raise a shout, by which means they thought that the enemy were terrified and their own men stimulated.

93 But when our men on the giving of the signal, had run forward with javelins levelled and had observed that the Pompeians were not advancing against them, profiting by the experience they had gained in former battles, they spontaneously checked their speed and halted in about the middle of the space, so that they might not approach the foe with their vigour exhausted; and after a brief interval, again renewing their rapid advance, they discharged their javelins and quickly drew their swords, according to Caesar's directions. Nor indeed did the Pompeians fail to meet the emergency. For they parried the shower of missiles and withstood the attack of the legions without breaking their ranks, and after discharging their javelins had recourse to their swords. At the same time the horse on Pompeius' left wing, according to orders, charged in a body, and the whole multitude of archers poured forth. Our cavalry, failing to withstand their attack, gradually quitted their position and retired. Pompeius' cavalry pressed forward all the more eagerly, and deploying by squadrons began to surround our lines on their exposed flank. Caesar, observing it, gave the signal to his fourth line, which he had composed of six cohorts. These advanced rapidly and with colours flying attacked Pompeius' horse with such fury that not one of them stood his ground, and all, wheeling round, not only quitted the position but forthwith in hurried flight made for the highest hills. When these were dislodged all the archers and slingers, left defenceless, without support, were slain. With the same onslaught the cohorts surrounded the left wing, the Pompeians still fighting and continuing their resistance in their lines, and attacked them in the rear.

94 At the same time Caesar ordered the third line, which had been undisturbed and up to that time had retained its position, to advance. So, as they had come up fresh and vigorous in place of the exhausted troops, while others were attacking in the rear, the Pompeians could not hold their

ground and turned to flight in mass. Nor was Caesar wrong in thinking that the victory would originate with those cohorts which had been posted opposite the cavalry in the fourth line, as he had himself stated in exhorting his troops; for it was by them that the cavalry was first repulsed, by them that the archers and slingers were slaughtered, by them that the Pompeian force was surrounded on the left and the rout first started. But Pompeius, when he saw his cavalry beaten back and that part of his force in which he had most confidence panic-stricken, mistrusting the rest also, left the field and straightway rode off to the camp. To the centurions whom he had placed on duty at the praetorian gate he exclaimed in a loud voice that the troops might hear: "Protect the camp and defend it carefully if anything goes amiss. I am going round the other gates and encouraging the guards of the camp." Having said this, he betook himself to the general's headquarters, mistrusting his fortunes and yet waiting to see the issue.

Source: Julius Caesar, *The Civil Wars*, 3.85, 88–94. Translated by A. G. Prescott. Loeb Classical Library (Cambridge, MA: Harvard University Press, 1914), 317–319, 323–331.

16. Galba, Roman versus Roman, Battle of Mutina

During the winter of 43, Antony had been declared an enemy and outlaw as he attacked Decimus Brutus at Mutina in the province of Cisalpine Gaul. The Senate, led by Cicero, sent the two consuls Hirtius and Pansa north with an army supported by Octavian to defeat Antony. The consuls ran into Antony's force on April 15 at Forum Gallorum, near Mutina. In the ensuing battle Antony was defeated and fled, but both consuls died of their wounds. It was the first Italian battle of the final civil war of the Roman Republic.

This passage comes from a letter written to Cicero by Servius Sulpicius Galba the day after the battle. As becomes clear in the letter, Galba was an officer in the consular army, and this was his eyewitness account of what happened. This letter is one of the few eyewitness accounts like it from the entire Roman Republic. Galba communicates the confusion of a battle in which both sides were veteran Roman soldiers, committed to victory. The way in which cavalry and infantry needed to support each other also emerges in the letter. The use of javelins in such a battle is clear from Galba's description. When he wrote it, no one could have known what would happen next; they just knew that Antony had been defeated soundly and had to withdraw. Galba's version of events carries an immediacy and sense of relief that is often lacking in the histories and commentaries written during the period.

CXXV. (*AD. FAM.* X.30.)
FROM SERVIUS SULPICIUS GALBA AT MUTINA
TO CICERO AT ROME.
April 16, 711 A.V.C. (43 B.C.)

On the 15th of April, the day on which Pansa was expected in the camp of Hirtius, I was in his company at the time, having marched a hundred miles to meet him and thereby hasten his arrival, when Antonius drew out two of his legions, the second and the thirty-fifth, and two cohorts of Guards, one of which was his own, while the other belonged to Silanus, and some of the reserve; and with this force advanced against us, because he imagined that we had only four legions of raw recruits. But Hirtius, in order that we might reach his quarters more safely, had sent us in the night the Martian legion, which I myself used generally to be in command of, and two cohorts of Guards. After Antonius' cavalry had once shown themselves it was impossible to keep either the Martian legion or the Guards in check, and we, since we could not keep them in control, began perforce to follow their lead. Antonius was keeping his main body still at Forum Gallorum, and did not want it to be known that he had any legions; he only showed his cavalry and light squadron. Pansa, seeing that the legion was advancing, however he might resist it, then ordered the two legions of recruits to follow him. After we had crossed a narrow strip between the woods and the marsh we formed in line, twelve cohorts in all—the two legions had not yet come. Suddenly Antonius deployed his forces from the village, and charged without waiting. At first the fighting was such that it could not possibly on either side have been more desperately contested, although the right wing where I was with eight cohorts of the Martian legion, had in the very first onset routed Antonius' thirty-fifth legion, so that it was some [five hundred] yards in advance of the line [and the spot where it had originally been drawn up]. Consequently, on the cavalry making an attempt to surround our wing, I began to draw back and throw the light-armed troops forward as a shield against the Moorish cavalry, lest they should attack our men in the rear. Meanwhile I find that I am entirely surrounded by troops of Antonius, and that Antonius himself is some little distance behind me.

Throwing my shield over my shoulder, I suddenly spurred my horse towards one of the legions of recruits, which was advancing from the camp. On come the Antonians in pursuit; our men are just about to hurl their javelins; so it must have been fate that somehow preserved me, because I was quickly recognised by our friends.

On the Aemilian road itself, where was the cohort of Caesar's Guards, the struggle was long. The wing to the left, which was comparatively weak, and where there were two cohorts of the Martian legion and a cohort of Guards, began to give ground, because they were being surrounded by the cavalry, in which perhaps the chief strength of Antonius lies. After all our lines had effected a retreat I myself began retiring last of all towards the camp. Antonius, who regarded himself as the victor, thought that he could take our camp; when he arrived there he lost many of his men at the place, and yet had no success. Hirtius on hearing of what had occurred took twenty cohorts of veterans, and met Antonius as he was returning to his own quarters; and cutting all his forces to pieces routed them on the same spot where the battle had been fought, at Forum Gallorum. Antonius about ten that night fell back upon his camp near Mutina; Hirtius returned to the camp which had been Pansa's quarters, where he had left the two legions which had been blockaded by Antonius. Thus Antonius has lost the greater portion of his veteran troops; that however could not be without some sacrifice of our own cohorts of the Guards and of the Martian legion. We have carried off from Antonius two legionary eagles and sixty standards. The result is in our favour.

The Camp, April 16.

Source: Marcus Tullius Cicero, *The Life and Letters of Marcus Tullius Cicero, Being a New Translation of the Letters Included in Mr. Watson's Selection.* Translated by Rev. G. E. Jeans (London: Macmillan, 1880), 399–401.

17. Appian, An End of Discipline during Civil War

Appian, a Roman Greek from Alexandria in the second century CE, wrote a history of the last century of the Roman Republic. Generally, his account reflects the accepted version of events as understood in his own day. He is important for his clear analysis and his use of some now-lost sources. In his analysis of the causes of the civil wars, he often blamed the soldiers and the politicians for what happened, a common elite view. The passage here draws attention to the various means that earlier leaders had used to control the soldiers and maintain discipline as well as how those tools had been ignored or undermined by the leaders of the Second Triumvirate.

17 Let these two instances out of many serve as examples of the prevailing insubordination. The cause was that the generals, for the most part, as is usually the case in civil wars, were not regularly chosen; that their armies were not drawn from the enrolment according to the custom of the fathers, nor for the benefit of their country; that they did not serve the public so much as they did the individuals who brought them together; and that they served these not by the force of law, but by reason of private promises; not against the common enemy, but against private foes; not against foreigners, but against fellow-citizens, their equals in rank. All these things impaired military discipline, and the soldiers thought that they were not so much serving in the army as lending assistance, by their own favour and judgment, to leaders who needed them for their own personal ends. Desertion, which had formerly been unpardonable, was now actually rewarded with gifts, and whole armies resorted to it, including some illustrious men, who did not consider it desertion to change to a like cause, for all parties were alike, since neither of them could be distinguished as battling against the common enemy of the Roman people. The common pretence of the generals that they were all striving for the good of the country made desertion easy in the thought that one could serve his country in any party. Understanding these facts the generals tolerated this behaviour, for they knew that their authority over their armies depended on donatives rather than on law.

Source: Appian, *Civil Wars,* 5.17. Translated by Horace White. Loeb Classical Library (London: Macmillan, 1913), 405–407.

Glossary

adnomen—A name added behind the original two or three name combination, usually for an honor, as in Publius Cornelius Scipio <u>Africanus</u>. Sometimes it was a nickname, as in Fabius Verrucosus Maximus <u>Cunctator</u>, that stayed with the person.

agger—Mound or earthwork, part of a fort.

auxilia—Military units from Roman allies outside Italy. These replaced *socii* completely after the Social War.

cognomen—The usual third name in a Roman's three names, as in Publius Cornelius <u>Scipio</u>. The name indicated the branch of his gens or clan. Not everyone had a cognomen, as in Gnaeus Pompeius.

coins—Romans adopted minting coins from the Greeks, probably in the fourth century, minting in silver and bronze, but minting was extremely irregular until the Second Punic War, when the standard silver coin, the denarius, emerged alongside the standard bronze fraction, the as. In the same currency reform, fractions included smaller silver coins, most of which were struck irregularly and on irregular standards. The denarius became the common silver coin in Rome after 211 BCE. One denarius originally was worth 10 asses, but after the coin reform of the 120s a denarius equaled 4 sesterces and 16 asses. Twenty-five denarii equaled one gold aureus. Sesterces and aurei were not regularly minted during the Roman Republic. The commission of moneyers, lesser magistrates, were in charge of minting coins. These men were in charge of production and choosing the coin types, so they often commemorated their family or patrons. Flamininus was the first living Roman whose bust appeared on a Greek coin, and Caesar's bust was the first to appear on a Roman coin. The connection between the adoption of coins and the need to pay armies and finance roads remains a topic of debate.

contio—An assembly to hear a speech. When commanders wished to address their men they would summon them to a *contio* unless they were about to enter battle.

cuirass—Metal breastplate that covered the entire torso. The cuirass was generally worn only by officers.

exempla—These were an important part of the history that Romans wrote. They are stories of individuals or specific deeds that provide an example of positive or negative behavior. The stories were selected or tweaked to conform to the tastes of the period in which they were written.

greaves—Bronze shin guards worn to protect a soldier's lower leg from debilitating injury in battle.

hastati—The first line in a manipular/Polybian legion. This line was made up of men in the lower 20s armed with sword, shield, and two *pila*.

imperator—An honorary title voted for a commander by his troops. The title carried no additional powers, only status.

lictors—These men were attendants on magistrates who held imperium. They carried on their shoulder fasces—a bundle of rods wrapped around a ax—as symbols of the magistrate's power. They walked before the magistrate in single file both as a mark of distinction and as status and protection. In a confrontation they would untie the bundle and use the rods as necessary. The magistrate with the most lictors would have precedence in any encounter between two groups of lictors. The lictors participated in triumphs and may have accompanied the magistrate when he left Rome, but not into battle.

lorica—Roman body armor that covered a soldier's torso. The type used during the Republic was *lorica hamata* (ring mail). Originally too expensive for any but the most wealthy soldiers, the price of *hamata* came down with equipment standardization. It seems to have been common among legionaries by the time of Caesar's Gallic Wars.

nomen— The middle name in a typical Roman's three names, as in Publius Cornelius Scipio. The nomen, which everyone had, indicated a person's clan. When a young man was adopted into another family he might take the name of his adoptive father and his original nomen to distinguish his original family line, as in Publius Cornelius Scipio Aemilianus or Gaius Julius Caesar Octavianus.

phalanx—The formation employed by Macedonian armies. Soldiers armed with 21-foot spears stood in close formation with the first five rows, lowering their spears to face forward. The soldiers in the phalanx, phalangites, wore limited body armor and carried a small shield strapped to their shoulder. They were an extremely effective formation on suitable terrain, but the strength of the phalanx depended on maintaining its cohesion, so it was often supported by other kinds of troops. The phalanx was organized by Philip II of Macedon and became the dominant military formation in the Hellenistic world.

pilum (**pl.** *pila*)—The heavy javelin with a wooden shaft and long metal point carried in legions and thrown before battle.

praemia—Cash bonus paid to soldiers. The first time that *praemia* was regularly paid was during the Second Triumvirate.

praetorium—The commander's headquarters in a military camp or fort, always in the center.

principes—The second line in a manipular/Polybian legion. This line included men in their upper 20s or early 30s. They were armed the same as the *hastati*.

prorogue—When the Senate extended a magistrate's term so that he could govern a province or take on another specific task, it was called prorogue. The extension usually required the magistrate to continue having the power of imperium, so the magistrates most commonly prorogued were consuls (proconsuls) and praetors (propraetors). These were common magistracies after the First Punic War. It was not unheard of for a quaestor to be extended as a proquaestor.

quadrireme/quinquireme—Ships larger than the trireme and probably invented by Phoenicians in the fourth century BCE. Sometimes called fours and fives to distinguish them from other ship sizes. It remains unclear how the oars and men were arranged, but the ships were larger, permitting more marines and cargo.

sortition—The process of drawing random lots to determine who would be selected.

suffect consul—A replacement consul (or any other magistrate). Suffect consuls were usually appointed by the Senate.

talent—A weight of precious metal that varied between cultures. The Roman talent weighed 71 pounds, whereas the Greek talent weighed 57 pounds. The talent is difficult to quantify, since the weight could apply to silver or gold and thus have different values. In the fifth century BCE, a talent of silver was the cost of equipping and maintaining an Athenian trireme for a month. The Romans typically used it for indemnities, which were usually measured in talents rather than coins. For example, Carthage paid an indemnity of 10,000 talents gold after the Second Punic War.

triarii—The third line in a manipular/Polybian legion. Made up of the oldest soldiers armed with a thrusting spear, a sword, and a shield.

Tribal Assembly—The popular assembly in Rome that voted based on the 35 tribes. Each tribe had one vote taken in random order so that the wealthy did not dominate this assembly the same way as the Comitia Centuriata. The Tribal Assembly had no military role but did pass laws, some of which could affect military practices. The assembly elected quaestors, aediles, and plebeian tribunes.

velites—The skirmishers in the manipular or Polybian legion. This line included the youngest men in the legion. They were armed with light round shields, a sword, and multiple light javelins.

Chronology

509 BCE	Traditional date for the revolt in Rome resulting in the creation of the Roman Republic.
508	Rome and Carthage conclude a treaty. Rome agrees not to trade west of Carthage, while Carthage agrees not to intervene in Latin territory.
507	Traditionally, Lars Porsenna, king of Etruscan Clusium, marches on Rome and besieges it. This event is possibly connected with the actual expulsion of the Tarquini. The Etruscans probably take Rome but remain there for only a brief time.
504	Traditionally, Rome and its Latin allies defeat Lars Porsenna in the Battle of Aricia.
499 OR 496	According to Roman tradition, a Roman army defeats the Latins in the Battle of Lake Regillus, resulting in a treaty of equality between the two.
483–474	First war with Veii. Rome and Veii clash over control of trade routes, the genuine beginning of the Etruscan Wars. The war ends in a draw and a 40-year treaty.
474	Battle of Cumae. The battle occurs in the Bay of Naples between Carthage and Hiero I of Syracuse allied with Cumae and effectively ends Etruscan influence in central Italy.
437–396	Second war with Veii. Rome declares war after the king of Veii murders Roman ambassadors. Fidenae fell in 435,

	and the siege of Veii begins in earnest the following year. Veii falls by 396 and is absorbed into Roman territory
390	The Gauls (Celts) move down the Po Valley from the north, laying waste to much of the territory as they proceed. They move on Rome itself, taking the entire city and sacking it except for the citadel on the Capitoline Hill. Marcus Furius Camillus secures the departure of the Gauls by giving them substantial tribute.
389–343	Recovering from the sack of their city by the Gauls, the Romans rapidly extend their influence throughout Latium and southern Etruria. Rome defeats the Aequians and Volsci in battle and forms the conquered cities into a confederation under its leadership.
367	New invasion by the Gauls. This time Camillus, again made Roman dictator, drives the Gauls from Rome.
358–351	New Etruscan war between Rome and the Etruscan city of Tarquinii, which was later supported by the Etruscan communities of Falerii and Caere.
347	Carthage and Rome conclude a treaty whereby Rome agrees to limit its trade to Italy, while Carthage agrees to keep out of Italy completely.
343–341	First Samnite War. The cities of Campania request Roman assistance against the Samnite hill tribes. The campaign ends with Rome establishing a protoprotectorate over Campania.
341–338	The cities of Latium, its colonies, and Campania rebel against Rome in the Latin War. Rome treats the defeated Latins generously, thereby ensuring future Latin loyalty.
327–304	The Second Samnite War is waged by Rome against Samnites in the central Apennines region.
321	The Samnites inflict a major military defeat on Rome in the Battle of the Caudine Forks.
316	The Romans lose to the Samnites at Lautulae.
315	The Romans defeat the Samnites in the Battle of Ciuna.
311	Etruscan cities attack the Roman colony at Sutrium in formerly Etruscan territory. Rome responds aggressively, forcing Perusia, Cortona, and Arretium to sign treaties the same year.

308	The Romans force the Etruscan city of Volsinii to make peace. Umbrians, Picentini, and Marsians of the southern Apennines all join the war on the side of the Samnites against Rome.
306	Carthage and Rome agree to limit their respective trading areas in the Mediterranean.
304	Roman consuls bring the Second Samnite War to a successful conclusion when all of Rome's Samnite enemies are forced to conclude peace.
298–290	Third Samnite War between Rome and the Samnites. An early Samnite military success in the Battle of Camerinum leads the Etruscans, followed by the Gauls and Umbrians, to join the fighting against Rome.
295	In the decisive Battle of Sentinum, Roman commanders Fabius Rullianus and Publius Decius Mus defeat a combined army of Etruscans, Gauls, and Samnites. Although their allies conclude peace as a result of this battle, the Samnites continue the struggle.
293	The Romans win a crushing victory over the Samnites in the Battle of Aquilonia. Rome makes them allies rather than subjects.
284	Etruscans and Gauls destroy a Roman army under Lucius Caecillus at Arretium.
283	Gaul/Etruscan invasion. Roman commander P. Cornelius Dolabella defeats a combined Gaul and Etruscan invasion at Lake Vadimo, north of Rome.
282	Rome brings to an end the revolt of the Etruscans and Gauls by defeating the Etruscans at Populonia.
281–280	Tarentum hires King Pyrrhus of Epirus to defend them against Rome.
280	Battle of Heraclea. Pyrrhus defeats a Roman army.
279	Pyrrhus of Epirus campaigns in Italy and attracts numerous supporters. The two armies meet near Ausculum, north of Heraclea.
278–276	Pyrrhus travels to Syracuse.
277	Carthage and Rome conclude an alliance against Pyrrhus.
275	Pyrrhus of Epirus returns to Italy, confronting the Romans in battle at Maleventum. A Roman army wins a decisive

victory over Pyrrhus, forcing him to depart. The Romans take Tarentum that same year.

273   Conquest of the Etruscan city of Caere and the end of the Etruscan Wars.

272–265   Rome consolidates its hold over the Greek city-states of southern Italy.

270   Rome takes Rhegium in southern Italy.

269   Rome defeats a Samnite rebellion to exercise unchallenged control of Italy south of the Arno River.

264   Effective beginning of the First Punic War when the Mamertines appeal for assistance to Carthage and Rome. The Carthaginians ally with Hiero II of Syracuse and besiege Messena. Rome declares war on Syracuse and drives them away. The siege of Syracuse begins.

263   Hiero II of Syracuse switches sides and allies with Rome against Carthage.

262–261   The Romans besiege the Carthaginian ally of Acragas. The Romans defeat a Carthaginian relief force under Hanno, but Hannibal Gisco and his army escape the city. Rome controls most of Sicily.

260   Battle of the Lipara Islands in which the Carthaginians defeat a Roman fleet.

A Roman commander wins a decisive naval victory over the Carthaginians in the Battle of Mylae.

256   Romans dispatch an expeditionary force from Sicily to Africa, winning a naval victory at Cape Economus before landing.

A Roman land force invades North Africa, winning a decisive victory over the Carthaginians in the Battle of Adys. Carthage hires the Spartan mercenary Xanthippus and his army.

255   Xanthippus reorganizes and retrains the Carthaginian Army and takes the field successfully against the Roman Army in the Battle of Tunis.

Roman ships recover the remaining Roman land forces after Tunis and sail for home. In a storm off Camarina, some 284 of 364 Roman ships are lost with all aboard, representing about 15 percent of all the available Roman adult manpower of fighting age. It takes two years to recover.

254   Following the naval disaster off Camarina the prior year, Carthage is able to reinforce its strongholds in Sicily and retake Acragas.

251   In the Battle of Panormus, Metellus defeats Hasdrubal in northwest Sicily.

249   A Roman fleet off Drepana is lost to a Carthaginian fleet under Adherbal.

247–242   Carthaginian commander Hamilcar Barca campaigns in western Sicily and effectively employs guerrilla tactics.

242   Reconstituting its sea power, Rome sends an expeditionary force to western Sicily. Gaius Lutatius Catulus captures the Carthaginian strongholds of Lilybaeum and Drepanum.

241   The Battle of the Aegates Islands leads to the end of the First Punic War after a Roman fleet wins a decisive victory over the Carthaginians. Rome gets Sicily in the treaty. The Revolt of Falerii is crushed the same year, ending the last Etruscan revolt.

238   Unpaid Carthaginian mercenaries revolt, thus beginning the Truceless War. Rome seizes the island of Sardinia from Carthage.

237   Rome occupies the island of Corsica.

235   For the first time in recorded history, the doors of the Temple of Juno, open when Rome is at war, are shut.

229–228   Greek states request Roman assistance in ending Illyrian piracy in the Adriatic and Ionian Seas, but when its ambassadors are murdered, Rome declares war.

228   Hasdrubal concludes the Ebro River Treaty with Rome, recognizing Carthaginian control of all Iberia south of the Ebro River.

225–222   A large force of Gauls invades central Italy, forcing Rome to mobilize. The Gauls are victorious in the Battle of Faesulae.

224	Roman armies win a victory over the Gauls in the Battle of Telamon.
222	At Clastidium, a Roman army defeats the remnants of the Gallic force.
219	Hannibal lays siege to Saguntum. Rome declares war. King Scerdilaidas of Illyria provokes a second Roman war against the Illyrians.
218	Hannibal leads his army from Spain into the Po Valley of northern Italy by way of the Alps. The battles at the Ticinus River and later at the Trebia River close the year.
217	After Rome loses a large battle at Lake Trasimene, the Senate appoints Quintus Fabius Maximus as dictator. Fabius adopts the strategy of avoiding direct battle in favor of harassing tactics. In the Battle of Geronium, Fabius rescues his colleague from a rout. Publius Scipio joins his brother Gnaeus in Spain to disrupt Carthaginian efforts to reinforce Hannibal.
216	Battle of Cannae (August 2). Rome assembles a large force and gives command of it to two new consuls, whom the Senate orders to combine their forces to defeat Hannibal once and for all. The troops first undergo a period of training, but by late summer they move to near Hannibal's base at Cannae in northern Apulia on the Adriatic coast. The two consuls alternate command daily, and on August 2 Varro, who then has the command, orders both armies to engage the Carthaginians. Cannae is a disaster for Rome, and it says much for the Roman state that it is able to recover from the defeat.
	Capua, the second-largest Italian city, and some other states defect. Although some Carthaginian reinforcements arrive at the end of the year, Hannibal receives little support. Marcellus repulses Hannibal's effort to take Nola in the first battle for that city in Campania.
	A Roman army is destroyed in an ambush by the Boii tribe in southern Gaul.
	The two Scipio brothers, Publius and Gnaeus, defeat Hasdrubal near the Ebro River.
215	Using Nola as a base of operations, Marcellus raids Hannibal's allies. Hannibal's attack fails when Marcellus

launches a counterattack. The bloody Second Battle of Nola ends in a draw. Hannibal then takes Casilinum, and Carthaginian reinforcements arrive at Lochi.

214

The Romans retake Casilinum. Hanno Barca loses to Tiberius Gracchus at Beneventum. Hannibal attacks Nola for a third time.

The First Macedonian War begins when Rome declares war on King Philip V of Macedon because he signed a treaty with Hannibal.

Syracuse allies with Carthage, and Marcus Claudius Marcellus arrives from Italy to begin Roman operations there.

213

Marcellus seizes Leontini and then commences siege operations against Syracuse, probably in the spring of 213. Epicydes flees Syracuse at the end of the year.

Syphax, the king of Numidia, revolts against Carthage, but Hasdrubal returns to North Africa and joins with Numidian prince Massinissa to defeat Syphax. Hannibal Barca concentrates on besieging Tarentum, while his brother Hanno defeats Roman commander Tiberius Gracchus at Bruttium.

212

Roman forces take the remainder of Syracuse, sacking it. Their victory at Syracuse solidifies Roman control over the island.

Hannibal captures Tarentum, and Rome begins the siege of Capua, which is already short of food.

Hasdrubal returns to Spain with reinforcements, including Massinissa's cavalry. Meanwhile, the Scipios recapture Saguntum in Spain.

Hannibal defends Capua and defeats the Romans in a battle outside the city. Hannibal's pursuit leads to his victories over two more Roman forces at Silarus and Herdonia. The consul, Flaccus, defeats Hanno at Beneventum.

211

Hasdrubal Barca, reinforced from Carthage, defeats Publius and Gnaeus Scipio in two separate battles in the Upper Baetis Valley. Both brothers are killed. These victories again give Carthage control of all of Spain south of the Ebro River.

In the Second Battle of Capua, Roman forces complete the investment of Capua. Following an appeal from Capua,

Hannibal marches north with 30,000 men and reaches the Roman lines but fails to relieve the city. Hoping to draw the Romans away and raise the siege of Capua, Hannibal marches on Rome. After a feint turns back, Capua still surrenders to Rome and is punished severely as an example.

210   Rome goes on the offensive against Hannibal, attempting to destroy his bases in southern Italy. Hannibal, however, continues to win victories, defeating a Roman army in the Second Battle of Herdonia and then another force in the Battle of Numistro.

Scipio Africanus establishes Roman control in Spain north of the Ebro River.

209   Africanus makes a rapid march against New Carthage, blockading it from the sea and taking it by assault.

Hannibal is victorious over Marcellus at Asculum, but the battle is indecisive strategically. Meanwhile, Fabius captures Tarentum.

208   Marcellus is killed in an ambush.

Africanus defeats Hasdrubal in the Battle of Baecula but does not stop him from marching to reinforce Hannibal. Marching to Gaul, Hasdrubal winters his army there, recruiting and training reinforcements.

207   Hasdrubal crosses the Alps via the Cenis Pass and arrives in the Po Valley of northern Italy in April 207. He initiates a siege of Placentia to draw the Roman armies north but then proceeds south to Fanum Fortunae. Nero defeats Hannibal at Grumentum. Leaving a force to keep watch on Hannibal, Nero marches north, linking with the Roman force at Fanum Fortunae. The combined Roman armies defeat Hasdrubal at the Metaurus River. This victory means the end of reinforcements for Hannibal.

206   Battle of Ilipa. Africanus outmaneuvers and double envelops a Carthaginian force at Ilipa. This decisive victory gives Rome control of all of Spain.

206–204   Roman forces pin down Hannibal in Bruttium. The fighting mostly consists of skirmishes.

205	Mago Barca lands at Genoum and marches into Gallic territory to stir up a revolt.
	The First Macedonian War ends after extended maneuvering accomplishes little. Philip signs a peace treaty.
204	Scipio Africanus invades North Africa and invests Utica but breaks off the siege after a large Carthaginian force under Hasdrubal Gisco and Syphax arrives. Scipio withdraws to a fortified camp on the coast, and both sides go into winter quarters.
203	Mago is defeated by the Roman allies at the Battle of Insubria.
	Africanus mounts a night attack on the Carthaginian and Numidian camps, destroying the two armies and burning the camps. He then renews the siege of Utica. Africanus later in the same year defeats a new Carthaginian army in the Battle of the Great Plains (Battle of Bagbrades), capturing Syphax. As a result, Carthage finally sues for peace with Rome, at the same time recalling Hannibal and Mago from Italy. Hannibal returns, but Mago dies in transit from wounds.
202	Carthage breaks the terms of the peace by seizing Roman supply ships scattered in a great storm. The final battle takes place in 202, probably in October, although its exact location remains in dispute. This time Scipio holds the upper hand. Just before the battle, Numidian king Masimissa joins the Romans, a fact unknown to Hannibal. Africanus wins a decisive victory. Hannibal escapes to Hadrumetum. Carthage signs a peace treaty.
202–191	Rome reconquers Cisalpine Gaul.
200	Roman forces are victorious against Gauls in the Battle of Cremona.
	Rome declares the Second Macedonian War against Philip V of Macedon an appeal for assistance by a number of Greek city-states, including Athens.
198	In the Battle of the Aous, Roman forces drive Macedonian forces from their strong defensive positions. Meanwhile, Roman diplomatic efforts undermine Philip's position in Greece.

197	Macedonian forces moving south in Thessaly under Philip V and Roman forces moving north unexpectedly collide at Cynoscephalae. The battle ends in overwhelming victory for the Romans.
	Indigenous Spanish tribes revolt against Rome, thus initiating the Spanish Wars.
196	Philip gives up all claim to Greece as well as his territories in Thrace, Asia Minor, and the Aegean.
195	Cato temporarily puts down a revolt in Iberia.
	After assisting the Achaean League against Sparta in the Battle of Gythium, Rome declares Greece to be independent and removes its troops from there.
194	Rome wins in Cisalpine Gaul at the Battle of Mutina.
191	Antiochus III of the Seleucid kingdom, invited by the Aetolian League, invades Greece. Rome declares the Syrian War. The Romans defeat Antiochus at Thermopylae.
190	The Romans win two naval battles. In the first, a Roman fleet assisted by Rhodes defeats a Syrian fleet under Hannibal at Eurymedon. It is Hannibal's only naval battle. In the second battle, at Myonnessus, Lucius defeats another Syrian fleet. Rome then invades Asia Minor to chastise Antiochus.
189	Celts of Galatia invade Pergamum in western Asia Minor. Gaius Manlius Volso leads a Roman army and assists Eumenes II in defeating the Celts.
	The Battle of Magnesia proves to be the turning point in the Syrian War. The Romans take control of almost all of western Asia Minor.
188	Under the peace terms, Antiochus III yields his possessions in Greece and in Anatolia west of the Taurus Mountains. Rome keeps only the islands of Cephalonia and Zacynthus, dividing the rest among its allies, Rhodes and Pergamum.
172	The Third Macedonian War between Rome and Macedon begins when King Perseus of Macedon seeks to expand influence. The Roman allies Eumenes II of Pergamum and the Achaean League request support.

171	Perseus defeats Rome in the Battle of Callicinus near Larissa.
171–168	Antiochus IV twice successfully invades Egypt (171–170 and 168). Rome warns Antiochus to withdraw from Egypt, and he complies.
170	Perseus defeats a second Roman legion in Thessaly.
169	Perseus defeats a third Roman invasion.
168	Rome sends reinforcements to Greece under Paullus, who restores discipline among the Roman forces in Greece and then takes the offensive against Perseus. In June 168 after maneuvering, the Roman force faces off against Perseus at Pydna. Paullus wins a total victory, ending the Third Macedonian War. Rome disarms the Macedonians, chasing down or sending to Italy all of those who have aided Perseus.
167	Macedon is split into four separate republics, all under Roman protection. Rome exercises control over Greece, establishes a protectorate over Anatolia, and reduces the power of Pergamum, as that state is no longer required as a counter to Macedon and Syria.
153	The Lusitanian and Celtiberian Wars begin in Spain.
152	The Fourth Macedonian War begins due to revolts. A pretender to the former throne, Andriscus, declares himself king and temporarily unites Macedon.
151	Long-standing disputes between Carthage and Massinissa of Numidia lead to war between the two states. Carthage declares war without permission from Rome and loses to Numidia at the Battle of Oroscopa.
149	Rome declares war against Carthage for breaking its treaty. The Roman Senate dispatches a force to Utica, beginning the war.
148	Rome defeats Andriscus and reestablishes peace before annexing the region as a province.
147	Scipio Aemilianus is sent to Africa to complete the siege of Carthage and rescue trapped Roman forces.
146	Scipio completes the siege. His army sacks the city, selling all survivors into slavery and razing the city. Spreading salt

on the ground is a ritual killing of the site. Africa now becomes a Roman province.

The Achaian League attacks Sparta, which is under Roman protection. Mummius defeats the Achaean League forces, sacking and razing Corinth. Rome makes Achaia part of the province of Macedonia.

144	Rome defeats the revolt of the Celtiberians.
139	A traitor assassinates the Lusitanian leader Viriathus. The revolt collapses, and the Lusitanians make peace.
137–133	Numantia, a city on the upper Durius River, becomes the center of a renewed effort by the Celtiberians to secure independence from Rome.
135–132	A slave uprising in Sicily grows into the First Servile War.
134	Rome gives command in Spain to Scipio Aemilianus. He defeats the Celtiberians and captures Numantia, ending the war in 133.
133	Aemilianus captures the Celtiberian stronghold at Numantia, ending the Spanish Wars.
132	The First Slave War ends after a Roman victory. Servile prisoners are crucified.
129	Willed to Rome by Attalus III on his death in 133, Pergamum becomes the Roman province of Asia.
125–121	Forces under Flaccus expand Rome's control into Transalpine Gaul.
124	Angered over the failure to extend citizenship to it and taking advantage of continuing unrest in Rome, Fregellae in Latium, the second-largest city in Italy, revolts against Rome. The Romans take and raze the city.
121	Roman forces allied with the Aedui tribe defeat the Arverni and the Allobroges. Rome organizes this territory as the province of Transalpine Gaul. Gallia Narbonensis, with Massilia as its key city, becomes a Roman province.
119	Jugurtha defeats Adherbal in a war over rule of Numidia. Rome intervenes, dividing Numidia between the two major claimants.
118–117	Roman armies campaign in Dalmatia.

113	The Cimbri, a Germanic tribe, reaches the Carnic Alps and defeats a Roman army in the Drava Valley and repulses subsequent Roman forays.
112	Rome declares war on Jugurtha. After Jugurtha wins a few minor military successes, a short truce is arranged in 111.
110	A Roman commander surrenders to Jugurtha, and war begins again.
109	The Cimbri and Teutones tribes arrive in southern Gaul and defeat a Roman army.
	Caecilius Metellus takes command against Jurgurtha and begins by training and reorganizing Roman forces in North Africa.
108	Rome defeats Jugurtha in the Battle of the Muthul, and Jugurtha pursues guerrilla war.
107	Gaius Marius is elected consul and accepts volunteers and proletarians into his army. He trains his army and captures Capsa.
106	Sulla arranges for Bochus, an African ally, to hand over Jugurtha, ending the war.
105	The Cimbri and Teutones defeat two consular army tribes in the Battle of Arausio.
104	The Cimbri and Teutones move across southern Gaul toward northern Spain but are rebuffed by the Celtiberians at the Pyrenees passes.
	Marius, reelected consul for the war against the Germanic tribes, initiates military reforms. At first avoiding pitched battle with the barbarians, he trains his forces and builds up his logistical support.
	The Second Servile War begins in Sicily.
102	When the Teutones move toward the Alpine passes, Marius pursues and defeats them in the ensuing Battle of Aquae Sextae. The Cimbri forces cross the Alps into northern Italy by way of the Brenner Pass, defeat a Roman army in the Adige Valley, and then winter in the Po Valley. Meanwhile, Marius hurries from Gaul with his legions to join his own forces with those under Catulus.

101	Roman forces in the region meet and destroy the Cimbri forces in the Battle of Vercellae. Prisoners are sold into slavery.
CA. **100**	Roman forces put down the Second Slave War in Sicily. Unclaimed survivors are crucified or sent to become gladiators.
93–92	A war takes place between Rome and Tigranes of Armenia, who invades the Roman province of Cappadocia in eastern Anatolia. Sulla, praetor of the Roman province of Asia, turns back Tigranes without assistance.
91	The Social War between Rome and most of its Italian allies begins due to Rome's refusal to share full citizenship. The rebels establish a new Italian republic at Corfinium and are at first successful militarily.
90	Rome offers full citizenship to any former ally that will stop fighting. Most Italians accept peace.
89	Italian holdouts win big at the Battle of Fucine Lake but lose to Rome in the Battle of Asculum. Sulla captures Pompeii.
88	The First Mithradatic War occurs between Rome and Mithradates VI of Pontus. Mithradates conquers Bithynia and Cappadocia and invades Asia, massacring Roman citizens. He then invades Greece.
	Sulla marches on Rome and executes Marius' supporters, initiating Civil War I. He then departs for Greece.
87	Cinna marches on Rome with Marius and supporters. They capture Rome and execute Sullan supporters. Cinna is elected consul for 86 with Marius.
	Sulla arrives in Greece and begins a siege of Athens and Piraeus while watching for Mithradates' stalled army in Thrace.
86	Sulla takes Athens and then Piraeus by storm. He moves into central Greece, defeating Archelaus' much larger forces at Chaeronea and Orchomenos.
85	Lucullus defeats a Mithradatic fleet in the Battle of Tenedos. Fimbria takes command of Flaccus' army and supports Sulla's operation.

85–84	Sulla billets his army in Asia. Leaving some forces in Asia under Lucullus, Sulla returns to Rome with the remainder.
83	Sulla lands with his legions at Brundisium. After defeating Marian troops at Mount Tifata near Capua, he spends the winter at Capua. Sulla sends Metellus and Pompey into Picenum.
83–82	The Second Mithradatic War is triggered as the result of an accidental clash between the forces of Mithradates VI and the Roman governor of Asia.
82	Sulla and his supporters maneuver around Italy, defeating Marian supporters. Sulla and Crassus capture Rome after the battle at the Colline Gate. The civil war ends except for mopping-up operations.
81	Sulla sends Pompey to Sicily and then on to Africa to crush the remaining Marian forces.
80–72	Sertorius, a Marian supporter, defeats the Roman governor of Nearer Spain in the Battle of the Baetis River in 80. Sullan commanders fight unsuccessfully against Sertorius until 72.
79–68	Rome carries out a series of antipirate naval operations in the Mediterranean but achieves limited success.
78	Tigranes of Armenia invades Roman Cappadocia, annexing it and consolidating his rule in the years immediately thereafter.
78–77	Marcus Aemilius Lepidus revolts against Sullan reforms. Defeated in battle, Lepidus flees with his supporters to Etruria, where Pompey destroys them in 77.
75	Nicomedes III of Bithynia wills his kingdom to Rome on his death. Roman troops occupy Bithynia.
74	Mithradates VI declares war on Rome (the Third Mithradatic War) and invades Cappadocia, Bithynia, and Paphlagonia. Mithradates defeats Cotta outside Chalcedon, driving his army back into the city and winning a battle at sea.
	Lucullus defeats Mithradates' commander near Brusa. Trapped between the two Roman armies, Mithradates

escapes by sea while his army cuts its way out. Lucullus pursues Mithradates into his home territory of Pontus.

73–72   Slaves led by Spartacus revolt against Rome. Establishing a base near Mount Vesuvius, they terrorize much of southern Italy. Defeating Roman forces sent against him, Spartacus' slave army ranges over Campania and in 72 over much of Italy.

72   Sertorius is assassinated by his chief subordinate Perperna, who then loses to Pompey, ending the last mopping-up campaign of the first civil war.

72–71   Lucullus utterly defeats Mithradates in the Battle of Cabira and completely conquers Pontus.

71   Mithradates flees to Armenia, ruled by his son-in-law and ally Tigranes.

Crassus defeats Spartacus in Lucania. Pompey crushes fugitives.

69   Lucullus invades Armenia, winning at Tigranocerta and Nisibis.

68   Advancing farther into Armenia, Lucullus wins at Artaxata, but his troops refuse to proceed farther. Mithradates invades Pontus. Lucullus is unpopular in Rome.

67   Mithradates wins at Zela. Rome calls for Lucullus' replacement. Pompey receives a three-year command against pirates but wins after three months. The Senate transfers Pompey's assignment to command against Mithradates.

66   Pompey utterly defeats Mithradates in the Battle of the Lycus and makes a deal with Parthia to invade Armenia. Mithradates escapes to the Crimea and there commits suicide in 63.

65   Tigranes of Armenia is captured by Parthia and forced to surrender all territory taken from Rome, ending the Mithradatic Wars.

65–62   Pompey remains in the east "settling affairs." He annexes Syria in 64 and captures Jerusalem in 63, adding Palestine to the empire.

63	Lucius Sergius Catilina (Catiline) incites a revolt in Rome and raises an army in Etruria.
62	Pompey returns to Italy, disbanding his army. Catiline is defeated and killed near Pistoria in January 62.
61–60	As praetor, Caesar suppresses an uprising in Spain and settles Lusitania.
60	Returning to Rome, Caesar forms the First Triumvirate with Pompey and Crassus.
58	Caesar takes up appointment as governor of Gaul. He defeats the Helvetii at the Battle of the Arar and the Battle of Bibracte. Caesar helps his Gallic allies by defeating Ariovistus at Vesontio.
57	Caesar campaigns against the Belgae, invading their territory. He wins a skirmish at Aisne and wins when attacked by the Nervii at the Sambre River. Caesar advances into Aduatuci territory and after a brief setback conquers them too.
56	After the Veneti tribe of Armorica seizes several ambassadors, Caesar moves against western Gaul. Decimus Brutus constructs ships and wins at the Battle of Morbihan Bay. Trebonius campaigns successfully in Normandy, while Crassus defeats the tribes in southern and southwestern Gaul. Afterward Caesar disperses the Morini and the Meapii. By the end of the campaign, he appears to have brought all of Gaul under Roman rule.
55	German tribes of the Usipetes and Tenceteri cross the Rhine into Gaul, so Caesar marches to the Meuse and mounts a preemptive strike during the negotiations. His men then swiftly bridge the Rhine so that Caesar can chastise several tribes. He then withdraws, destroying the bridge after him.
	Caesar invades Britain with two legions. Moving inland, he remains in Britain for three weeks before extracting his forces and returning to Gaul.
54	Crassus, governor of Syria, campaigns against Parthia, moving to the Euphrates and capturing several towns, but he has to return to Syria for cash and supplies.

Caesar returns to Britain, moving inland and crossing the Thames. Receiving nominal submission of the Britons, he returns to Gaul. During the winter, the Eburones tribe attacks the winter camp of Sabinus and Cotta and then ambushes them as they march away, annihilating the Roman units. Revolt spreads quickly. The Nervii try the same trick against another camp, but the commander is less gullible.

53   Caesar marches out and rescues the besieged winter quarters, defeating a large Belgae force in the process. Once able to do so, Caesar goes on the offense, subduing the Belgae and crushing the Eburones. Caesar again bridges the Rhine, carries out a raid, and withdraws. By the end of the summer he again seems to be master of northern Gaul, but southern Gaul remains rebellious.

Crassus moves against Parthia but is defeated and dies in the Battle of Carrhae. Cassius survives and defends Syria against Parthian cavalry raids.

52   Vercingetorix leads a revolt and recruits a large army in the south. Caesar captures Avaricum in March and moves south against the Arverni capital of Gergovia, which he fails to capture. After much maneuvering, Vercingetorix occupies Alesia, and Caesar invests it with walls of contravallation and circumvallation. A vast Gallic relief force besieges the besiegers but is unable to break through. Vercingetorix surrenders in October. The Gallic defeat at Alesia effectively ends the revolt.

51   Caesar impresses upon the Gauls the futility of further resistance, crushing the remaining pockets of revolt.

Parthia invades Syria.

49   Caesar crosses the Rubicon with his army into Italy proper, triggering civil war. Pompey and many senators quickly abandon Rome and eventually raise an army in Greece. Before he can march against Pompey, Caesar defeats a Pompeian army in Spain at Ilerda in August. Caesar captures Massilia on his return to Brundisium.

After capturing Sardinia and Sicily, Curio sails for North Africa. Though initially triumphant near Utica, he is subsequently defeated.

48   Caesar crosses the Adriatic and invests Pompey near
            Dyracchium after Antony arrives. Pompey breaks the
            siege and forces Caesar to withdraw. Moving into Thessaly,
            Caesar camps at Pharsalus, and Pompey follows. He ac-
            cepts battle on August 9, but Caesar's veterans and flexi-
            ble lines prove superior. Pompey loses decisively and flees
            to Egypt, where he is murdered by Ptolemy XII.

            Caesar, following Pompey, becomes embroiled in a local
            war. King Ptolemy besieges Caesar at Alexandria.
            Although victorious in two desperate naval battles outside
            the harbor, Caesar loses a land battle on the harbor mole
            and a third naval battle nearby.

47   After allied reinforcements arrive, Caesar defeats Ptolemy
            and Arsinoe in February at the Battle of the Nile. Caesar
            relieves his forces in Alexandria and after some more rest
            moves north against Pharnaces of Bosporus, who has con-
            quered much of Anatolia. Caesar defeats him in the Battle
            of Zela in May, sending the message to Rome "Veni, vidi,
            vici" ("I came, I saw, I conquered").

            Returning to Rome, Caesar subdues a mutiny from among
            his troops. He convinces them to accompany him to
            Africa, where the Pompeian forces have concentrated.
            Caesar invades North Africa and after some initial diffi-
            culties establishes a base.

46   Pompeian forces in Africa outnumber Caesar, but he at-
            tacks Thapsus and wins a climactic battle in April. The
            remaining Pompeians now flee to Spain, where the sons of
            Pompey have taken advantage of anti-Roman feelings to
            raise a revolt. Caesar, meanwhile, returns to Rome.

45   Caesar moves against Pompey's sons in Spain, maneuver-
            ing for advantage. Caesar and Pompey meet in battle on
            the plains of Munda in southern Spain, where Caesar wins
            decisively. Munda and Corduba both fall after siege.
            Sextus Pompey escapes Corduba, but the war is effectively
            over. Caesar returns to Rome to prepare for a Parthian war.

44   A conspiracy of senators assassinates Caesar on March
            15. The assassins, realizing their unpopularity, gradually
            depart Rome for provincial assignments. Antony and

Octavian vie for control of the city, with Antony departing Rome in November.

43   Octavian receives imperium and supports the consuls marching against Antony, who has been declared a public enemy. Antony loses two battles at Mutina and flees to Gaul, where he joins Lepidus. In November they join Octavian and form a triumvirate to defeat the assassins. Antony, Lepidus, and Octavian promise their soldiers bounties and proscribe their enemies.

42   Brutus and Cassius have established firm control over the Roman east, raising an army and marching into Thrace. Octavian and Antony invade Greece, and the armies meet in two engagements at Philippi in October. Antony wins the first engagement, and Cassius commits suicide. Twenty days later Antony and Octavian defeat Brutus, who also commits suicide. Antony goes east to raise money to pay the soldiers' bounties while Octavian settles the troops.

Sextus captures Sicily and starts using it as a base against the triumvirs.

41–40   Octavian settles the discharged troops. Antony's brother, Lucius, and wife, Fulvia, raise a revolt against Octavian called the Perusine War. Both sides raise legions, but Octavian catches Lucius in Perusia and sieges the city, taking it in 40.

40   Parthian forces invade Syria and push all the way across Anatolia.

Antony and Octavian barely avoid renewed war at Brundisium, but their troops intercede, and they make a pact. They redivide the empire. Octavian receives Italy, Dalmatia, Sardinia, Spain, and Gaul; Antony receives the entire eastern region; and Lepidus is left with Africa.

39   Sextus blockades Italy, forcing Antony and Octavian to make the Pact of Misenum and share power.

Ventidius defeats Parthian forces in Cilicia at the Battle of the Cilician Gates and the Battle of the Amanus Pass.

38   Ventidius defeats Parthia at the Battle of Gandarus in northern Syria. Antony captures Samosata.

There is renewed fighting between Sextus and Octavian after an alleged treaty violation. Octavian loses a naval battle at the Straits of Messana.

Agrippa eliminates threats to Roman Gaul, even marching across the Rhine.

37   Antony and Octavian agree on the Pact of Tarentum in which each gives the other military support and renews the triumvirate. Agrippa arranges for a new navy and training facilities in Italy.

36   From June to October, Antony attacks Parthia, marching through Armenia into Media Atropatene. He loses an engagement at Phraaspa and has to withdraw under harassing fire.

Octavian invades Sicily with support from Lepidus. Octavian loses a naval engagement in August. Agrippa wins several naval engagements and a decisive victory at Naulochus on September 3. Lepidus captures Messana, but then Octavian deposes him after a disagreement about taking sole credit for the victory.

35   Octavian campaigns in Illyria against the Iapudes tribes.

34   Octavian campaigns in Dalmatia, Illyricum, and Pannonia.

Antony invades Parthia, capturing Armenia and Media. He marries Cleopatra.

32   In the spring, Antony and Cleopatra move with a powerful army and fleet to Greece, setting up positions in western Greece.

32–31   Taking advantage of the fighting between Antony and Octavian, Parthian ruler Phraates IV reconquers much of the region.

31   Agrippa leads successful naval maneuvers, capturing Methone and other coastal points. He and Octavian outmaneuver his opponent's fleet, gradually forcing Antony's land and naval forces into the Bay of Actium. On September 3 they try to break out of the blockade at sea. Although some ships get away, Antony and Cleopatra lose tremendously as the bulk of their fleet and the entire army surrender or are captured. Afterward Octavian dominates the military situation in the Mediterranean, but the war continues.

30   Following up his victories at Actium, Octavian invades Egypt. Antony's attempts to resist fail when his forces defect to Octavian. Antony kills himself, and a week later Cleopatra is also dead. Octavian takes possession of Egypt, and Civil War III ends. The Roman Republic is over also, although this will not be formalized until 27 BCE.

Bibliography

Astin, A. E. *Scipio Aemilianus*. Oxford: Oxford University Press, 1967.

Badian, Ernst. *Lucius Sulla: The Deadly Reformer.* Sydney, Australia: Sydney University Press, 1970.

Beard, Mary. *The Roman Triumph*. Cambridge, MA: Belknap, 2009.

Bishop, M. C., and J. C. Coulston. *Roman Military Equipment: From the Punic Wars to the Fall of Rome*. 2nd ed. Oxford, UK: Oxbow, 2011.

Boatright, Mary, Daniel Gargola, Noel Lenski, and Richard Talbert. *The Romans: From Village to Empire*. 2nd ed. Oxford: Oxford University Press, 2012.

Bradley, Guy. *Early Rome to 290 B.C.: The Beginnings of the City and the Rise of the Republic*. Edinburgh, UK: Edinburgh University Press, 2013.

Brand, C. E. *Roman Military Law*. Austin: University of Texas Press, 1968.

Breed, Brian, Cynthia Damon, and Andreola Rossi, eds. *Citizens of Discord: Rome and Its Civil Wars*. Oxford: Oxford University Press, 2010.

Brice, Lee L. "Discharging Pullo and Vorenus: Veterans in *Rome.*" In *Rome Season Two: Trial & Triumph,* edited by Monica Cyrino. Edinburgh, UK: Edinburgh University Press, 2014.

Brice, Lee L. "Disciplining Octavian: An Aspect of Roman Military Culture during the Triumviral Wars, 44–30 BCE." In *Warfare and Culture in World History,* edited by Wayne Lee, 35–60. New York: New York University Press, 2011.

Brice, Lee L. *Holding a Wolf by the Ears: Mutiny and Military Unrest in the Roman Army, 90 BCE–70 CE*. Baltimore: Johns Hopkins University Press, forthcoming 2015.

Brice, Lee L. "Second Chance for Valor: Restoration of Order after Mutinies and Indiscipline in the Roman Military." In *Aspects of Ancient*

Institutions and Geography, edited by L. L. Brice and D. Slöötjes, 23–34. Leiden: Brill, 2014.

Brice, Lee L., ed. *New Approaches to Greco-Roman Warfare.* Oxford, UK: Wiley-Blackwell, 2014.

Brice, Lee L., and J. Roberts, eds. *Recent Directions in the Military History of the Ancient World.* Claremont, CA: Regina, 2011.

Brunt, P. A. "The Army and the Land in the Roman Revolution." In *The Fall of the Roman Republic and Related Essays,* 240–275. Oxford, UK: Clarendon, 1988.

Caesar. *War Commentaries of Caesar.* Translated by Rex Warner. New York: New American Library, 1960.

Carter, J. M. *The Battle of Actium: The Rise and Triumph of Augustus Caesar.* London: Hamish Hamilton, 1970.

Charles, M. B. "African Forest Elephants and Turrets in the Ancient World." *Phoenix* 62(3–4) (2008): 338–362.

Clarke, M. L. *The Noblest Roman: Marcus Brutus and His Reputation.* Ithaca, NY: Cornell University Press, 1981.

Cooley, Allison, trans. and ed. *Res Gestae Divi Augustae.* Cambridge: Cambridge University Press, 2009.

Cornell, T. J. *The Beginnings of Rome: Italy and Rome from the Bronze Age to the Punic Wars (1000–264 BC).* London: Routledge, 1995.

Cornell, Tim, Boris Rankov, and Philip Sabin, eds. *The Second Punic War: A Reappraisal.* London: Institute for Classical Studies, 1996.

Daly, G. *Cannae: The Experience of Battle in the Second Punic War.* London: Routledge, 2001.

Davies, R. W. "Joining the Roman Army." In *Service in the Roman Army,* edited by D. Breeze and V. Maxfield, 3–32. New York: Columbia University Press, 1989.

de Souza, Philip. *Piracy in the Graeco-Roman World.* Cambridge: Cambridge University Press, 2002.

de Souza, Philip. "Rome's Contribution to Piracy." In *The Maritime World of Ancient Rome,* edited by Robert L. Hohlfelder, 71–96. Ann Arbor: University of Michigan Press, 2008.

Eck, Werner. *The Age of Augustus.* 2nd. ed. Oxford, UK: Wiley-Blackwell, 2007.

Eckstein, Arthur. *Rome Enters the Greek East: From Anarchy to Hierarchy in the Hellenistic Mediterranean, 230–170 BC.* Oxford, UK: Wiley-Blackwell, 2008.

Erdkamp, P., ed. *A Companion to the Roman Army.* Oxford, UK: Wiley-Blackwell, 2011.

Evans, Richard J. *Gaius Marius: A Political Biography.* Pretoria: University of South Africa Press, 1994.

Feldherr, A., ed. *Cambridge Companion to the Roman Historians.* Cambridge: Cambridge University Press, 2009.

Frere, S. *Britannia: A History of Roman Britain.* 3rd ed. London: Routledge, 1987.

Galinsky, Karl. *Augustus: Introduction to the Life of an Emperor.* Cambridge: Cambridge University Press, 2012.

Gelzer, M. *Caesar: Politician and Statesman.* Translated by P. Needham. Cambridge, MA: Harvard University Press, 1968.

Gibson, Bruce, and Thomas Harrison, eds. *Polybius and His World: Essays in Memory of F. W. Walbank.* Oxford: Oxford University Press, 2013.

Glover, R. F. "The Tactical Handling of the Elephant." *Greece and Rome* 17(49) (1948): 1–11.

Goldsworthy, A. K. *The Army at War, 100 B.C.–A.D. 200.* Oxford, UK: Clarendon, 1996.

Goldsworthy, A. K. *Caesar: Life of a Colossus.* New Haven, CT: Yale University Press, 2006.

Goldsworthy, A. K. *Caesar's Civil Wars, 49–44 BC.* Oxford, UK: Osprey, 2002.

Goldsworthy, A. K. *The Punic Wars.* London: Cassell, 2000.

Grainger, John D. *The Roman War of Antiochos the Great: Mnemosyne, Bibliotheca Classica Batava Supplementum.* Leiden: Brill.

Griffin, Marian, ed. *A Companion to Julius Caesar.* Oxford, UK: Wiley-Blackwell, 2009.

Gruen, Erich. *The Last Generation of the Roman Republic.* Berkeley: University of California Press, 1995.

Hammond, N. G. L. "Battle of Pydna." *Journal of Hellenic Studies* 104 (1984): 31–47.

Hammond, N. G. L. "The Campaign and the Battle of Cynoscephalae in 197 B.C." *Journal of Hellenic Studies* 108 (1988): 60–82.

Harris, W. V. *War and Imperialism in Republican Rome, 327–70 B.C.* Oxford: Oxford University Press, 1985.

Hoyos, Dexter. *The Carthaginians.* London: Routledge, 2010.

Hoyos, Dexter, ed. *A Companion to the Punic Wars.* Oxford, UK: Wiley-Blackwell, 2011.

Hoyos, Dexter, ed. *A Companion to Roman Imperialism.* Leiden: Brill, 2013.

James, Simon. *Rome and the Sword: How Warriors and Weapons Shaped Roman History.* London: Thames and Hudson, 2011.

James, Simon. *The World of the Celts.* London: Thames and Hudson, 2005.

Joshel, Sandra. *Slavery in the Roman World.* Cambridge: Cambridge University Press, 2010.

Keaveney, Arthur. *The Army in the Roman Revolution.* London: Routledge, 2007.

Keaveney, Arthur. *Sulla, the Last Republican.* 2nd ed. London: Routledge, 2005.

Keegan, John. *Face of Battle.* New York: Penguin, 1976.

Keppie, L. J. F. *The Making of the Roman Army, From Republic to Empire.* Updated ed. Norman: University of Oklahoma Press, 1998.

Konrad, C. F. *Plutarch's Sertorius: A Historical Commentary.* Chapel Hill: University of North Carolina Press, 1994.

Lamberton, Robert. *Plutarch.* New Haven, CT: Yale University Press, 2001.

Lazenby, J. F. *The First Punic War.* London: Routledge, 1996.

Lazenby, J. F. *Hannibal's War: A Military History of the Second Punic War.* Norman: University of Oklahoma Press, 1998.

Lendon, J. E. *Soldiers and Ghosts: A History of Battle in Classical Antiquity.* New Haven, CT: Yale University Press, 2006.

Levithan, J. *Roman Siege Warfare.* Ann Arbor: University of Michigan Press, 2014.

Levithan, J. "Roman Siege Warfare: Moral and Morale." In *New Approaches to Greco-Roman Warfare,* edited by Lee L. Brice, 127–148. Oxford, UK: Wiley-Blackwell, 2014.

Ligt, Luuk de. *Peasants, Citizens and Soldiers: Studies in Demographic History of Roman Italy, 225 BC–AD 100.* Cambridge: Cambridge University Press, 2012.

Lintott, A. *The Constitution of the Roman Republic.* Oxford: Oxford University Press, 1999.

Livy. *History of Rome.* 14 vols. Translated by B. O. Foster. Loeb Classical Library. Cambridge, MA: Harvard University Press, 1919.

Lovano, M. *The Age of Cinna: Crucible of Late Republican Rome.* Stuttgart: Steiner, 2002.

Lowe, B. *Roman Spain: Economy, Society and Culture.* London: Gerald Duckworth, 2009.

Ma, John. *Antiochus III and the Cities of Western Asia Minor.* Oxford: Oxford University Press, 2000.

MacKay, C. *The Breakdown of the Roman Republic: From Oligarchy to Empire.* Cambridge: Cambridge University Press, 2009.

Manning, J. G. *The Last Pharaohs: Egypt under the Ptolemies, 305–30 BC.* Princeton, NJ: Princeton University Press, 2012.

Marincola, John, ed. *A Companion to Greek and Roman Historiography.* Oxford, UK: Wiley-Blackwell, 2007.

Marsden, Eric W. *Greek and Roman Artillery: Historical Development.* Oxford, UK: Clarendon, 1969.

Matyszak, P. *Sertorius and the Struggle for Spain.* Barnsley, UK: Pen and Sword Military, 2013.

Maxfield, V. *Military Decorations of the Roman Army.* Berkeley: University of California Press, 1981.

Mayor, Adrienne. *The Poison King: Life and Legend of Mithradates, Rome's Deadliest Enemy.* Princeton, NJ: Princeton University Press, 2011.

McCall, J. *The Cavalry of the Roman Republic: Cavalry Combat and Elite Reputations in the Middle and Late Republic.* London: Routledge, 2002.

McGing, B. *Polybius: The Histories.* Oxford: Oxford University Press, 2010.

McGing, B. "Subjection and Resistance: To the Death of Mithradates." In *A Companion to the Hellenistic World,* edited by A. Erskine, 71–89. Oxford, UK: Blackwell, 2005.

Meckler, Michael. *Classical Antiquity and the Politics of America.* Waco, TX: Baylor University Press, 2006.

Morrison, J. S. *Greek and Roman Oared Warships.* Oxford, UK: Oxbow, 1996.

Murray, William. *The Age of Titans: The Rise and Fall of Great Hellenistic Navies.* Oxford: Oxford University Press, 2012.

Murray, William M., and P. M. Petsas. *Octavian's Campsite Memorial for the Actium War: Transactions of the American Philosophical Society,* Vol. 79. Philadelphia: American Philosophical Society, 1989.

Nicolet, Claude. *The World of the Citizen in Republican Rome.* Translated by P. S. Falla. Berkeley: University of California Press, 1980.

Osgood, Josiah. *Caesar's Legacy: Civil War and the Emergence of the Roman Empire.* Cambridge: Cambridge University Press, 2006.

Phang, S. E. *Roman Military Service: Ideologies of Discipline in the Late Republic and Early Empire.* Cambridge: Cambridge University Press, 2008.

Plutarch. *Lives.* 11 vols. Translated by B. Perrin. Cambridge, MA: Harvard University Press, 1919.

Pollard, N. *Soldiers, Cities, and Civilians in Roman Syria.* Ann Arbor: University of Michigan Press, 2000.

Pollard, N., and J. Berry. *The Complete Roman Legions*. London: Thames and Hudson, 2012.

Polybius. *Histories*. Translated by R. Waterfield and B. McGing. Oxford: Oxford University Press, 2010.

Potter, D. "The Roman Army and Navy." In *The Cambridge Companion to the Roman Republic,* edited by H. I. Flower, 66–88. Cambridge: Cambridge University Press, 2004.

Powell, Anton, and Kathryn Welch, eds. *Sextus Pompey*. Swansea, UK: Classical Press of Wales, 2002.

Rankin, David. *Celts and the Classical World*. 2nd ed. London: Routledge, 1996.

Rich, J., and G. Shipley, eds. *War and Society in the Roman World*. London: Routledge, 1993.

Roddaz, Jean-Michel. *Marcus Agrippa*. Rome: École Française de Rome, 1984.

Roller, Duane. *Cleopatra: A Biography*. Oxford: Oxford University Press, 2010.

Rosenstein, N. *Rome and the Mediterranean, 290–146 BC: The Imperial Republic*. Edinburgh, UK: Edinburgh University Press, 2012.

Rosenstein, N., and R. Morstein-Marx, eds. *A Companion to the Roman Republic*. Oxford, UK: Blackwell, 2010.

Sabin, Philip. "The Face of Roman Battle." *JRS* 90 (2000): 1–17.

Sabin, Philip, Hans Van Wees, and Michael Whitby, eds. *The Cambridge History of Greek and Roman Warfare*. 2 vols. Cambridge: Cambridge University Press, 2007.

Sage, Michael M. *The Republican Roman Army: A Sourcebook*. London: Routledge, 2008.

Scullard, Howard H. *Scipio Africanus: Soldier and Politician*. London: Thames and Hudson, 1970.

Seager, Robin. *Pompey the Great*. Oxford, UK: Blackwell, 2002.

Shaw, Brent. *Spartacus and the Slave Wars: A Brief History*. Boston: Bedford/St. Martin's, 2001.

Silva, L. *Viriathus and the Lusitanian Resistance to Rome, 155–139 BCE*. Barnsley, UK: Pen and Sword Military, 2013.

Smith, Christopher, and John Serrati, eds. *Sicily from Aeaneas to Augustus: New Approaches in Archaeology and History*. Edinburgh, UK: Edinburgh University Press, 2000.

Southern, Patricia. *Mark Antony*. Charleston, SC: Tempus, 1998.

Strauss, Barry. *Masters of Command: Alexander, Hannibal, Caesar and the Genius of Command*. New York: Simon and Schuster, 2012.

Syme, R. *The Roman Revolution.* Oxford: Oxford University Press, 1938.

Tritle, Lawrence A., and J. Brian Campbell, eds. *The Oxford Handbook of Classical Military History.* Oxford: Oxford University Press, 2012.

Walker, Susan, and Peter Higgs. *Cleopatra of Egypt: From History to Myth.* Princeton, NJ: Princeton University Press, 2001.

Ward, A. M. *Marcus Crassus and the Late Roman Republic.* Columbia: University of Missouri Press, 1977.

Weigel, Richard. *Lepidus, the Tarnished Triumvir.* London: Routledge, 1992.

Welch, Kathryn. *Magnus Pius: Sextus Pompeius and the Transformation of the Roman Republic.* Swansea, UK: Classical Press of Wales, 2012.

Wheeler, Everett. "Greece: Mad Hatters and March Hares." In *Recent Directions in the Military History of the Ancient World,* edited by Lee L. Brice and Jennifer Roberts, 53–104. Claremont, CA: Regina, 2011.

Winkler, M. M., ed. *Spartacus: Film and History.* Oxford, UK: Blackwell, 2007.

Zhmodikov, A. "Roman Republican Heavy Infantrymen in Battle (IV–II Centuries B.C.)." *Historia* 49 (1999): 67–78.

About the Author

Lee L. Brice, PhD, is Professor of history at Western Illinois University, where he has been teaching for 11 years since he completed his doctorate at the University of North Carolina at Chapel Hill. He is the editor of *Greek Warfare: From Marathon the the Conquests of Alexander the Great,* the coeditor of *Recent Directions in the Military History of the Ancient World,* and the author of articles on Philip II and Alexander the Great of Macedon, Octavian Caesar of Rome, the coins of Greek Corinth, and the Roman Army in film. Brice is currently working on a study of mutinies in the ancient world.

List of Contributors

Dr. Lee L. Brice
Professor of Ancient History
Western Illinois University

Mike Dixon-Kennedy
Independent Scholar

Dr. James Emmons
Independent Scholar

Christina Girod
Independent Scholar

Mark Haviland
Independent Scholar

Dr. Rosemary Moore
Lecturer, Ancient History
University of Iowa

Dr. Junius P. Rodriguez
Associate Professor of History
Eureka College, Illinois

Dr. Joyce Salisbury
Frankenthal Professor of History
University of Wisconsin–Green Bay

Dr. Tom Sizgorich
Associate Professor of History
University of California, Irvine

Dr. Spencer C. Tucker
Senior Fellow
Military History, ABC-CLIO, LLC

Categorical Index

Index

Note: Page numbers in **bold** indicate main entries in the text.